TO BALANCE OR NOT TO BALANCE

In loving memory of Stanley Miller

To Balance or Not to Balance
Alignment Theory and the Commonwealth of Independent States

ERIC A. MILLER
National Institute for Public Policy, USA
and
Institute for European, Russian and Eurasian Studies,
George Washington University, USA

ASHGATE

Published by
Ashgate Publishing Limited
Gower House
Croft Road
Aldershot
Hampshire GU11 3HR
England

Ashgate Publishing Company
Suite 420
101 Cherry Street
Burlington, VT 05401-4405
USA

Ashgate website: http://www.ashgate.com

British Library Cataloguing in Publication Data
Miller, Eric
    To balance or not to balance: alignment theory and the
    Commonwealth of Independent States
    1. Russia (Federation) - Foreign relations - Ukraine
    2. Ukraine - Foreign relations - Russia (Federation)
    3. Ukraine - Foreign relations - 1991- 4. Russia (Federation)
    - Foreign relations - Uzbekistan 5. Uzbekistan - Foreign
    relations - Russia (Federation) 6. Ukraine - Politics and
    government - 1991- 7. Uzbekistan - Politics and government -
    1991-
    I. Title
    327.4'7'0477

Library of Congress Cataloging-in-Publication Data
Miller, Eric A.
    To balance or not to balance : alignment theory and the Commonwealth of Independent
States / by Eric A. Miller.
        p. cm.
    Includes bibliographical references and index.
    ISBN 0-7546-4334-4
    1. Commonwealth of Independent States 2. Nonalignment--Former Soviet republics. 3.
Former Soviet republics--Politics and government. I. Title.

    DK1.5.M55 2006
    320.94709'049--dc22

                                                                                    2005032388

ISBN 0 7546 4334 4

Printed and bound by Athenaeum Press Ltd,
Gateshead, Tyne & Wear.

Contents

List of Tables

List of Figures

About the Author

Dr. Eric A. Miller is an International Affairs Analyst with the National Institute for Public Policy in Fairfax, Virginia and a Research Associate at the Institute of European, Russian, and Eurasian Studies at George Washington University in Washington, D.C. He currently provides on-site support for the Missile Defense Agency's International Support Directorate, where he focuses on missile defense issues pertaining to Russia, Ukraine, the Caucasus, and Central Asia. While at National Institute, he has authored studies on U.S. nuclear policy, U.S.-Russian relations, the future of ballistic missiles, efforts to democratize the national security structures of the Republic of Georgia, and Iranian domestic politics and security policy. He also serves as Program Director for the Georgia Forum, a Washington D.C.-based forum dedicated to supporting Georgia's political and economic development and promoting stronger U.S.-Georgian relations. He has also served as a consultant and analyst for the Defense Intelligence Agency, U.S. Coast Guard, and Joint Forces Staff College, and held teaching positions at Old Dominion University and Christopher Newport University. His articles, commentary, and reviews on Russia and the Commonwealth of Independent States, U.S. foreign and defense policy, and international relations theory have appeared in leading publications, such as *Astropolitics*, *Defense News*, *European Security*, *Financial Times*, *Janes's Intelligence Review*, *Presidential Studies Quarterly*, *Problems of Post-Communism*, and *Security Studies*. He holds a B.A. in Political Science from the University of Florida with a certificate in Russian and Slavic Studies, and an M.A. and Ph.D. from Old Dominion University in Norfolk, Virginia.

Acknowledgements

This book would not have been possible without the assistance and support of a wide range of colleagues, family members, and friends. My colleagues at Old Dominion University were the first to shape and guide the present work. Steve Yetiv was an enduring supporter and critic which forced me to push the bounds of my own theoretical understanding and to challenge long-standing assumptions in international relations theory. Glen Sussman, Stephen Medvic, and Francis Adams were equally challenging colleagues and never let me get too comfortable. Simon Serfaty and David Smith both left indelible marks on my intellectual and professional development, without which this project and many like it could never have been realized. National Institute for Public Policy, under the leadership of Keith Payne, has been a wonderful intellectual home after graduate school, providing me ample time and space to refine this book. Amy Joseph at NIPP was also wonderfully helpful in the final stages of the manuscript. Other colleagues have read portions of this work in various forms, and for their insights I am forever indebted: Rawi Abdelal, Tor Bukkvoll, Stacy Closson, Steven David, Kurt Taylor Gaubatz, Henry Hale, Richard Harknett, Fiona Hill, Charles King, Deborah Sanders, Joanne Tompkins and Cory Welt. For her tireless support and willingness to endure endless drafts, I owe a special debt of gratitude to Dr. Daneta Billau for all that she has given me professionally and personally. Finally, without my parents, Ron and Kathy, I would not be who I am today, and Meredith, Jim, Ryan, Renee, and especially Pooh, have kept my spirits up over the years and my feet firmly on the ground.

Chapter 1

Introduction

With the collapse of the Soviet Union in December 1991, fifteen newly independent states were thrust onto the international stage – some more ready and able than others. All had been part of the Soviet Union for most of the twentieth century (and many integrated during the Tsarist period in the nineteenth century). That is to say, all but one – Russia – had been subjugated to a Russian-dominated empire. Nonetheless, vast cultural, historical, and geographical differences existed, and the political and economic trajectories of these countries were anything but clear. Since independence, some states of the former Soviet Union embraced their newfound independence, while others were reluctant to step from the "shadow of the bear."[1] This book focuses primary attention on those states that decided to remain in the Commonwealth of Independent States (CIS), the loosely-associated political, military, and economic union that succeeded the Soviet Union.[2]

Despite the importance of the former Soviet region and the unprecedented independence of these new states, few studies have sought to understand their foreign policy in a theoretical and conceptual fashion.[3] A growing body of literature examines the foreign policies of former Soviet republics, but these studies tend to focus on bilateral or regional dynamics as opposed to developing broader frameworks that are applicable throughout the region.[4] Thus, while some have argued that a new "geopolitical pluralism" emerged within the former Soviet Union, our knowledge and understanding of the forces underlying such developments remain underdeveloped.[5] This book explores why some CIS states cooperated with Russia while others did not – in particular, by focusing on alignment patterns between these states and Russia.

Objectives of the Book

This book has two interrelated objectives. First, it develops an original framework for understanding alignment patterns between CIS states and Russia – one that differs from traditional alignment theories such as balance of power and balance of threat theories – and then tests the framework against the empirical behavior of Uzbekistan and Ukraine. In the process, it provides a new alignment explanation as to why some states cooperated with Russia and others did not. The second objective adds to the international relations theory debate on alignment outcomes. Before turning to the theoretical and empirical phases of this book, it is first

important to outline the main research questions that guide the present study and
how they are addressed.

This book addresses seminal questions in the study of international relations,
and more specifically alignment patterns. Why do states align? What factors are
most influential in alignment calculations? In the context of the CIS, balance of
power and balance of threat theories lead us astray when seeking answers to these
questions, but the framework developed in this book reveals straight-forward
answers. The present framework steps away from the standard state-centric
approach of balance of power and balance of threats theories that emphasizes the
distribution of power and threats in the international system. Instead, it explains
alignment outcomes by examining CIS states themselves and focusing on domestic
political and economic variables. Such an effort is important given the difficulty
traditional alignment theories have in explaining post-Soviet alignment patterns.

Balance of power and balance of threat theories suggest that states are most
likely to balance other more powerful or threatening states as opposed to
bandwagoning with them.[6] Kenneth Waltz's theory of neorealism is the most
refined articulation of balance of power theory. However, Waltz points out that his
theory is intended to explain international outcomes, not the foreign policies of
particular states, suggesting "the behavior of states and statesmen is
indeterminate."[7] This is not entirely convincing, though, since the international
structure provides opportunities and constraints that significantly shape state
behavior. Waltz himself noted that "neorealist, or structural, theory leads one to
believe that the placement of states in the international system accounts for a good
deal of their behavior."[8] Moreover, balance of power theory can (and has) been
interpreted and applied by generating simple deductions from the theory's causal
logic.[9]

This book does not refute Waltzian neorealism per se, but rather it takes issue
with the explanatory capability of balance of power and balance of threat theories.
In applying inferences derived from these theories, former Soviet republics are
systemically constrained by Russia's overwhelming capabilities. Therefore, Russia
is inevitably perceived as the most significant threat, based on its aggregate power,
geographic proximity, ability to engage in offensive military operations, and
inclination to act upon its "neoimperial" ambitions.[10] In such an "anarchic"
environment, traditional alignment theories would suggest that former Soviet
republics are likely to balance Russia.[11]

Yet this proposition has not played out in reality. For instance, the resource-
rich and culturally distinctive states of Muslim Central Asia embarked on
predominantly pro-Russian policies, while Ukraine, the most populous and
militarily strong of the former Soviet republics, adopted an anti-Russian stance
immediately after independence but then shifted to pro-Russian policies. These
alignment outcomes are inconsistent with traditional alignment theories and raise
an unanswered empirical question: Why did CIS states not balance Russia?

To answer this question, this book develops a framework for understanding
the alignment patterns of CIS states vis-à-vis Russia. I argue that CIS alignments

vis-à-vis Russia are best explained by two factors: 1) internal political threats to leaders, and 2) economic dependence on Russia.

By design, the framework focuses less on Russian behavior and more on political and economic developments within CIS states themselves and how these forces shaped alignment decisions towards Russia.[12] Based on traditional power indices, such as military and economic power, Russian aggregate power has been a defining characteristic within the former Soviet space, and this asymmetry has changed little since independence. (See Table 1.1.) Furthermore, Moscow retained ambitions to consolidate its hegemonic position throughout the region whenever and wherever possible – a relative constant that shaped Russian relations with its former periphery under both Boris Yeltsin and Vladimir Putin. Indeed, of late, Putin's proclivity to articulate these ambitions draws additional attention to an impulse that was often downplayed in Moscow's political rhetoric in previous years.[13] This reality suggests that a more interesting avenue of analysis is not how Russia attempted to dominate its former republics, but rather how and why CIS leaders responded to systemic and domestic constraints the way they did – where some willingly acquiesced to and even sought Russian hegemony.

Table 1.1 Traditional Power Indices for the Commonwealth of Independent States[14]

| | 1994 | | | 1999 | | |
	Pop (mill)	GDP (bill)	Armed Forces (thous)	Pop (mill)	GDP (bill)	Armed Forces (thous)
Armenia	3.8	2.3	60.0	3.8	1.9	42.3
Azerbaijan	7.6	2.9	86.7	7.3	4.5	72.1
Belarus	10.4	22.0	98.4	10.0	9.3	83.1
Georgia	5.4	1.5	29.0	5.5	2.5	26.9
Kazakhstan	16.8	14.0	40.0	15.0	14.5	64.0
Kyrgyzstan	4.6	3.4	7.0	4.9	1.1	9.0
Moldova	4.4	1.0	11.9	4.4	1.1	9.5
Russia	150.4	400.2	2,030.0	146.0	1,100.0	1,004.0
Tajikistan	6.0	2.2	2.5	6.1	1.2	6.0
Turkmenistan	4.1	5.8	11.0	5.0	3.3	17.5
Ukraine	51.9	39.0	452.3	50.0	49.0	303.8
Uzbekistan	23.0	13.8	41.0	24.1	15.9	59.1

The present framework departs from traditional alignment theories in two distinct ways. First, it suggests CIS leaders are the principal actors and focuses on their particular motivations. Traditional alignment theories assume states are unitary actors that act in rational ways based on national rather than individual interest. It is misleading to assume that CIS leaders were primarily motivated by national interests, or what was best for the state, because in the transition period they tended to prioritize their own personal self-interest and often sought to ensure their political positions at any cost. To that end, most CIS states developed strong executive branches, which legitimated and institutionalized the power of the respective leader. In short, many of the theoretical assumptions realists make offer especially poor guidance in the post-Soviet context, which warrants a more "leader-centric" analysis.

Second, the framework incorporates an economic variable – economic dependence on Russia – to explain alignment outcomes.[15] This is particularly important for CIS states because they were integrated into the Soviet command economy, placing Russia at the center of all Soviet economic activity. Leaders in Moscow made allocation decisions that forced specialization on each republic. Indeed, all former Soviet republics were dependent on Russia to some degree, but they did not face the same level of economic dependence and were not dependent on the same items. Thus, with some states left in better relative economic positions, understanding the extent of economic dependence on Russia helps define the economic constraints CIS leaders faced. Before addressing these theoretical issues, the next section reinforces the importance of the former Soviet Union to international security and stability and underscores why the region remains militarily, geopolitically, politically, and economically relevant today.

Why the Former Soviet Union Matters

The former Soviet Union is a prime laboratory for testing and examining various theories and approaches to international relations. But beyond this academic interest, the region quickly came to the fore after the terrorist attack in New York and Washington, D.C. on 11 September 2001. Few could have named even one Central Asian state before then, but with the beginning of military operations in Afghanistan and the George W. Bush administration's "war on terrorism," international attention focused on this often overlooked region.[16]

To support military operations in Afghanistan, Washington courted regional leaders, especially those in Central Asia and the Caucasus. The U.S. military acquired temporary forward basing rights in Uzbekistan and Kyrgyzstan, and access to airspace and restricted use of bases in Kazakhstan and Tajikistan. Coalition aircraft en route to Afghanistan and Central Asia were allowed to overfly and refuel in the South Caucasus states, namely Georgia and Azerbaijan, providing the only realistic air corridor through which military aircraft could travel. And regional governments became an essential source of intelligence to support operations in Afghanistan. Indeed, the entrance of the U.S. military in the former Soviet space was of historic and unprecedented significance. As Vladimir Socor pointed out, these accomplishments were historic: one signifying the setting foot of Western forces in the heartland of Asia, formerly the exclusive preserve of land empires.[17]

After the 5 October 2001 visit of Secretary of Defense Donald Rumsfeld to Tashkent, Uzbekistan signed an agreement with the United States allowing approximately 1,500 military personnel to operate out of the Karshi Khanabad airbase in southern Uzbekistan in exchange for security guarantees and U.S. agreement to target training camps in Afghanistan known to harbor Islamic Movement of Uzbekistan (IMU) militants.[18] Then in March 2002 the United States and Uzbekistan signed a strategic partnership: in exchange for allowing the United States to remain in Uzbekistan as along as necessary to complete its antiterrorism operations in Afghanistan, the United States would "regard with grave concern any external threat to Uzbekistan."[19] A significant increase in U.S. assistance was also part of this package deal. In 2002, for instance, a one-time payment of $100 million bolstered the $60 million annual aid package to Uzbekistan.[20] Despite this initial boom in U.S.-Uzbek security cooperation, the Andijon massacre in May 2005, where Uzbek security services shot hundreds of civilian protesters without warning, and subsequent international and U.S. pressure on the Uzbek government, prompted Tashkent to give the U.S. military 180 days to withdraw from its base at Karshi Khanabad.[21]

After this recent eviction, the base in neighboring Kyrgyzstan became even more important. On 5 December 2001 U.S. and Kyrgyz officials signed a one year basing access agreement, allowing U.S. and coalition forces to use the Manas airport outside of the country's capital, Bishkek. The agreement was then prolonged for a second year, and on 5 June 2003, Kyrgyzstan committed to a three year extension. Approximately, 1,000 U.S. troops are stationed at the base, which sends aerial tankers to Afghanistan daily, as well as regular transport of food, medical supplies, equipment, ammunition, and coalition troops into Afghanistan.[22] The domestic economic impact of the airbase has also been substantial, serving as an additional bonus for Kyrgyz support.[23] The loss of the Uzbek base further underscores the importance of access to the Manas base, prompting a July 2005 visit by Rumsfeld to secure assurances that the U.S. military could stay in Kyrgyzstan as long as necessary.[24]

Tajikistan and Kazakhstan also played a support role in these basing efforts. Tajikistan allowed the U.S. military to use the Dushanbe airport on a contingency basis, mostly for refueling, and granted the United States overflight rights.[25] Similarly, Kazakhstan provided overflight rights and allowed transshipments of supplies over its territory destined for bases in Uzbekistan and Kyrgyzstan. Yet, unlike the airbases in Uzbekistan and Kyrgyzstan, no U.S. military personnel were actively deployed in either country.

Beyond their logistical support for operations in Afghanistan, Georgia and Azerbaijan have also been active participants in the war on terrorism. When al Qaeda terrorists were reportedly identified in Georgia's Pankisi Gorge in 2002, Washington launched a two-year $64 million Georgian Train and Equip Program (GTEP), answering Tbilisi's request for assistance in building up its counter-terrorism capabilities. GTEP has been the cornerstone of U.S. efforts to strengthen Georgia's beleaguered armed forces by creating an anti-terrorist force of 2,000 troops to serve as the core of a revitalized Georgian military.[26] This effort was also a means to alleviate tensions between Moscow and Tbilisi over sporadic Chechen presence in the Pankisi Gorge. Similarly, Washington pledged $10 million to Azerbaijan to strengthen its border security, improve its communications infrastructure, and help its government carry out security operations aimed at countering the spread of weapons of mass destruction.[27] U.S. defense planners have also openly spoken with Azerbaijani leaders about the possibility of establishing a major, cooperative military training program and a base for U.S. forces in the country, although no decision has been made on either side.[28] While the war on terrorism had been the main driver of U.S. engagement after 11 September, other geopolitical, political, and economic interests retain U.S. attention.

From a geopolitical perspective, the continued expansion of the North Atlantic Treaty Organization (NATO) at the November 2002 Prague summit further shattered the Cold War lines dividing East from West. The latest round of enlargement included East European states, such as Romania, Bulgaria, Slovakia, and Slovenia, which had not received invitations at the 1997 Madrid summit when Poland, Hungary, and the Czech Republic joined the alliance. But perhaps even more provocatively, for the first time in NATO's history, the alliance welcomed three new members that had been part of the Soviet Union itself – Estonia, Latvia, and Lithuania. As a result of the eastward shift of NATO's borders and the entrance of the first post-Soviet republics, several other NATO aspirants have emerged. In Prague, for instance, former Georgian President Eduard Shevardnadze openly declared Georgia's ambition of joining the alliance. Similarly, at the April 2005 summit in Vilnius, Lithuania, NATO invited Ukraine to begin an intensified dialogue on possible membership – an objective Bush openly supported during Ukrainian President Viktor Yushchenko's official visit to Washington, D.C. the same month. While it is unclear when, how, or if ever, these states can fulfill the necessary obligations to join the alliance, NATO expansion serves as a reminder that the former Soviet Union is no longer an exclusive Russian condominium.

Furthermore, the spread of democracy throughout the world has become an important objective for the Bush administration. As Bush recently noted,

> From Germany and Japan after World War II, to Latin America, to Asia, and Central and Eastern Europe, and now to the broader Middle East, the advance of freedom is the great story of our age. And in this history, there are important lessons. We have learned that free nations grow stronger with time, because they rise on the creativity and enterprise of their people. We have learned that governments accountable to citizens are peaceful, while dictatorships stir resentments and hatred to cover their own failings. We have learned that the skeptics and pessimists are often wrong, because men and women in every culture, when given the chance, will choose liberty. . . . We seek democracy [in the Middle East] for the same reasons we spent decades working for democracy in Europe – because freedom is the only reliable path to peace. . . . We have learned our lesson; no one's liberty is expendable. In the long-run, our security and true stability depend on the freedom of others. And so, with confidence and resolve, we will stand for freedom.[29]

While in many respects this democratization movement grew out of the military campaign to oust Saddam Hussein from Iraq, the former Soviet Union has proven a fertile ground for these ideals. Whether the Rose Revolution in Georgia in November 2003, the Orange Revolution in Ukraine in December 2004, or the Tulip Revolution in Kyrgyzstan in March 2005, the citizens of these respective countries have proven their dedication to a more free and fair democratic process through largely non-violent revolutions. Ironically, the democratic wave was not directly attributable to U.S. actions and efforts, but rather grew from the resentment felt by the citizens of these countries – a resentment born from the pervasive corruption and inability of these leaders to provide for the future of their countries in any meaningful fashion. These revolutions were organic and largely homegrown expressions of free will from citizens fed up with corrupt and selfish leaders, and Washington has stated it will not lose sight of these compelling steps. As Bush emphasized to the Georgian people in May 2005:

> The path of freedom you have chosen is not easy, but you will not travel it alone. Americans respect your courageous choice for liberty. And as you build a free and democratic Georgia, the American people will stand with you. . . . You are making many important contributions to freedom's cause, but your most important contribution is your example. . . Your courage is inspiring democratic reformers and sending a message that echoes across the world: Freedom will be the future of every nation and every people on earth.[30]

Economic interests are another driving force for U.S. and Western involvement in the region. The most important economic element of this picture involves the export of oil and gas supplies, a consideration that gained more attention after 9/11 with concerns over maintaining a sufficient flow of oil at reasonable prices. Indeed, according to some estimates, total CIS oil exports could equal Saudi oil exports within four years, although the CIS still lacks a highly efficient infrastructure, namely inadequate pipelines and port facilities.[31]

Moreover, the long-awaited construction of the Baku-Tbilisi-Ceyhan (BTC) oil pipeline through the Caucasus, which officially opened on 25 May 2005, and the Baku-Tbilisi-Erzurum gas pipeline, scheduled to open in 2006, have raised considerable hopes from Washington and within the region. As U.S. Energy Secretary Samuel Bodmen stated during the formal opening ceremony, the oil pipeline may "defuse the current tension on world oil markets."[32] While this optimistic claim may not come to fruition for several years, the BTC opening remains significant. Georgian president Mikheil Saakashvili characterized the opening as a "geopolitical victory" for Caspian basin nations, since the pipeline stands to break Russia's virtual monopoly in regional export routes. It will also enhance prospects for regional economic growth and development, and enable Georgian and Azerbaijan to more effectively resist geopolitical pressure exerted by Russia. During the opening ceremony, Azerbaijani President Ilham Aliyev stated firmly that BTC marked a "serious step forward" for his country's economic development. Meanwhile, Bodman affirmed the positive benefits likely from the pipeline: "It will open up new economic opportunities for [Caspian Basin states], boost energy independence and supply additional fuel necessary for the developing economies."[33]

In the end, the former Soviet Union has emerged as an area of vital interest to U.S. and international security. The myriad security, geopolitical, political, and economic interests at stake for the United State and the Euro-Atlantic community are unlikely to waiver. Because these compelling interests will not change in the foreseeable future, strengthening our understanding of the factors influencing politics within and between CIS states, as well as their relations with the larger international system is particularly important to both the academic and policy communities.

Structure of the Book

The remainder of this book is divided into eight chapters. Chapter 2 outlines the framework for understanding CIS alignment patterns vis-à-vis Russia developed in this book. I refer to it as the internal threat/economic dependence (IT/ED) framework, comparing it to balance of power and balance of threat theories, and demonstrating how it builds on the work of Steven David's theory of omnibalancing.[34] I do not suggest that balance of power and balance of threat theories are void of all merit, but where traditional approaches fail is in their inability to recognize contextual and situational variables often more influential in a leader's alignment calculations.

In subsequent chapters, I articulate the argument in detail for the two case studies of Uzbekistan (Chapters 3-5) and Ukraine (Chapters 6-8). The findings for each case study are divided into three chapters that examine security relations since independence, internal threats to leaders, and economic dependence on Russia, respectively. These chapters are based on a variety of primary and secondary documents, as well as Russian and Ukrainian language sources.

One of the principal findings of this research is that internal threats to CIS leaders have a stronger impact on alignment calculations towards Russia than economic dependence on Russia. This is primarily because the former has a direct influence on a leader's political security, while the latter tends to exert an indirect impact on a leader's political survival. Thus, while economic dependence may constrain a leader's alignment choice, the presence of internal threats tends to exert the strongest impact on a leader's decision to align with Russia. Chapter 9 concludes with a more thorough assessment of the theoretical and empirical findings of this book in the two case studies of Uzbekistan and Ukraine. It also offers the theoretical and policy implications of the work.

Notes

1. Rajan Menon, "In the Shadow of the Bear: Security in Post-Soviet Central Asia," *International Security* 20, no. 1 (1995): 149-81.
2. The Baltic states (Latvia, Lithuania, and Estonia) were the only three former Soviet republics that chose not to join the CIS in any fashion. The remaining twelve republics, including Russia, joined the CIS albeit to varying degrees. For good overviews of CIS integration, see Mark Webber, *CIS Integration Trends: Russia and the Former Soviet South* (London: Royal Institute of International Affairs, 1997); and Martha Brill Olcott, Anders Aslund, and Sherman W. Garnett, *Getting It Wrong: Regional Cooperation and the Commonwealth of Independent States* (Washington: Carnegie Endowment for International Peace, 1999).
3. Notable exceptions are Hendrik Spruyt, "The Prospects for Neo-Imperial and Nonimperial Outcomes in the Former Soviet Space," in *The End of Empire? The Transformation of the USSR in Comparative Perspective*, ed. Karen Dawisha and Bruce Parrott (Armonk, NY: M. E. Sharpe, 1997), 315-37; and Philip G. Roeder, "From Hierarchy to Hegemony: The Post-Soviet Security Complex," in *Regional Orders*, ed. David A. Lake and Patrick M. Morgan (University Park, PA: Pennsylvania State University Press, 1997), 219-44.
4. See, for example, Henry Hale, "Islam, State Building, and Uzbekistan Foreign Policy," in *The New Geopolitics of Central Asia and Its Borderlands*, ed. Ali Banuazizi and Myron Weiner (Bloomington, Indiana University Press, 1994), 136-172; Adeed Dawisha and Karen Dawisha, *The Making of Foreign Policy in Russia and the New States of Eurasia* (Armonk, NY: M. E. Sharpe, 1995); Rajan Menon and Hendrik Spruyt, "Possibilities for Conflict and Conflict Resolution in Post-Soviet Central Asia," in. *Post-Soviet Political Order: Conflict and State Building*, ed. Jack Snyder and Barnett R. Rubin (London, Routledge, 1998), 104-127; Ilya Prizel, *National Identity and Foreign Policy: Nationalism and Leadership in Poland, Russia, and Ukraine* (Cambridge: Cambridge University Press, 1998); Paul J. D'Anieri, *Economic Interdependence in Ukrainian-Russian Relations* (Albany: State University of New York Press, 1999); Rajan Menon, Yuri E. Fedorov, and Ghia Nodia, eds., *Russia, the Caucasus, and Central Asia: The 21st Century Security Environment* (Armonk, NY: M. E. Sharpe, 1999); and Jennifer D. P. Moroney, Taras Kuzio, and Mikhail Molchanov, ed., *Ukrainian Foreign and Security Policy: Theoretical and Comparative Perspectives* (Westport, CT: Praeger, 2002).
5. Taras Kuzio, "Geopolitical Pluarlism in the CIS: The Emergence of GUUAM," *European Security* 9, no. 2 (2000): 81-114.
6. Kenneth N. Waltz, *Theory of International Politics* (Reading, MA: Addison-Wesley, 1979); and Stephen M. Walt, *Origins of Alliances* (Ithaca: Cornell University Press, 1987).
7. Waltz, *Theory of International Politics*, 68.
8. Kenneth N. Waltz, "The Emerging Structure of International Politics," *International Security* 18, no. 2 (1993): 45.
9. John J. Mearsheimer, "Back to the Future: Instability in Europe After the Cold War," *International Security* 15, no. 1 (1990): 5-56; Christopher Layne, "The Unipolar Illusion: Why New Great Powers Will Rise," *International Security* 17, no. 4 (1993): 5-51; Colin Elman, "Horses for Courses: Why *Not* Neorealist Theories of Foreign Policy," *Security Studies* 6, no. 1 (1996): 7-53; David Priess, "Balance-of-Threat Theory and the Genesis of the Gulf Cooperation Council: An Interpretative Case

Study," *Security Studies*, 5, no. 4 (1996): 143-71; and Michael Mastanduno, "Preserving the Unipolar Moment: Realist Theories and U.S. Grand Strategy after the Cold War," *International Security* 21, no. 4 (1997): 5-58.

10. For more on Russian interests and the perception of Russian intentions, see Spruyt, "The Prospects for Neo-Imperial and Nonimperial Outcomes in the Former Soviet Space"; Roeder, "From Hierarchy to Hegemony"; and Daniel W. Drezner, *The Sanctions Paradox: Economic Statecraft and International Relations* (Cambridge: Cambridge University Press, 1999).

11. For more on using neorealist theory in understanding foreign policy see, Elman, "Horses for Courses."

12. For good theoretical discussions that incorporate Russian behavior see, Drezner, *The Sanctions Paradox*; Spruyt, "The Prospects for Neo-Imperial and Nonimperial Outcomes in the Former Soviet Space"; and Roeder, "From Hierarchy to Hegemony."

13. In his State of the Nation Address on 25 April 2005, Putin stated, "The demise of the Soviet Union was the greatest geopolitical catastrophe of the century." He went on to add, "The civilizing mission of the Russian nation on the Eurasian continent should continue. This means that democratic values multiplied by national interests should enrich and strengthen our historical unity." Vladimir Putin, Annual Address to the Federal Assembly, 25 April 2005, http://www.kremlin.ru/eng/speeches/2005/04/25/2031_type70029_87086.shtml.

14. International Institute for Strategic Studies, *The Military Balance, 1995-1996* (London: IISS, 1995); and International Institute for Strategic Studies, *The Military Balance, 2000-2001* (London: IISS, 2000).

15. For similar efforts see, Paul A. Papayoanou, *Power Ties: Interdependence, Balancing, and War* (Ann Arbor: University of Michigan Press, 1999); and Dale C. Copeland, "Economic Interdependence and War: A Theory of Trade Expectations," *International Security* 20, no. 4 (1996): 5-41.

16. For a good recent overview see, Ariel Cohen, ed., *Eurasia in Balance: The U.S. and the Regional Power Shift* (Aldershot, UK: Ashgate Publishing, 2005).

17. Vladimir Socor, "Cheek by Jowl in Kyrgyzstan," *Wall Street Journal*, 8 August 2003.

18. According to a 12 October 2001 U.S.-Uzbekistan joint statement, the two states would "consult on an urgent basis about appropriate steps to address the situation in the event of a direct threat to the security or territorial integrity of the Republic of Uzbekistan." "Joint Statement between the Government of the United States of America and the Government of the Republic of Uzbekistan," 12 October 2001, http://www.state.gov/r/pa/prs/ps/2001/5354.htm; Eric Schmitt and James Dao, "U.S. is Building Up Its Military Bases in Afghan Region," *New York Times*, 9 January 2001, A10. From an operational perspective, however, Karimov requested that aircraft based at Karshi Khanabad were to be used primarily for humanitarian and search-and-rescue purposes, not combat operations. Tamara Makarenko and Daphne Billouri, "Central Asian States to Pay the Price of US Strikes," *Jane's Intelligence Review*, 19 October 2001.

19. See "United States-Uzbekistan Declaration on the Strategic Partnership and Cooperation Framework," March 12, 2002, http://www.fas.org/terrorism/at/docs/2002/US-Uzbek_Declaration.htm.

20. Svante E. Cornell, "The United States and Central Asia: In the Steppes to Stay?" *Cambridge Review of International Affairs* 17, no. 2 (2004): 241.

21. Ariel Cohen, "Washington Grapples with Uzbekistan's Eviction Notice," *Eurasianet*,

16 August 2005.

22. Early into operations in Afghanistan, the Manas base was very much a multinational facility including French, Australian, Norwegian, Dutch, Italian, South Korean, and Danish forces. However, with the exception of a handful of Spanish transport crewmen, the force is entirely American. Alexander Cooley, "Depoliticizing Manas: The Domestic Consequences of the U.S. Military Presence in Kyrgyzstan," PONARS Policy Memo 362 (February 2005), 2; and Elizabeth Wishnick, *Strategic Consequences of the Iraq War: U.S. Security Interests in Central Asia Reassessed* (Carlisle, PA: Strategic Studies Institute, U.S. Army War College, May 2004), 3.

23. Exact figures are not available, but different informed observers estimate the impact of all base-related exchanges at $150,000 to $200,000 a day. This is broadly consistent with the figure of a net $40 million a year impact on the Kyrgyz economy reported by U.S. authorities, which amounts to about 5 percent of Kyrgyzstan's small real gross domestic product. Cooley, "Depoliticizing Manas," 2-3.

24. "Rumsfeld's Visit May Only Temporarily Relieve Pressure on U.S. Forces in Central Asia to Leave," *Eurasianet*, 28 July 2005.

25. "Tajikistan Will Cooperate with Military Strikes, but Fearful of the Consequences," *RFE/RL Central Asia Report*, 28 September 2001; and "Dushanbe Reverses its Stance on Military Strikes, Hosts CIS Meeting," *RFE/RL Central Asia Report*, 11 October 2001.

26. Eric A. Miller, "Morale of U.S. Trained Troops in Georgia is High, But U.S. Advisors Concerned About Sustainability," *Eurasianet*, 5 May 2003.

27. "United States Signs Agreement With Azerbaijan to Help Ex-Soviet Republic Strengthen Its Borders," Associated Press, 3 January 2004; and "Azerbaijan, U.S. Sign Agreement on WMD," *RFE/RL Newsline*, 6 January 2004.

28. Alman Mir Islmail, "A Base or Not a Base for Azerbaijan?" *Eurasianet*, 12 September 2005; Alman Talyshli, "Rumsfeld's Baku Trip Stirs Controversy," *Eurasianet*, 13 April 2005; and "Azerbaijan, U.S. Discuss Military Cooperation," *RFE/RL Newsline*, 24 November 2003.

29. "President Discussed Freedom and Democracy in Latvia," 7 May 2005, http://www.whitehouse.gov/news/releases/2005/05/20050507-8.html.

30. "President Address and Thanks Citizens in Tbilisi, Georgia," 10 May 2005, http://www.whitehouse.gov/news/releases/2005/05/20050510-2.html.

31. Edward L. Morse and James Richard, "The Battle for Energy Dominance," *Foreign Affairs* 81, no. 2 (2002): 16, 24-25. For an assessment of Russian export potential see, Fiona Hill and Florence Fee, "Fueling the Future: The Prospects for Russian Oil and Gas," *Demokratizatsiya* 10, no. 4 (2002): 462-87.

32. "Caspian Basin Leaders Hail Opening of Baku-Tbilisi-Ceyhan Pipeline," *Eurasianet*, 25 May 2005.

33. Ibid.

34. Steven R. David, "Explaining Third World Alignment," *World Politics* 43, no. 2 (1991): 233-57; and idem, *Choosing Sides: Alignment and Realignment in the Third World* (Baltimore: Johns Hopkins University Press, 1991).

Chapter 2

Threats, Dependence, and
Alignment Patterns

This chapter serves several purposes. First, it sets out existing alignment explanations and shows why they are inadequate for understanding the alignment choices of CIS states, followed by a discussion of the contributions of this book. Next I lay out the logic of the internal threat/economic dependence (IT/ED) framework at great length, demonstrating how the framework differs from traditional alignment explanations. The reasons for choosing these particular independent variables are offered, paying special attention to the impact of the Soviet experience on CIS leaders and states and how it shaped the immediate political and economic environment leaders faced after independence. I also provide a rationale for why other alternative variables were not chosen. The methodology for this book is then put forth including indicators used to estimate the independent and dependent variables as well as testable hypotheses and the rationale underlying them. The justification for why Uzbekistan and Ukraine are chosen as principal case studies is also offered. The chapter concludes with some of the limitations of the proposed framework.

Alignment Theory

The study of alignments has long been defined by various realist explanations. Systemic explanations identify a state's relative position in the structure of the international system as the primary determinant of alignment outcomes. Balance of power theory highlights the distribution of capabilities as the most critical variable in determining alignment behavior. These theorists suggest that states tend to balance for two reasons. First, by aligning against the strongest power and potential hegemon, states ensure that no one state will dominate the system, which stabilizes the system and creates a new equilibrium or balance. The traditional British role of continental balancer is indicative of this strategy. As Winston Churchill explained joining the stronger side was at times both easy and tempting, however, "we always took the harder course, joined with the less strong Powers,. . .and thus defeated and frustrated the Continental military tyrant whoever he was. . .".[1] Based on this propensity to balance power, scholars in the post-Cold War applied this rationale to U.S. grand strategy. For instance, Christopher Layne championed the neorealist cause, arguing that the post-Cold war unipolarity is an illusion that is destined to fade within a few decades as other great powers rise up to balance Washington's preeminent position.[2]

Second, by joining the weaker and more vulnerable side, states increase their relative influence in the weaker coalition. As Kenneth Waltz theorizes, "secondary states, if they are free to choose, flock to the weaker side; for it is the stronger side that threatens them. On the weaker side, they are both more appreciated and safer, provided, of course, that the coalition they join achieves enough defensive or deterrent strength to dissuade adversaries from attacking."[3] For example, by joining forces at the turn of the eighteenth century with England, the United Provinces, and the major German states, Austria illustrates this motivation leading up to the War of Spanish Succession. Austria was more appreciated because the successful repulsion of Turkish forces on their Balkan flank allowed for a more active role in the anti-French coalition; and they were safer given the accession of Louis' grandson, Philip V, to the Spanish throne in 1700, greatly increasing the potency of the Bourbon bloc.[4]

This rationale is prefaced on a strong belief in the anarchic structure of the international system. States are seen as the primary actors in world affairs, and they interact in a system that lacks an effective government above states, an international policing force, and a widely accepted body of international law. Thus, states find themselves locked into a perpetual structure from which, much like Jean Paul Sartre's conception of hell, there is "no exit." As a consequence of this socialization to anarchy, states seek self-preservation and pursue security to ensure their survival.[5]

In a refinement of balance of power theory, Stephen Walt argues that states ally to balance against threats rather than against power alone.[6] Walt sees the level of external threat as a function of four factors including: the distribution of capabilities, geographic proximity, offensive capabilities, and perceived aggressive intentions. Thus, a state might not necessarily balance against the most powerful state, but consider through these factors which state poses the greatest threat and balance accordingly. Nonetheless, Waltz and Walt are in agreement that the dominant behavior of states is to balance, although they disagree as to the reason why balancing would occur (power vs. threat).

Under some circumstances, states may find that the distribution of capabilities favors an alignment with the stronger power. Bandwagoning theory suggests that states may join the stronger side in order to avoid immediate attack and divert it elsewhere or in hopes of sharing in the spoils of victory with the stronger side.[7] The Nazi-Soviet Pact of 1939 illustrates the dual usage of the term. Through his alliance with Adolf Hitler, Joseph Stalin was able to divert any immediate attack on the Soviet Union.[8] The domestic turmoil caused by industrialization, forced collectivization, and the Stalinist purges of the 1930s left the Soviet Union unprepared for combat with Nazi Germany. Time was needed to mobilize the Soviet economy for war production and strengthen the depleted officer corps of the Red Army. Simultaneously, Stalin, through his appeasement of Hitler, was granted a buffer zone between the Soviet Union and the Third Reich. The dismemberment of Poland provided breathing space for Stalin and allowed Hitler to expand his position with relative ease.

In considering weak states that are often fragile, Waltz and Walt both conclude that bandwagoning is the most likely occurrence. As Waltz writes, "the power of the strong may deter the weak from asserting their claims, not because the weak recognize a kind of rightfulness of rule on the part of the strong, but simply because it is not sensible to tangle with them."[9] For his part, Walt reasons that because weak states offer little to a rival coalition and have limited affect on the outcome of a war they are forced to bandwagon.[10] Therefore, it is rational for weak states to balance power only when their capabilities can affect the outcome.[11]

In building upon Walt's argument, Steven David argues states are more concerned with threats than power alone, but he argues that the most pressing threats are domestic rather than external.[12] David acknowledges that in an anarchic international system external security threats to state survival cannot be dismissed, but it is the interaction between the distribution of systemic and domestic threats that determines a state's alignment behavior.[13] Ultimately, the most powerful determinant of alignments in the Third World is the "rational calculation of Third World leaders as to which outside power is most likely to do whatever necessary to keep them in power."[14] When the most pressing threat is internal (e.g., coup, revolution, insurgency),[15] leaders will seek an external alignment that will assist in eliminating domestic threats, even if a state must align with another state it considers an external, although secondary, security threat. As David writes, leaders may even "protect themselves at the expense of promoting the long-term security of the state and the general welfare of its inhabitants."[16] This behavior of aligning with the strongest, yet secondary, threat would be identified as a superficial form of bandwagoning by balance of power and balance of threat theories.[17] A bandwagoning explanation, however, would mischaracterize the true motivations behind an alignment, which would be to balance a leader's more pressing internal threats.

David qualifies his argument and acknowledges that his theory of omnibalancing was rooted in the distinctive character of Third World states and prefaced on two conditions: 1) that leaders are weak and illegitimate, and 2) that the stakes for domestic politics are very high.[18] This article accepts these established conditions as to when internal threats may exist (and subsequently when they are most illustrative in explaining alignment calculations). That is, in countries where political legitimacy is weak and power is concentrated in a strong state apparatus, there is a greater likelihood that internal threats to leaders may exist.[19] After the Soviet collapse, these dynamics were prevalent throughout the CIS, which provides an opportunity to test these causal relationships.

David's work highlights domestic factors that traditional alignment explanations fail to identify. First, David recognizes that a great deal of conflict occurs within states as well as between them. In many regions of the world, this form of conflict is more common than the invasion of a foreign army.[20] Leaders must react to the immediate security environment in which they exist, and they often prioritize domestic considerations in their alignment calculations. Systemic explanations like balance of power theory do not capture such calculations because of their focus on factors largely external to the state, predominantly the distribution of international power.

Second, David correctly asserts that in many countries political legitimacy does not exist. Fareed Zakaria coined the phrase "illiberal democracies" to describe countries in which "democratically elected regimes, often ones that have been reelected or reaffirmed through referenda, routinely [ignore] constitutional limits on their power depriving their citizens of basic rights and freedoms."[21] Pluralist and institutional arguments assume that political competition takes place in an accepted policy arena.[22] That is, actors and groups influence the policy process in a routine, peaceful, and bureaucratized manner. This political process enables the state's decisions to be seen as legitimate. Yet, pluralist and institutional approaches (many of which are rooted in the study of foreign economic policy) fail to capture the intensity of internal threats to leaders common in states where leaders possess questionable political legitimacy.

Richard Harknett and Jeffrey VanDenBerg refined David's theory of omnibalancing. Whereas David stressed that leaders balanced their most pressing threats (which tended to be domestic in origin), they suggested that interrelated threats require leaders to keep an eye on external *and* internal forces, and that balancing and bandwagoning are the basic responses to these threats.[23] Thus, leaders do not always balance their internal threats and may bandwagon with them. As we will see, CIS leaders in quasi-democratic systems, where some open political process existed, relied more on the bandwagoning technique to ensure their political survival. They forged political alliances with important and powerful constituents to secure political support. This coopted approach tended to prevent or limit the more intense internal political challengers from emerging. In contrast, authoritarian leaders intimidated and repressed domestic opponents. These leaders preferred to balance and often eliminate their internal threats, as opposed to bandwagoning with them.

In sum, various scholars provide insight into why states choose particular alignment patterns and what factors influence those decisions. Balance of power theory focuses on the distribution of power within the international system, while balance of threat theory includes systemic and domestic level variables, namely the perceived aggressiveness of another state's intentions. These theories seek to abstract away from a range of variables to offer parsimony, but the parsimony itself creates problems of explanation, especially in countries, such as those of the CIS. Indeed, David challenged these theories in the context of alignment patterns in the Third World, arguing that internal threats to leaders tend to exert a stronger influence on a leader's alignment choices. The framework outlined below, which builds on David's work, is parsimonious and offers greater explanatory value for CIS alignment patterns vis-à-vis Russia.

Contributions to the Literature

This book makes an original contribution to the study of the international relations (IR) of the CIS in four key ways. First, it addresses theoretical questions central to the IR and security studies literature. Why do states align? What types of threats (external or internal) are most influential in alignment calculations? Traditional alignment theories, such as balance of power and balance of threats theories, focus primarily on the distribution of power in the internal system or the level of perceived aggression from other states. Yet, the present framework holds prospects for refining traditional alignment theories in its incorporation of domestic political and economic variables. That is, traditional approaches privilege factors exogenous to the state, whereas the present framework bridges the artificial divide between domestic and international politics. In so doing it provides a more compelling explanation of the dynamics underlying alignments within the CIS. Indeed, IR theorists tend to give priority to either international or domestic level factors, although, not surprisingly, both are likely to influence a particular decision.[24]

Moreover, this book addresses the concerns of other IR theorists, who encourage richer theoretical understandings about international relations.[25] This falls in line with Fareed Zakaria's plea for scholars to "develop a tolerance for more limited – but also more accurate – generalizations," by developing theories of international affairs that draw on both internal and external factors to explain state behavior.[26] What is lost in theoretical parsimony is more than made up for in the empirical explanatory capability.

Second, the present work develops a framework that incorporates key political *and* economic factors and their impact on foreign alignments. The work of Paul Papayoanou on economic interdependence and the balance of power is an excellent example of this approach. Papayoanou's findings reveal that firm balancing policies conducive to peace in the international system are most likely when there are extensive economic ties among status quo powers and few or no such links between them and perceived threatening powers. When economic interdependence is not significant between status quo powers or if status quo powers have strong economic links with threatening powers, weaker balancing postures and conciliatory policies by status quo powers, and aggression by aspiring revisionist powers, are more likely.[27]

Within IR theory, however, theorists tend to privilege one set of issues over the other. Realist theorists tend to focus on security and military issues, while liberal scholars focus more on economic issues. Even scholars that appreciate the connection between the two fields often focus on how economic and security matters determine, respectively, security or economic outcomes.[28] Furthermore, our understanding of the nexus between security studies and international political economy remains underdeveloped.[29] With the wider notions of security after the Cold War, this research path has not gone unnoticed, but more work is needed to increase our overall appreciation for how both political and economic factors shape international politics and, more specifically, the international politics within the CIS.

Third, this book fills a gap in the literature on the foreign relations between Russia and its former Soviet republics. Some scholars have focused on the importance and pervasiveness of nationalism and national identity in shaping a country's foreign and economic policies towards Russia.[30] Daniel Drezner analyzed Russian economic coercion against other former Soviet republics, arguing that states that expected conflict with Russia (what he calls a "conflict expectations hypothesis") influenced the ability of Russia to use other states' economic dependence to coerce their leaders.[31] Similar to the framework developed here, other scholars have examined various domestic political factors that influence a country's foreign policy towards Russia, such as leadership survival, social mobilization, and political institutionalization.[32] Other early studies theorized about the prospects for imperial revival and provided conceptual treatments of how these relations may unfold.[33]

However, no study to date has applied balance of power theory, balance of threat theory, or omnibalancing specifically against the empirical behavior of CIS states.[34] No study has differentiated beyond different types of internal threats that leaders face, and the varying ways in which they influence alignment patterns within the CIS.[35] Finally, no study has conceptualized or tested the framework offered in this book that integrates the impact of internal threats and economic dependence on Russia on alignment choices of the post-Soviet states.

Fourth, there is an increasingly important body of literature that addresses the more complex security environment of the former Soviet space.[36] This literature focuses on the non-military security threats that post-Soviet states face. These real security considerations include, among other things, domestic threats such as dislocations within and among states brought on by economic change, civil strife driven by nationalist sentiment and disputed borders, and the erosion of the stability and political legitimacy of states by the drug trade, organized crime, and pervasive corruption. This book builds on the above scholarship and attempts to bridge the concerns of both. That is, it seeks a causal explanation for why CIS states adopt particular alignment patterns towards Russia by focusing on domestic political and economic variables *and* it assesses the foreign policy implications of non-state centric security threats. The next section outlines the importance of internal threats and economic dependence in the minds of CIS leaders, and explains their roots stemming from the Soviet experience.

The Importance of Internal Threats and Economic Dependence

This section briefly explains why these variables – internal threats and economic dependence on Russia – are particularly relevant for the study of the CIS and why they are highlighted in this book. The reasons stem from the previous Soviet experience. First, by the way in which the Communist Party maintained and upheld the political system, and second, by the way in which party leaders in Moscow made economic decisions that influenced the allocation of resources, bringing about the narrow specialization of Soviet republics. A final explanation is offered as to why other variables were not chosen.

FSU Leaders and Political Survival

Politically, most post-Soviet leaders faced a precarious situation amid their newfound independence. The Communist Party had for many years legitimated (and guaranteed through force when necessary) their leadership, but with this formidable presence gone, the rules of the political game were unclear. CIS leaders were keenly aware that such an environment offered the opportunity for extended political survival, provided the right domestic strategies were chosen. Because of this propensity, and the difficulties associated with the post-Soviet transition, internal threats were powerful motives driving the alignment calculations of leaders.

As I argue, CIS leaders seek political survival as their primary goal, and are, therefore, mindful of domestic threats that can influence their careers and positions.[37] Political survival is a first-order goal, much in the same way that realists identify the survival of the state as a first-order goal.[38] The empirical record during the post-Soviet transition and initial steps towards democratization supports this assertion that most CIS leaders have been primarily concerned with ensuring their political positions.[39] Indeed, to help ensure this survival many CIS states developed strong executive branches, which legitimated and institutionalized the power of the respective leader.[40] Much of this tendency is rooted in the Soviet system in which most post-Soviet leaders were well versed and experienced.

Indeed, the focus on leaders and their political survival factors in the unique political system established and maintained by the Communist Party. This political system was based on formal recognition of power as well as informal bargaining practices that were necessary for the command economy to work. Formally, the Soviet system was based on various union-wide and republic-level ministries, organs, and agencies that were all part of an intricate and encompassing bureaucracy. Officially the Communist Party allocated resources to meet the needs of the larger Union. However, what began to emerge after Stalin's death was a bargaining system in which informal networks (often based on personal exchange) permeated the policy making process. What was important and necessary to succeed politically was having the right connections and patronage networks to ensure a person's bureaucratic position while facilitating advancement. The pervasiveness of informal networks, coupled with Moscow's ineffective oversight, contributed to the power of regional leaders and various bureaucratic administrators who were able to distribute positions and resources for their political benefit (based on traditional social loyalties and affiliations).[41] Sharaf Rashidov, the leader of the Uzbek Communist Party from 1959-83, is one of many examples. Upon his death in 1983, KGB officials conducted a full investigation of the regime. Among the many charges levied were widespread bribery, nepotism, large-scale embezzlement from inaccurate cotton output statistics, and general economic mismanagement. Ironically, in Uzbekistan today, Rashidov is remembered warmly not for his corrupt practices but for his deception of Moscow leaders.[42]

After the decentralization of Gorbachev's *perestroika*, this bargaining system gained even more momentum. As Maxim Boycko, Andrei Shleifer, and Robert Vishny point out, while the state formally owned property and assets, regional leaders, bureaucrats, managers, and other economic agents exercised *de facto* control over resources.[43] This enabled regional leaders to distribute resources in ways that would maximize their political tenure. By the Soviet collapse, regional leaders were well versed in these bureaucratic bargaining games, and those that lacked such political skill were more times than not left out of the new political systems, or out maneuvered by more cunning politicians. In this sense, the Communist legacy shaped the experiences of the initial ruling elites of the new post-Soviet states, many of whom were attached in some way to the party apparatus and were trained in such bureaucratic wrangling. Beyond these entrenched practices and concerns with political survival, there were also structures in place left over from the Soviet era, such as an extensive secret police force, which allowed leaders to further control their political opponents and clamp down on any source of discontent directed at the leadership.[44] This leads to a related point about the importance of focusing on leaders, and hence the political threats they faced.

From a theoretical perspective, there are other compelling reasons to adopt a "leader-centric" approach when examining the CIS. Traditional alignment theories assume states are unitary actors that act in rational ways based on national rather than individual interest. In this regard, realist theories tend to assume away the problem of anarchy at the state level while making it the central problem at the international level. But during the post-Soviet transition, political turmoil and change in CIS states were common, and assuming that these states act in rational and unitary fashions, as realist theories would suggest, poses an important challenge. Moreover, assuming CIS leaders were primarily motivated by the national interest or what was best for the state is misleading, because in the transition period they tended to prioritize their own self-interest and often sought to ensure their political positions at any cost. In the words of Philip Roeder, "post-Soviet politics is dominated by self-interested politicians who seek to maximize their control over the policy process."[45] Thus, many of the theoretical assumptions that realists make about the nation-state, sovereignty, and the consistency of foreign and domestic preferences offer especially poor guidance in the post-Soviet context, which warrants a closer analysis of CIS leaders.[46]

This effort coincides with another intellectual approach within IR to bring the leaders back into the analytical focus. Indeed, there has been a growing call by some political scientists to refocus our attention on leaders and domestic affairs as the centerpiece for understanding world affairs. The logic behind such an effort is understandable. As Bruce Bueno de Mesquita suggested:

> Leaders, not states, choose actions. Leaders and their subjects enjoy the fruits and suffer the ills that follow from their decisions. Alas, leaders seem to be motivated by

their own well-being and not by the welfare of the state. The state's immortality beyond their own is secondary to the quest of leaders for personal political survival....When we construct theories in which the state is the focal actor we miss all of the institutional and political incentives that shape the policies leaders choose. And yet it is those policies – decisions to align or not, decisions to build up armament or promote economic growth at home, and so forth – that determine whether the international system is balanced or not, bipolar or not, and on and on.[47]

This book addresses these larger concerns of political scientists and attempts to bring the leaders back into the theoretical and analytical fold.[48] In his study of regime change in the postcommunist world, Michael McFaul takes a similar actor-centric approach:

Inert, invisible structures do not make democracies or dictatorships. People do. Structural factors such as economic development, cultural influences, and historical institutional arrangements influence the formation of actors' preferences and power but ultimately these forces have causal significance only if translated into human action. Individuals and the decisions they make are especially important for explaining how divergent outcomes result from similar structural contexts.[49]

This book, therefore, sheds light on these larger concerns for the IR literature on leaders and foreign policy outcomes, especially those with a regional interest in the international and domestic politics of the CIS.

Soviet Legacies and Economic Dependence

Much like internal threats to leaders, the nature of economic dependence on Russia is critical for understanding alignment patterns in the CIS. This is true for myriad reasons, most of which are rooted in Soviet economic planning. First, because all economic decisions were made in Moscow and implemented in various republics, Russia became the hub of the Soviet economy.[50] Despite efforts by Gorbachev to restructure the economy in the late 1980s, Russia remained at the center of the economy. Independence did not necessarily alter these preexisting relationships either.

This pervasive economic dependence was particularly evident in the creation of the ruble zone. After independence many countries (with the exception of the Baltic states and Ukraine) sought to maintain their existing currency arrangement with Russia for fear of sparking rampant inflation and overall economic instability. The belief also existed that there was greater security in working with other CIS states because most firms lacked the comparative advantage to compete on world markets. But, in July 1993 Russia's plans to reform the monetary system placed pressure on CIS states, prompting Azerbaijan, Georgia, Moldova, and Turkmenistan to issue their own independent currencies. It was only after Russia clarified its terms for membership in the new ruble zone in November 1993 that the remaining states (Armenia, Belarus, Kazakhstan, Tajikistan, and Uzbekistan) decided to opt out of the new arrangement.[51] Among the more stringent conditions,

Russia insisted that ruble zone states deposit hard currency or gold worth 50 percent of the value of the ruble "loan" in the Central Bank of Russia, that member states could trade their old rubles for new rubles at a rate of approximately three to one, and that member states could not issue an independent currency for a period of five years. Clearly Russia felt it was in a strong bargaining position to insist on such conditions, given the existing dependence on the Russian monetary system, despite the fact that these countries eventually were forced from the zone. As Rawi Abdelal contends, "Russia had changed from a generous leader of post-Soviet monetary cooperation seeking to pay post-Soviet republics for their political acquiescence to a self-interested hegemon intent on either profiting from the ruble zone or destroying it."[52] Monetary relations between Russia and CIS states were thus illustrative of how some leaders dealt with their initial economic dependence on Russia while others sought to sever their ties with Russia altogether by pursuing alternative markets and trading partners.

Second, leaders in Moscow made decisions for the command economy that allowed some republics to enjoy full or near-full monopolies in the production of various goods For example, Uzbekistan specialized in cotton production, Latvia in electronics, and Azerbaijan in oil industry equipment. Communist leaders in Moscow made allocation decisions, in that each republic performed different economic functions, while every republic was integrated into the larger Soviet command economy. It mattered little if a republic had to import all of its energy needs or consumer goods, because the command economy would presumably allocate resources to fulfill these needs, although as we saw above, informal exchanges were as important (and sometimes more so) than formal exchanges between Moscow and regional leaders. This also meant that while some republics were well endowed with vast natural resources, they did not always have the facilities necessary to refine such goods, which relegated them to the producer of raw materials for production in Russia with little or no infrastructure to produce and finish goods independent of Russia. Hence, some states were left in better relative economic positions at the time of independence, and understanding the level of economic dependence a state has on Russia is helpful in defining the economic constraints CIS leaders faced. It is also important to note that while all the former Soviet republics were dependent on Russia to some degree, this did not imply that all states faced the same level of economic dependence, or that they were all dependent for the same items.

Third, this book focuses on energy dependence on Russia as a critical indicator in understanding the alignment preferences of CIS states. Accordingly, it is important to note that some republics within the Soviet system were energy exporters, while others were energy importers, or in other words there were the energy haves and have-nots.[53] This was not a problem during the Soviet period, but it did pose considerable problems for these countries if they sought to adopt independent policies from Russia. Countries such as Russia, Kazakhstan, Uzbekistan, Turkmenistan, and Azerbaijan were the principal sources of energy within the Soviet system, most of which was dominated by Russia and heavily subsidized. Other republics, thus, were left to import their energy needs from these countries, and Russia tended to dominate this trade after the Soviet collapse.

A related issue concerning energy resources and dependence has to do with the issue of pipelines. Without pipelines a country that is rich in oil and gas supplies is still unable to capitalize on this domestic resource because they cannot get the goods to the international market. This places countries, such as Kazakhstan, in extremely vulnerable positions, and they then have to work with Russia for the use of preexisting pipelines or else accept that their most important export commodity will remain in the country. Ukraine has at times also used this method of coercion against Russia, since a tremendous amount of Russian natural gas is transported across Ukrainian pipelines on its way to European markets.

Fourth, the severity of a country's economic dependence on Russia can also directly influence the level of internal threats to leaders. That is, when countries that are heavily dependent on Russia attempt to change or alter these relations, economic decline and collapse is always possible. When economic conditions begin to deteriorate rapidly, there is a greater likelihood that internal threats to leaders will emerge as a result of large-scale dissatisfaction with leaders. In the most severe case, economic crisis may even bring about a regime change.[54] For instance, Ukrainian leaders attempted to sever the countries economic dependence on Russia in the early 1990s, but they grossly underestimated both the extent of that dependence and their ability to find alternative trading partners, especially when it came to energy resources. As a result, Ukraine faced a dire energy crisis in 1993-94 that exacerbated the domestic political challenges to the incumbent leaders. In the end, that leader was removed from office later that year during presidential elections. For these reasons, economic dependence is seen as a critical and important variable in understanding the alignment strategies available to CIS leaders vis-à-vis Russia.

Alternative Variables Not Chosen

The IT/ED framework offers a bivariate analysis of alignment strategies vis-à-vis Russia, focusing on internal threats to leaders and economic dependence on Russia. These variables are chosen because they highlight the critical role that leaders play in the alignment decisions of their respective countries, but critics may suggest that other variables played a role in alignment calculations. While this is a fair observation, many of the most compelling alternative variables are either subsumed by the logic of the IT/ED framework or they are considered less explanatory. Other alternative variables include: 1) the presence of Russian minorities in a given country, 2) external pressures from the West, 3) leadership personalities, 4) the nature of a state's government (whether democratic or authoritarian), and 5) ideological similarities between leaders and/or countries. A final discussion is offered about the rationale for excluding Russia's policies towards CIS states in the IT/ED framework.

The presence of significant Russian minorities throughout the former Soviet Union is a legacy of the Soviet era.[55] To increase their influence throughout the former republics, Moscow encouraged and at times directed ethnic Russians to move to republics, especially to republican capitals, to strengthen the imperial grip on these regions and ensure Moscow's interests. The presence of minorities is widespread, but their distribution is not consistently felt. (See Table 2.1.) In countries like Kazakhstan (the most Russian of all republics) ethnic Russians made up almost half of the population at the time of independence, ranging to other republics such as Armenia, where ethnic Russians totaled only about 2 percent of the population.

Table 2.1 Russian Minorities in CIS States as of 1989 Census[56]
(as percentage of total population)

	Dominant Nationality	Russian
Armenia	94	2
Azerbaijan	83	6
Belarus	76	13
Georgia	70	6
Kazakhstan	40	38
Kyrgyzstan	52	22
Moldova	64	13
Tajikistan	62	8
Turkmenistan	72	10
Ukraine	73	22
Uzbekistan	71	8

From a theoretical point of view, it could be hypothesized that the greater the percentage of ethnic Russians living in a country, the more likely a pro-Russian alignment would be adopted. While this provides another descriptive variable, it is unnecessary to integrate this variable formally into the IT/ED framework. This is in large part because the issue of ethnic Russians living in a country is part of the domestic political games that leaders play and therefore is subsumed within the discussion of internal threats. For instance, in Kazakhstan the capital was moved from the southern part of the country predominated by ethnic Kazakhs to the northern part of the country, where ethnic Russians reside, presumably to shore up any irredentist claims that could be made by the Russian government. Clearly, if a leader adopts a very anti-Russian alignment in a country where there are significant ethnic Russians, this is likely to spark opposition to a leader and inherently increase a leader's internal threats. As we will see in the case of Ukraine, this was an important factor in the domestic and international political strategies of Ukrainian leaders, and influenced (and at times limited) Kyiv's ability to adopt a strong pro-Western orientation or a strong pro-Russian alignment. Accordingly, this variable is seen more as a subset under the internal threat variable and can be explained using that logic as opposed to a formalized introduction into the IT/ED framework.

The potential for external pressure from the West is similarly an explanation that is subsumed by the logic of the framework, and one that warrants qualification given the empirical realities of U.S. and Western policy. The idea that Western action influences alignments strategies is well founded and incorporated into the IT/ED framework. This is most evident in the discussion of economic dependence and how available Western economic resources are. As argued, the main factor influencing access to alternatives resources from the West is the implementation of reform. When countries did this, then Western aid was likely to follow. When comprehensive reform continued over the years, this was the most compelling manner to reorient a country's economy away from Russia, such as in the case of Eastern Europe and the Baltic states.

Moreover, positive inducements were the most common form of Western statecraft towards the CIS, as opposed to economic sanctions or other negative pressures.[57] The William J. Clinton administration sought to assist these countries in their political and economic transition as opposed to pressuring them into adopting various policy decisions.[58] As we will see in Chapter 6, the one exception to this pattern was found in the case of Ukrainian nuclear disarmament. The first George Bush administration placed a tremendous amount of attention on Ukrainian leaders to adhere to the Non Proliferation Treaty (NPT) and sign on to Strategic Arms Reductions Talks (START). However, at the same time the policy was not one of pure sanctions and pressure, and in fact positive inducements were very influential in the overall process of Ukrainian nuclear disarmament, along with agreements that addressed the real security concerns of Ukraine. In the end, positive inducements and not negative sanctions were the preferred method of statecraft the United States, especially under the Clinton administration, and other Western nations employed, and this consideration is integrated into the IT/ED framework.

The personalities of individual leaders may also be relevant at times to the alignment decisions of leaders.[59] For instance, in recent encounters between U.S. President George W. Bush and Russian President Vladimir Putin, Bush claimed to have seen into Putin's soul and therefore cooperation, whether on the war against terrorism or in the field of strategic offensive weapons reductions, is more credible and possible. Similarly, tensions between Putin and Georgian President Eduard Shevardnadze in the summer of 2002 concerning Chechen guerrillas in the Pankisi Gorge was driven by a general hatred and contempt for Shevardnadze. Russians see the former Soviet Foreign Minister, along with former Soviet Premier Gorbachev, as the principal architects of the Soviet demise and to blame for much of the countries problems.[60]

However, the analysis of personality does not warrant fuller explication beyond what the IT/ED framework offers. Leaders do matter, which is a central consideration of the present framework, but calculating for their actual personalities does not add much to the framework's explanatory capability, and instead it would raise other methodological issues that would hinder the parsimonious nature of the IT/ED framework. By design the IT/ED framework views leaders as self-interested actors that prioritize their security over the security of the country. To factor in different personality measures would lessen the ability to generalize across the CIS, and such an analysis would be driven by considerations of political psychology, an endeavor that goes well beyond the present discussion.

Many IR theorists have also placed emphasis on the nature of a government and its impact on foreign policy. The democratic peace thesis is perhaps the most often cited in this genre of research.[61] In short, democracies are less prone to fight other democracies, in contrast to dyads in which one country is democratic and the other non-democratic or both countries are non-democratic.

While the IT/ED framework does not tackle such questions head on, it does factor in the importance of regime type. First, the framework attempts to explain alignment decisions in countries that are either authoritarian or quasi-democratic. Second, from a theoretical standpoint, leaders in different types of regimes are expected to respond to internal threats differently. Authoritarian leaders are more likely to balance internal threats because of their willingness and ability to repress domestic political opposition. On the other hand, leaders in quasi-democratic states are more likely to bandwagon with the most powerful groups in the state because of their inability to crackdown openly on opposition. Thus, while some could point to regime type as a factor that influences alignment decisions, the IT/ED framework includes this consideration into its theoretical treatment of alignment calculations vis-à-vis Russia.

Ideological considerations could also be highlighted as important factors in bringing about stronger policies between a country and Russia. Yet, unlike the above alternative variables, this factor is largely discounted in the present work and not incorporated in any fashion into the IT/ED framework.

The most significant analytical problem is that CIS leaders did not consistently adhere to any preconceived ideology. In large part ideology became less relevant after the collapse of Soviet communism. As Francis Fukuyama suggested, the century ended with a triumph for liberal democracy over its communist and fascist rivals, signaling the "end of history," or at least the end of ideological clashes.[62] But, very few leaders in the CIS openly and sincerely embraced the precept of this ideology. It could be argued that the Baltic states have, and this would explain why their trajectory has been a linear one towards the West. The same cannot be said for other CIS countries, where leaders did what was best for them with little or no preconceived ideological underpinnings. Moreover, if a leader professed a particular ideology one day, this did not ensure that a few days later the same ideology would be upheld. All of this suggests that ideological factors played little role in explaining relations between CIS countries and Russia, and therefore the variable is not considered an important explanatory factor.

Finally, the IT/ED framework does not incorporate Russian interests and actions into the framework for two primary reasons. First, Russian policy as an explanatory factor is largely seen as a constant variable. While Russian policy did fluctuate over the past decade, Russia by in large sought to maintain (and at times extend) its influence in the CIS, both formally and informally. The region was treated by Western policy makers and seen by Russian policy makers as part of Russia's larger sphere of influence. U.S. policy generally took a back seat to Russian interests in these various regions, although in the wake of the terrorist attacks of 11 September the United States has dramatically increased its military presence in regions such as Central Asia and the Caucasus. In short, Russia is seen a country that wants to maintain its hegemonial status in its former empire, and therefore other countries in the region are likely to see this as neo-imperial in some respect. Because this was a constant since independence, it is less important analytically (although there was some limited change over those years as Russian cabinet officials were replaced).

Second, by design the framework is more interested in the forces that are driving policies in Russia's former periphery as opposed to what is driving policy from Moscow. Much attention in the early 1990s focused on Russia's role in the region depicting CIS states as relatively passive actors to the exclusion of the many domestic factors that drove policies towards Russia. The IT/ED framework is more interested with alignments vis-à-vis Russia, and examining the underlying motives for why leaders chose alignment towards Russia and not the other way around. In the next section the methodology of the IT/ED framework is outlined.

Internal Threat/Economic Dependence Framework

Internal political threats and economic dependence on Russia vary considerably across the CIS. When considered together, they provide a framework for understanding the dynamic nature of alignments within the CIS. These two variables are not exhaustive but illustrate the core logic of the present argument: CIS leaders prioritize domestic threats to their political positions and are constrained by their country's economic dependence on Russia.

The next three sections introduce the IT/ED framework as a general explanation of alignment outcomes. I begin with definitions of key terms and then provide testable hypotheses along with the rationale underlying each alignment strategy. Justification for the selection of the two cases (albeit with six different alignment periods) is then offered.

Alignment

An alliance with Russia, or a strong pro-Russian alignment, is estimated in a number of ways including: 1) whether the country signed onto the CIS Collective Security Treaty (CST), 2) whether the country allowed Russian bases on its soil, and 3) whether the country signed a bilateral security treaty with Russia. For purposes of definitional clarity, I focus on the more binding concept of an alliance with Russia, but alignment theorists, such as Walt and David, have also used the less binding term of alignment as their dependent variable. They define an alignment as a relationship between two or more states, which involves mutual expectations of some degree of policy coordination on security issues under certain conditions in the future.[63]

If a CIS state formed an alliance with Russia, as described above, this would clearly be an indicator of a much stronger security relationship, then if there was simply security cooperation on a given issue. Yet, focusing narrowly on the former to the exclusion of the latter would miss an important element of security relations between CIS states and Russia. Accordingly, I acknowledge increased levels of security cooperation with Russia as an indicator of a pro-Russian alignment, although this is not as strong of a relationship as the formation of a formal alliance with Russia. However, such security cooperation is particularly relevant for the present discussion when it focuses on or is the result of a leader's response to internal threats. Indicators of increased security cooperation may include more frequent high-level military meetings, joint training of personnel, and military hardware transfers. In the end, the rationale for CIS leaders to align with Russia stems from the belief that Moscow presumably would be willing to back these leaders (e.g., through direct military assistance to secure borders or crackdown on domestic opponents or through financial contributions to the political machines that sustain a leader's power base), notwithstanding the fact that in some instances Russia was the primary source of funding for those forces that threatened the leader in the first place.

Internal Threats

Internal threats to leaders are estimated in two ways. First, as David suggests, they constitute those actors that jeopardize the political position (and often the livelihood) of a leader, such as assassination attempts, coups, civil wars, and secessionist movements. These types of internal threats have been present throughout the CIS over the years, albeit to varying degrees. Faced with such domestic threats, leaders find it necessary to focus on these more pressing internal challenges in contrast to external threats to the state. This often leads leaders to align with states that would otherwise be seen as external security challenges (i.e., Russia in the context of the CIS), and as Karen Dawisha argued, that alignment may even involve ceding over portion's of a country's sovereignty.[64] For instance, the Emomali Rakhmonov government in Tajikistan turned to Russia for military assistance in an effort to protect the regime from being toppled during the country's five year civil war. In exchange for Russia's help in securing the Tajik-Afghan border, supporting the Rakhmonov government, and at times taking the lead on domestic military questions, Dushanbe readily joined the CST and welcomed Russian military forces into the country, which served ostensibly as CIS peacekeepers.[65] But, if we focus narrowly on David's conceptualization, then we would miss a variety of other types of domestic actors that also threatened (or were at least perceived to be a threat to) the political positions of CIS leaders. My usage of internal threats builds on his more narrow definition associated with threats to a leader's survival (and often life).

Accordingly, I broaden David's definition to include a "galvanizing" opposition leader or party as an internal threat to CIS leaders. The likelihood of such a galvanizing force emerging is greatest when the country faces an acute state crisis, potential collapse or when a leader's political legitimacy is in question. For instance, if a country faces economic collapse in part due to a leader's inability or unwillingness to enact and implement reform, address the country's basic economic needs, or perhaps because of outright corruption and graft, then the likelihood of such an opposition force emerging is greater. That is not to say that it has to emerge, but rather that the conditions facilitating such a rise are greatest when state collapse/failure is occurring or imminent or when a leader's political legitimacy is called into question.

The term galvanizing is both meaningful and intentional. Throughout the CIS, political parties exist, but the state apparatus frequently controls these parties, or at a minimum, their ability to challenge the government is largely curtailed, either through outright repression, the threat of repression, or by limiting the resources available to them (e.g., lack of a free press or media). But when a leader or party has the ability to galvanize an opposition movement against the leader, often in times when the country faces deep systemic problems or acute political/ economic crisis, such a force is likely to be seen as a threat to a leader's position. For CIS leaders, many of whom gained their political experience in the former Soviet apparatus, the concern is that a galvanizing opposition leader or party could serve as a potent threat is left unchecked.

Georgian President Shevardnadze's ouster from power in November 2003 is a case in point. Georgia had for several years faced a deep political and economic crisis, and increasingly the opposition movement focused on the Shevardnadze government as the root of the problem. Over the years opposition leaders and parties played an active role in Georgian politics and voiced their criticism of Shevardnadze through a relatively free mass media. This open political space strengthened the opposition's ability to mobilize its supporters, especially after the fraudulent November parliamentary election demonstrated the extent to which Shevardnadze would go to secure his political support and position, even if it meant rigging elections closely monitored by the international community. This political openness enabled a galvanizing opposition movement to emerge, which sparked the successful "revolution of roses" and led to Shevardnadze's political demise.[66] Ukraine's Orange Revolution in December 2004, discussed at greater length in subsequent chapters, took a similar trajectory as the Georgian experience, where a fraudulent election served as a catalyst for the rise of a galvanizing opposition movement to challenge the legitimacy of the dubiously-elected president. But, as was seen in Kyrgyzstan's Tulip Revolution in March 2005, there is not always a tremendous amount of planning and protesting that may occur. What happened there was a much more spontaneous and reactionary change of regime that surprised many in how quickly and how successfully it led to the ouster of the existing president.[67] Thus, for many leaders the preferred course is to limit domestic opposition altogether, or at the very least to ensure that no galvanizing opposition leader or party can emerge to challenge them.

If leaders are concerned with a rising domestic challenge, then we might anticipate them to take a variety of actions. For instance, they might rig elections, jail opposition leaders, crack down on opposition media outlets, etc. In contrast to the first type of internal threat described by David, when facing these kinds of threats, leaders may have the resources available to them domestically to balance such opposition forces, especially given the extensive networks of secret police that post-Soviet republics inherited after the Soviet collapse.[68] However, heavy-handed tactics are also likely to isolate them politically from the West, which placed a higher value on political freedom and reform after independence than Russia. In this regard, CIS leaders may have a personal need to feel welcome as state leaders internationally, and when they are denied this in the West, they may turn to Russia for such recognition. They may also require financial assistance from Russia to support their personal political networks, without which their ability to maintain the loyalty of influential elites within the country may diminish.

Economic Dependence on Russia

Economic dependence is defined as a condition of significant asymmetry in which two conditions emerge: 1) country B has valuable resources that A lacks and 2) country A has few if any alternate or substitute relationships to which to turn.[69] This differs from asymmetrical interdependence, which is a relationship in which country A needs country B more than B needs A. Economic dependence suggests that a major imbalance of need exists between two states, which tends to leave the dependent country in a vulnerable situation.[70]

Economic dependence on Russia is estimated using three indicators. These include: 1) an examination of a state's exports and imports with Russia as a percentage of its total trade, 2) the availability of energy supplies, and 3) a country's access to alternative (or substitute) economic resources, predominantly from Western countries and institutions. The first two indicators are commonly used in the statistical study of economic interdependence.[71] Tables 2.2 and 2.3 offer data to demonstrate how these measures varied throughout the CIS.

The third indicator is also important, since dependence is a function of a country's ability to find substitutes or alternatives to a dependent relationship. If alternatives can be found in the West, then countries are less vulnerable in their economic relationship with Russia. Assistance can be either in the form of bilateral transfers from individual countries or multilateral, channeled through such financial institutions as the International Monetary Fund (IMF), the World Bank, and the European Bank for Reconstruction and Development.

The main factor influencing the third indicator (access to Western alternatives) was the willingness of leaders to implement economic reform.[72] Economic reform was not the only manner by which resources could be acquired, but the present effort is to highlight its implications for the accumulation of Western economic resources.[73]

Table 2.2 Structure of Trade with Russia[74]
(*as percentage of total trade*)

| | Exports | | Imports | |
	1994	1998	1994	1998
Armenia	35	18	28	21
Azerbaijan	22	17	15	18
Belarus	47	65	63	55
Georgia	33	17	8	9
Kazakhstan	43	30	36	39
Kyrgyzstan	17	16	22	24
Moldova	51	54	47	22
Tajikistan	9	8	11	14
Turkmenistan	5	5	14	13
Ukraine	40	23	54	48
Uzbekistan	39	14	36	13

Table 2.3 Energy Dependence on Russia, 1992[75]
(*as percentage of total consumption*)

	Oil	Gas
Armenia	*	0
Azerbaijan	14	0
Belarus	91	100
Georgia	82	27
Kazakhstan	0	0
Kyrgyzstan	*	0
Moldova	*	100
Tajikistan	*	0
Turkmenistan	16	0
Ukraine	89	56
Uzbekistan	55	0

*   These countries have no oil refineries and import refined oil products, primarily from Russia.

The implementation of economic reform is seen as influencing access to Western resources in a straightforward manner. The more radical the implementation of economic reform, the more likely a state will obtain Western economic assistance. The term radical here is most associated with the idea of "shock therapy," a term popularized by Harvard economist Jeffrey Sachs, where countries should not only embark on a comprehensive strategy of economic reform, but that it should be done in as swift a time frame as possible. The explicit purpose of this therapy was to tear down the institutional apparatus of the former regime, and pave the way for a new economic system.[76] The present framework does not make any prior assumptions about the effectiveness of shock therapy. Rather, the principal concern is to draw attention to the fact that if countries "enacted" *and* "implemented" economic reform, then Western economic resources were more available to leaders, which could help sever or mitigate a country's economic dependence on Russia.[77] It should also be noted that economic reform programs often altered the existing economic relationships between leaders and their powerful constituents, and thus if they were sustained the interests of a leader's power base could be threatened, which subsequently could increase the internal threats to a leader.[78]

Hypotheses: IT/ED and Alignment Outcomes

This section explores the logic of four distinct alignment strategies derived from the combination of the two independent variables, and the rationale underlying these particular outcomes. Because of the dynamism of the political and economic environment, CIS leaders tended to adopt a variety of alignment strategies based on variations of the independent variables. Thus, it is not uncommon for a leader to exhibit the logic of one alignment pattern, while adopting a different alignment pattern a short time later, and so on and so forth. The critical factor is how leaders dealt with political threats and economic dependence over time. The expected relationship of internal threats and economic dependence to alignment outcomes is summarized in Figure 2.1.

H1: *When internal threats are high and economic dependence is high, leaders are more likely to adopt a strong pro-Russian alignment.*

RATIONALE. Leaders that face internal threats and govern countries that are economically dependent on Russia generally have few alternatives and adopt strong pro-Russian alignments. Leaders choosing this strong pro-Russian alignment tend to face the most intense form of internal threats (e.g., assassination attempts, armed minorities and secessionist movements, and radical Islamic extremism). In some cases the drive for political survival can prompt a leader to cede over aspects of a country's sovereignty (to the detriment and subjugation of the state) in exchange for domestic support and political backing.[79]

Russia is the likely alignment option because few countries were available or willing to assist leaders in their attempt to maintain power. Russian assistance may come in a variety of ways such as direct military assistance to secure borders or crackdown on domestic opponents and financial contributions to the political machines that sustain a leader's power base. Leaders may also have a personal need to feel welcome as state leaders internationally, and when they are denied this in the West, they may turn to Russia for such recognition.

H2: *When internal threats are high and economic dependence is low, leaders are more likely to adopt a moderate pro-Russian alignment.*

RATIONALE. When leaders face internal threats, and are therefore concerned with their political survival, they tend to adopt moderate pro-Russian alignments, although because dependence is low the intensity of that alignment is not as strong as H1, but stronger than H3. This is because in the IT/ED framework, internal threats, which have a direct impact on a leader's political survival, have a much stronger impact of alignment decisions, whereas economic dependence merely constrains a leader's alignment options. A leader can adopt a more independent alignment (H4) if they successfully address their internal threats, either through their own actions or through Russian assistance.

H3: *When internal threats are low and economic dependence is high, leaders are more likely to adopt a weak pro-Russian alignment.*

RATIONALE. Leaders that are relatively secure in their political position, in that they do not face many internal threats, do not find strong pro-Russian alignments necessary. However, in this hypothesis leaders are still constrained by the high level of economic dependence on Russia, and they must continue to work with Russia, prompting a weak pro-Russian alignment.

The ability of a leader to address a country's economic dependence on Russia influences this alignment strategy over time. For instance, a country that was dependent at independence could develop its own domestic resources if available or it could implement reform and obtain Western economic resources. This may lessen the extent of dependence and enable a leader to adopt a more independent alignment (H4). The inverse can be true as well. A leader who faces little domestic political opposition may attempt to sever the country's economic dependence on Russia (H3), through radical reform, trade restructuring, or other domestic strategies. If these strategies are unsuccessful, they may backfire and provoke greater domestic political opposition, which would likely prompt a stronger pro-Russian alignment (H1), as leaders look to once again secure their political positions. Nonetheless in the H3 outcome, because leaders are politically secure, their alignment is constrained only by the country's dependence on Russia, and a greater degree of flexibility in terms of foreign policy choices is possible.

H4: *When internal threats are low and economic dependence is low, leaders are more likely to adopt a strong pro-independence alignment.*

RATIONALE. In this alignment strategy, leaders face few political threats and are able to address their economic dependence on Russia through domestic self-sufficiency or by finding substitutes to Russia. Because there is little need for Russian assistance, leaders tend to adopt more independent policies.

This alignment is not necessarily anti-Russian, but it is often perceived that way in Moscow. That is, by adopting policies independent of Russia, a leader may be seen as pursuing an anti-Russian alignment although this is not necessarily his intent. For example, economic cooperation between Georgia, Uzbekistan, Ukraine, Azerbaijan, and Moldova, the so-called GUUAM countries, is indicative of this pattern. These leaders have consistently and publicly stated that their cooperative efforts are not anti-Russian and are aimed only at increasing the economic interaction between the respective members. But, many Russia policy makers question this neutral status.

		Internal Political Threats	
		High	Low
Economic Dependence on Russia	High	Strong Pro-Russian (H1)	Weak Pro-Russian (H3)
	Low	Moderate Pro-Russian (H2)	Strong Pro-Independence (Anti-Russian) (H4)

Figure 2.1 Leader Alignment Strategies towards Russia

Case Study Selection

While there are eleven potential cases (the total number of non-Russian republics in the CIS), this book undertakes close examination of only two countries – Ukraine and Uzbekistan. These case studies should be seen as plausibility studies. If the framework accurately predicts alignment outcomes, then it would be plausible to study other CIS states at greater length to determine how successful the framework is in explaining their alignment strategies. If the findings are not robust against the empirical matter, then the framework either needs revising or is largely misplaced in its assumptions. Moreover, the present analysis requires reasonably detailed case study analysis and lends itself to an in-depth qualitative approach, and as we will see below, coding data for a quantitative assessment involves many methodological challenges.

Ukraine and Uzbekistan are appropriate case studies to explore for at least four reasons. One rationale for case study selection is that rival theories, in this case balance of power and balance of threat theories, have difficulty explaining alignment patterns and generate predictions that are inconsistent with empirical behavior. These states are prime examples of countries that should follow balance of power and balance of threat logic, as they are some of the largest CIS states in terms of military strength, geographical size, economic resources, and population, and are therefore some of the strongest countries based on a traditional assessment of their capabilities. As traditional alignment theories suggest, stronger states are more likely to balance against Russia to ensure their security than weaker states.[80]

However, this balancing behavior did not occur in any meaningful fashion. Ukraine went from a strong pro-independence alignment in the early 1990s (H4), to a weak pro-Russian alignment in the mid 1990s (H3), and then to a strong pro-Russian alignment beginning in 2000 (H1). On the other hand, Uzbekistan went from a strong pro-Russian alignment in the early 1990s (H1) to a strong pro-independent alignment in the mid 1990s (H4), and then to a more moderate Russian alignment by 2000 (H2). Thus, these two cases provide ample variation in the independent and dependent variables.[81] And while only two cases are chosen for detailed analysis, six alignment patterns are observed when the cases are divided into different time periods.

Second, these countries enhance the comparative dimension in that they possess different political systems. Ukraine is a quasi-democratic state that allows opposition parties to register and run for elected office, including the presidency. On the other hand, Uzbekistan is an authoritarian regime in which little if any domestic political opposition exists. By drawing on these different cases, the various ways in which leaders can address domestic opposition becomes clearer, which allows for more general discussion across the CIS. If only authoritarian cases were selected (or, alternatively, only quasi-democratic states), then the ability to generalize based on domestic political systems would be diminished.

Third, these cases allow for greater generalization across regions of the CIS. Indeed, much of the work on the international relations of the CIS remains at the regional or bilateral level, and therefore our understanding of broader patterns remains understudied.[82] Finally, as Arend Lijphart pointed out, case study selection can be made "because of an interest in the case rather than an interest in the formulation of general theory."[83] Besides Russia, Ukraine and Uzbekistan are arguably the most important countries in the CIS from a geopolitical perspective, and both are vital to the security and stability of Eurasia and central to U.S. policy concerns. For instance, Ukraine, one of the largest countries on the European continent, has been described as the "keystone in the arch" of Europe and the "lynchpin of European security" and today finds itself at the forefront of the eastern expansion of NATO.[84] Similarly, Uzbekistan is essential to the stability of Central Asia and became an important partner in the war against terrorism, and more specifically, in the U.S.-led military campaign in Afghanistan.[85] More recently, concerns over the rising Islamic extremist threat in the region, in general, and in the country, in particular, including bombings in March and July 2004, have brought greater attention to Uzbekistan and its importance to Eurasian security.[86]

Limitations of the IT/ED Framework

The application of the IT/ED framework in this book is not without limitations. The first limitation of the framework involves the problem of inferring a leader's intent from political statements. Leaders may use rhetoric or tailor public speeches and statements for the consumption of a variety of audiences, whether domestic, vis-à-vis Russia, or the international community at large. From an analytical point of view, therefore, one cannot assume that just because a leader makes a particular statement about a given subject it is necessarily an accurate depiction of what that leader truly believes. Moreover, CIS agreements are often symbolic in nature, and little tangible effort is expended to implement them. But it is in the symbolic nature that these agreements should be seen. That is, the willingness of a leader to align even if only symbolically, is still an important international statement of a country's foreign orientation.

While this methodological hurdle cannot be overcome completely, the use of public statements provides at the very least a starting point to infer about a leader's intent. Moreover, one indirect method can be used to assess intent from statements. That is, if a leader makes a public statement and then adopts a policy in line with the statement, then that leader's statement is seen as representative of intent. On the other hand, if a leader makes a particular statement, but then does not back it up with some type of policy decision, then the statement is seen less as a measure of true intent (unless there are mitigating factors that inhibit a leader from adopting a particular policy). For instance, if a leader makes anti-Russian statements, but then quietly signs cooperative agreements with Russia, the initial statement is less compelling than a leader that refuses to engage in cooperation. While this is not a perfect solution to the problem, it does lessen the difficulty associated with using public statements, especially since other first-hand accounts are impossible to obtain and the sensitivity of the topics discussed inhibit interviewing leaders.

The second limitation of this work lies in the rigor of the methodology. The IT/ED framework is not a purely quantitative or statistical assessment of the impact of internal threats and economic dependence on alignments with Russia. That is, data is not coded to provide a precise measure for internal threats to leaders or economic dependence that could then be plotted on a particular grid. Instead, the IT/ED framework uses some quantitative indicators to provide the researcher with a baseline to make a qualitative assessment of the extent of internal threats and economic dependence.

With respect to internal threats, coding data would not necessarily strengthen the overall argument because of the need to qualify and explain the data under certain circumstances. For example, a measure of the number of political parties in a country may or may not provide insight into the extent of political opposition a leader faces. We could hypothesize that more parties would mean more opposition, but this might fracture opposition and make a cohesive opposition less likely to emerge. This could be identified as hyper-pluralism and was seen in some CIS countries as parties sprouted up along vast, compartmentalized interests. In some cases electoral laws were adopted to promote party cohesion, for instance, by providing greater benefits to parties that received a certain percentage of the popular vote. More parties do not necessarily mean that there will be a stronger opposition. Moreover, in many authoritarian countries political parties were often government sponsored and did not really represent any opposition to the leader at all. They were used to provide a democratic façade to an otherwise undemocratic regime and largely rubber-stamped what the leader wanted to do.

The same could be said for political protest. A country may have several small protests that do little in terms of mobilizing opposition to a leader, but if they were quantified it might provide a different picture. However, a country may experience one or two significant protests that ultimately bring about the collapse of the system, but a quantified protest variable may not accurately reflect such a reality.[87] The recent example of regime change in Kyrgyzstan in 2005 and how quickly it occurred, in contrast to the larger and longer duration protests in Georgia in 2003 and Ukraine in 2004, is a case in point. Another consideration that would be difficult to control for in a more statistical assessment of political protest involves who is actually protesting. In some cases in the CIS, protesters were not out in the streets because of their open opposition to a given leader, but because they were paid by various officials that wanted to put on an illusion of protest, once again complicating a measure that may be taken out of context. In such instances, qualitative assessments provide a more accurate depiction of political opposition than quantitative measures.

Similarly, when discussing traditional internal threats outlined by David, such as assassination attempts, may provide some insight into the extent of internal threats facing a leader, but groups themselves may pose a challenge for quantification. In particular, the size of an anti-state group may not reveal itself because it has been forced underground, so it would be difficult to measure accurately the size of a group. Also, in the case of religious extremists or secessionist movements, a smaller number of individuals may be extremely effective, such as that seen in the 11 September terrorist attacks, in which sheer numbers may be misleading. The resolve of such groups would also pose a problem for quantification since the willingness of a group to continue the struggle to the last man or woman could never be measured accurately. The relatively small numbers of Chechen guerillas fighting against Russian forces demonstrate the important distinction between numbers and resolve. Indeed, the systematic cleansing of Chechen men had two direct impacts on the Chechen movement: 1) the resolve of those remaining men was only strengthened, and 2) women have become more active in the insurgency and in their willingness to serve as suicide bombers for terrorist attacks, many of which have struck Moscow directly.

Economic dependence on Russia is not as difficult to operationalize and therefore the indicators used to estimate the variable are more straightforward. The one difficulty associated with these indicators, however, is that reliable data is not always available, especially with respect to trade statistics generated by the countries themselves. Accordingly, two steps are taken to address this dilemma. First, original data is checked against other sources to see how well it correlates with Western figures; and second, the primary sources used in this study are from the IMF. Yet, these statistics themselves are estimates and are not put forth as definitive measures, but merely as accurate as Western assessments can be though crosschecking trade with other states.

It should also be noted that the two independent variables of the IT/ED framework can influence one another. This is mitigated in one aspect because the variables are cast at different levels of analysis. Internal threats focus on the individual level and address what factors leaders see as most threatening to their positions. Economic dependence on Russia, on the other hand, emphasizes the interaction between states. This is evident in the indicators used to estimate a country's dependence on Russia (e.g., trade, energy dependence, and access to Western economic resources). We would not speak of a leader being economically dependent on Russia; rather a leader may govern a country that is economically dependent. This contrasts with internal threats where the leader is the focal point of analysis.

That being said, the most likely scenario in which the variables influence one another is one in which economic dependence influences internal threats. A state that is economically dependent on Russia often faces few alternatives, and under such conditions, economic decline or collapse is possible, in which case internal pressures to leaders are more likely to occur. When countries face a dire economic situation, the populace and other domestic opponents, both mainstream and others seeking more radical regime change, may challenge the present leader blaming them or their policies for such turmoil, hence there is a rise in the level of internal threats to leaders. Economic dependence and subsequent economic pressure creates a reciprocal political pressure, forcing leaders either to crackdown on opposition or prompting them to adopt even stronger pro-Russian policies.

Similarly, if leaders adopt economic reform, but the measures fail to provide short-term benefits, then there is a greater likelihood that leaders will face additional internal threats seeking to remove them from office. These are the most plausible (and empirically consistent) instances in which the two independent variables influence one another. Thus, when dependence is severe and the economy declines rapidly or collapses altogether or when economic reform is unsuccessful in the short-term, there is a greater likelihood that internal threats to leaders will increase. Internal threats, however, do not influence economic dependence in any straightforward manner.

Finally, internal threats and economic dependence are not really dichotomous variables, in the sense that they are either high or low values. Instead, this should be seen more as a continuum that can fluctuate over time and as a result of leader's responses to these threats. The decision to discuss the variables in a dichotomous fashion is warranted because it provides the IT/ED framework with its four testable hypotheses.

In the end, the IT/ED framework does not provide a highly quantified rendering of its variables, but instead uses basic indicators to provide the researcher with some factors to allow for a qualitative assessment. This is both sensible and reasonable given the subject matter, and it still provides for a detailed and sophisticated account of these variables and their impact of alignment patterns vis-à-vis Russia. The framework therefore meets the challenge of being rigorous but not so rigorous that the method becomes the problem. The remainder of this book turns to a more explicit examination of the IT/ED framework against the empirical behavior of Uzbekistan and Ukraine.

Notes

1. Winston Churchill, *The Second World War*, vol. 1 (Boston: Houghton Mifflin, 1948), 208.
2. Layne, "The Unipolar Illusion." In addition, scholars have begun to put forth the concept of "soft balancing" in contrast to the more commonly used definition. These soft balancing measures do not directly challenge U.S. military preponderance but use international institutions, economic statecraft, and diplomatic arrangements to delay, frustrate, and undermine U.S. policies. For more this recent literature see, Robert A. Pape, "Soft Balancing against the United States," *International Security* 30, no. 1 (2005): 7-45; T.V. Paul, "Soft Balancing in the Age of Primacy," *International Security* 30, no. 1 (2005): 46-71; Stephen G. Brooks and William C. Wohlforth, "Hard Times for Soft Balancing," *International Security* 30, no. 1 (2005): 72-108; and Keir A. Lieber and Gerard Alexander, "Waiting for Balancing: Why the World is Not Pushing Back," *International Security* 30, no. 1 (2005): 109-39.
3. Waltz, *Theory of International Politics*, 127.
4. John B. Wolf, *The Emergence of the Great Powers, 1685-1715* (New York: Harper, 1951), chaps. 1-7; and Paul Kennedy, *The Rise and Fall of Great Powers: Economic Change and Military Conflict from 1500 to 2000* (New York: Random House, 1987), chap. 3.
5. Within the realist school, there is also an ongoing debate between offensive and defensive realists. Offensive realism predicts that states try to maximize their influence in the international system, especially when they feel that they have the power and capability to do so. Defensive realism predicts that when leaders feel threatened and insecure, they will tend to increase their security by pursuing ambitious military and diplomatic strategies. In short, offensive realism suggests that states are "power maximizers," whereas defensive realism argues that states are "security maximizers." For examples of offensive realism see, John J. Mearsheimer, *The Tragedy of Great Power Politics* (New York: W.W. Norton, 2003); Eric J. Labs, "Beyond Victory: Offensive Realism and the Expansion of War Aims," *Security Studies* 6, no. 4 (1997): 1-49; and Robert Gilpin, *War and Change in World Politics* (Cambridge: Cambridge University Press, 1981). Important examples of defensive realism include Steven Van Evera, *Causes of War*, Vol. 1, *The Structure of Power and the Roots of War* (Ithaca: Cornell University Press, 1999); Barry R. Posen, *The Sources of Military Doctrine: France, Britain, and Germany between the World Wars* (Ithaca: Cornell University Press, 1984); Jack Snyder, *Myths of Empire: Domestic Politics and International Ambition* (Ithaca: Cornell University Press, 1991); and Charles L. Glaser, "Realists as

Optimists: Cooperation as Self-Help," *International Security* 19, no. 3 (1994/95): 50-90.

6. Walt, *Origins of Alliances*, 5; and Walt, "Testing Theories of Alliance Formation: The Case of Southeast Asia," *International Organization* 42, no. 2 (1988): 277.

7. Bandwagoning has also been described as a form of appeasement or capitulation in Walt, *Origins of Alliances*, 19-21. Randall L. Schweller argues that states may "bandwagon for profit" in that they seek to reap the benefits of a revisionist state's aggression in "Bandwagoning for Profit: Bringing the Revisionist State Back In," *International Security* 19, no. 1 (1994): 72-107. See also Robert Jervis and Jack Snyder, ed., *Dominoes and Bandwagons: Strategic Beliefs and Great Power Competition in the Eurasian Rimland* (New York: Oxford University Press, 1991); and Arnold Wolfers, *Discord and Collaboration: Essays on International Politics* (Baltimore: Johns Hopkins University Press, 1962), 124.

8. Adam B. Ulam, *Expansion and Coexistance* (New York: Praeger, 1972), 276-77; and Isaac Deutscher, *Stalin: A Political Biography* (London: Pelican Books, 1966), 437-43.

9. Waltz, *Theory of International Politics*, 113.

10. Walt, *Origins of Alliances*, 29-31.

11. Robert L. Rothstein, *Alliances and Small Powers* (New York: Columbia University Press, 1968), 11.

12. David, *Choosing Sides*; and idem, "Explaining Third World Alignment."

13. For recent work that blends systemic theories with other domestic factors see, Richard J. Harknett and Jeffrey A. VanDenBerg, "Alignment Theory and Interrelated Threats: Jordan and the Persian Gulf Crisis," *Security Studies* 6, no. 3 (1997): 112-53; Jack S. Levy and Michael N. Barnett, "Alliance Formation, Domestic Political Economy, and Third World Security," *Jerusalem Journal of International Relations* 14, no. 4 (1992): 19-40; Michael N. Barnett and Jack S. Levy, "Domestic Sources of Alliances and Alignments: The Case of Egypt, 1962-1973," *International Organization* 45, no. 3 (1991): 369-95; Robert G. Kaufman, "To Balance or to Bandwagon? Alignment Decisions in 1930s Europe," *Security Studies* 1, no. 3 (1992): 417-47; and Laurie A. Brand, "Economics and Shifting Alliances: Jordan's Relations with Syria and Iraq, 1975-1981," *International Journal of Middle East Studies* 26, no. 3 (1994): 393-413.

14. David, *Choosing Sides*, 6.

15. Michael E. Brown provides a similar and more comprehensive definition of internal conflict that includes events such as violent power struggles involving civilian or military leaders; armed ethnic conflicts and secessionist campaigns; challenges by criminal organizations to state sovereignty; armed ideological struggles; and revolutions in *The International Dimensions of Internal Conflict*, ed. Michael E. Brown (Cambridge: MIT Press, 1996), 1.

16. David, *Choosing Sides*, 7.

17. David, "Explaining Third World Alignment," 236.

18. Richard Harknett and Jeffrey VanDenBerg identified three more specific conditions that contribute to internal threats including: competing national allegiances, a lack of political legitimacy for the leadership, and a state apparatus that possesses the predominant source of wealth in society. Harknett and VanDenBerg, "Alignment Theory and Interrelated Threats," 120-28.

19. Author's correspondence with Richard Harknett, 15 June 2001.

20. Ted Robert Gurr, *People Versus States: Minorities at Risk in the New Century* (Washington, D.C.: U.S. Institute of Peace Press, 2000), 43-44.

21. Fareed Zakaria, "The Rise of Illiberal Democracy," *Foreign Affairs* 76, no. 6 (1997): 22.
22. See, for example, David Skidmore and Valerie Hudson, ed., *The Limits of State Autonomy: Societal Groups and Foreign Policy Formulation* (Boulder, CO: Westview, 1993), 1-22; Peter Gourevitch, *Politics in Hard Times* (Ithaca: Cornell University Press, 1986); G. John Ikenberry, "The State and Strategies of International Adjustment," *World Politics* 39, no. 1 (1986): 53-77; and Peter Katzenstein, "International Relations and Domestic Structures," *International Organization* 30, no. 1 (1976): 1-45.
23. Harknett and VanDenBerg, "Alignment Theory and Interrelated Threats."
24. For a seminal study see, Robert D. Putnam, "Diplomacy and Domestic Politics: The Logic of Two-Level Games," *International Organization* 42, no. 3 (1988): 427-60.
25. Other studies attempt to create a link between domestic and international pressures and incentives in explaining state action in security matters. See Fareed Zakaria, *From Wealth to Power: The Unusual Origins of America's World Role* (Princeton: Princeton University Press, 1998); Bruce Bueno de Mesquita and David Lalman, *War and Reason: Domestic and International Imperatives* (New Haven: Yale University Press, 1992); Richard Rosecrance and Arthur A. Stein, ed., *The Domestic Bases of Grand Strategy* (Ithaca: Cornell University Press, 1993); Jack Snyder, *Myths of Empire: Domestic Politics and International Ambitions* (Ithaca: Cornell University Press, 1991); and Matthew Evangelista, "Issue-Area and Foreign Policy Revisited," *International Organization* 43, no. 1 (1989): 147-71. For a good literature review see, Gideon Rose, "Neoclassical Realism and Theories of Foreign Policy," *World Politics* 51, no. 1 (1998): 144-72.
26. Fareed Zakaria, "Realism and Domestic Politics: A Review Essay," *International Security* 17, no. 1 (1992): 179.
27. Paul A. Papayoanou, "Economic Interdependence and the Balance of Power," *International Studies Quarterly* 41, no. 1 (1997): 113-40.
28. Papayoanou, *Power Ties*, 160.
29. Jean-Marc F. Blanchard, Edward D. Mansfield, and Norrin M. Ripsman, ed., *Power and the Purse: Economic Statecraft, Interdependence, and National Security* (London: Frank Cass, 2000). For seminal studies see, Klaus Knorr and Frank N. Trager, ed., *Economic Issues and National Security* (Lawrence, KS: Regents Press of Kansas, 1977); and Klaus Eugen Knorr, *Power and Wealth: The Political Economy of International Power* (New York: Basic Books, 1973).
30. Henry E. Hale, "Statehood at Stake: Democratization, Secession, and the Collapse of the Union of Soviet Socialist Republics" (Ph.D. diss., Harvard University, 1998); Rawi Abdelal, *National Purpose in the World Economy: Post-Soviet States in Comparative Perspective* (Ithaca: Cornell University Press, 2001); and Andrei P. Tsygankov, *Pathways After Empire: National Identity and Foreign Economic Policy in the Post Soviet World* (Lanham: Rowman & Littlefield, 2002).
31. Drezner, *The Sanctions Paradox*.
32. Hale, "Islam, State-Building, and Uzbekistan Foreign Policy"; Menon and Spruyt, "Possibilities for Conflict and Conflict Resolution in Post-Soviet Central Asia"; and Roeder, "From Hierarchy to Hegemony."
33. For his part Spruyt suggested an eightfold taxonomy that speculated on possible policy outcomes within the former Soviet Union based on the insights of theories of imperialism and systems-level theories of integration. Dawisha forwarded her concept

of autocolonization or a process by which peripheral elites welcomed Russian power and were willing to accept a diminution of the state's sovereignty in exchange for enhanced security and material benefits. Spruyt, "The Prospects for Neo-Imperial and Nonimperial Outcomes in the Former Soviet Space," and Karen Dawisha, "Constructing and Deconstructing Empire in the Post-Soviet Space," in *The End of Empire?*

34. For a theoretically informed discussion of bilateralism and multilateralism in the FSU see, Paul J. D'Anieri, "International Cooperation Among Unequal Partners: The Emergence of Bilateralism in the Former Soviet Union," *International Politics* 34, no. 4 (1997): 417-48. For the application of these theories in different regional contexts see, Priess, "Balance-of-Threat Theory and the Genesis of the Gulf Cooperation Council: An Interpretive Case Study"; and Mastanduno, "Preserving the Unipolar Moment."

35. Some scholars have focused on leadership survival, but they do not draw an analytical distinction between various types of threats to leaders. Roeder, "From Hierarchy to Hegemony"; and Hale, "Statehood at Stake."

36. Menon, Fedorov, and Nodia, ed., *Russia, the Caucasus, and Central Asia*; and Roy Allison and Lena Jonson, ed., *Central Asian Security: The New International Context* (Washington, D.C.. Brookings Institution Press, 2001).

37. Other studies have made similar assumptions about leaders. Bruce Bueno De Mesquita and Randolph M. Siverson, "War and the Survival of Political Leaders: A Comparative Study of Regime Types and Political Accountability," *American Political Science Review* 89, no. 4 (1995): 841-55; and Randolph M. Siverson, ed., *Strategic Politicians, Institutions, and Foreign Policy* (Ann Arbor: University of Michigan Press, 1998).

38. As Colton pointed out, assuming preferences for post-Communist politicians is problematic and very complex. Assuming that leaders maximize power by attaining office is a necessary simplification that may not fit for all actors, but it seems a plausible assumption since there are fewer leaders than politicians and many leaders that were in power prior to the collapse of the Soviet Union remain there today. Timothy J. Colton, "Professional Engagement and Role Definition among Post-Soviet Deputies," in *Parliaments in Transition*, ed. T.F. Remington (Boulder, CO: Westview, 1994), 55-73.

39. See Philip G. Roeder, "Varieties of Post-Soviet Authoritarian Regimes," *Post-Soviet Affairs* 10, no. 1 (1994): 61-101; and Michael McFaul, "The Fourth Wave of Democracy and Dictatorship: Noncooperative Transitions in the Postcommunist World," *World Politics* 54, no. 2 (2002): 212-44.

40. As Timothy Frye concluded from his work on post-Communist presidents, political institutions can be analyzed as the by-products of power-seeking politicians making choices under varying degrees of uncertainty. Despite the great uncertainty of the transition, actors understood their interests and strategies, which prompted them to hedge their bets when designing political institutions. Frye, "A Politics of Institutional Choice: Post-Communist Presidencies," *Comparative Political Studies* 30, no. 5 (1997): 523-52.

41. Alena V. Ledeneva, *Russia's Economy of Favours: Blat, Networking, and Informal Exchange* (New York: Cambridge University Press, 1998).

42. Dilip Hiro, *Between Marx and Muhammad: The Changing Face of Central Asia* (London: Harper Collins, Publishers, 1996), 161.

43. Maxim Boycko, Andrei Shleifer, and Robert Vishny, *Privatizing Russia* (Cambridge:

MIT Press, 1995), chaps. 2-3.

44. For a good overview see, Amy Knight, *Spies without Cloaks: The KGB's Successors* (Princeton: Princeton University Press, 1996), 181-90.

45. Roeder, "Varieties of Post-Soviet Authoritarian Regimes," 61.

46. For a good discussion of "weak" states that share similar characteristics see, Robert H. Jackson and Carl G. Rosberg, "Why Africa's Weak States Persist: The Empirical and Juridical in Statehood," *World Politics* 35 (October 1982): 1-24; and Robert H. Jackson, *Quasi-States: Sovereignty, International Relations, and the Third World* (Cambridge: Cambridge University Press, 1990).

47. Bruce Bueno de Mesquita, "Domestic Politics and International Relations," *International Studies Quarterly* 46, no. 1 (2002): 4, 8.

48. For a theoretical discussion of the impact of individuals on international relations and the conditions in which they are most likely to be influential see, Daniel L. Byman and Kenneth M. Pollack, "Let Us Now Praise Great Men: Bringing the Statesman Back In," *International Security* 25, no. 4 (2001): 107-46.

49. McFaul, "The Fourth Wave," 214.

50. For classic studies see, Paul Gregory and Robert Stuart, *Soviet and Post-Soviet Economic Structure and Performance*, 5th ed. (New York: Harper Collins, 1994); and Alev Nove, *The Soviet Economic System* (Boston: Allen & Unwin, 1986).

51. Turkmenistan and Moldova officially left the ruble zone in November 1993. Tajikistan exited in May 1995.

52. Abdelal, *National Purpose in the World Economy*, 58.

53. For an excellent overview see, Robert E. Ebel, *Energy Choices in the Near Abroad: The Haves and Have-nots Face the Future* (Washington, D.C.: Center for Strategic and International Studies, 1997).

54. For a good overview of this literature see, Barbara Wejnert, ed., *Transition to Democracy in Eastern Europe and Russia: Impact on Politics, Economy, and Culture* (Westport, CT: Praeger, 2002); James F. Hollifield and Calvin Jillson, ed., *Pathways to Democracy: The Political Economy of Democratic Transitions* (New York: Routledge, 2000); Lisa Anderson, ed., *Transitions to Democracy* (New York: Columbia University Press, 1999); and Stephen Haggard and Robert Kaufman, *The Political Economy of Democratic Transitions* (Princeton; Princeton University Press, 1995).

55. Aurel Brown, "All Quiet on the Russian Front? Russia, Its Neighbors, and the Russian Diaspora," in *The New European Diasporas: National Minorities and Conflict in Eastern Europe*, ed. Michael Mandelbaum (New York: Council of Foreign Relations Press, 2000).

56. Soviet census data from 1989 cited in Ian Bremmer and Ray Taras, ed., *Nations and Politics in the Soviet Successor States* (Cambridge: Cambridge University Press, 1993), 550-60.

57. For a discussion of positive versus negative sanctions see, David A. Baldwin, *Economic Statecraft* (Princeton: Princeton University Press, 1985).

58. Stephen F. Cohen, *Failed Crusade: America and the Tragedy of Post-Communist Russia* (New York: W.W. Norton & Company, 2000); and Janine R. Wedel, *Collision and Collusion: The Strange Case of Western Aid to Eastern Europe, 1989-1998* (New York: St. Martin's Press, 1998).

59. Not surprisingly most scholarly attentions has focused on Russian leaders. See, for example, George W. Breslauer, *Gorbachev and Yeltsin as Leaders* (Cambridge: Cambridge University Press, 2002); and Archie Brown and Liliia Fedorovna

Shevtsova, *Gorbachev, Yeltsin, and Putin: Political Leadership in Russia's Transition* (Washington, D.C.: Carnegie Endowment for International Peace, 2001).

60. Vladimir Socor, "Putin's New Tune: I've Got Georgia on My Mind," *Wall Street Journal*, 14 August 2002, A12.

61. Michael E. Brown, Sean M. Lynn-Jones, and Steven E. Miller, ed., *Debating the Democratic Peace* (Cambridge: MIT Press, 1996).

62. Francis Fukuyama, "The End of History?" *The National Interest*, no. 16 (1989): 3-18.

63. For this definition of an alignment see, Walt, *Origins of Alliances*, 1; David, *Choosing Sides*, 29; and Barnett and Levy, "Domestic Sources of Alliances and Alignments," 370. For a sample of definitions of alignment and alliance in the literature see, Rothstein, *Alliances and Small Powers*, 46-64; George Modelski, "The Study of Alliances: A Review," in *Alliance in International Politics*, ed. Julien Friedman, Christopher Bladen, and Steven Rosen (Boston: Allyn and Bacon, 1970), 63-75; Robert A. Kann, "Alliances versus Ententes," *World Politics* 28, no. 4 (1976): 611-21; and Robert V. Dingman, "Theories of, and Approaches to, Alliance Politics," in *Diplomacy: New Approaches in Theory, History, and Policy*, ed. Paul Gordon Lauren (New York: Free Press, 1979).

64. Dawisha, "Constructing and Deconstructing Empire in the Post-Soviet Space."

65. For good overviews see, Barnett R. Rubin, "Tajikistan: From Soviet Republic to Russian-Uzbek Protectorate," in *Central Asia and the World*, ed. Michael Mandelbaum (New York: Council of Foreign Relations Press, 1994), 207-24; and Dov Lynch, *Russian Peacekeeping Strategies in the CIS: The Cases of Moldova, Georgia and Tajikistan* (New York: St. Martin's Press, 2000).

66. For more on these developments see Eric A. Miller, "Smelling the Roses: Eduard Shevardnadze's End and Georgia's Future," *Problems of Post-Communism* 51, no. 2 (2004): 12-21.

67. For a good overview of the revolutionary tide in the former Soviet Union see, Henry E. Hale, "Democracy and Revolution in the Postcommunist World: From Chasing Events to Building Theory," PONARS Working Paper no. 24 (April 2005).

68. For a good overview see, Knight, *Spies Without Cloaks*, 181-90.

69. This discussion is based largely on Robert O. Keohane and Joseph S. Nye, *Power and Interdependence*, 3rd ed. (New York: Longman, 2001). For other definitions of economic dependence see, Albert O. Hirschman, *National Power and the Structure of Foreign Trade* (Berkeley: University of California Press, 1969); David A. Baldwin, "Interdependence and Power: A Conceptual Analysis," *International Organization* 34, no. 4 (1980): 471-506; and James A. Caporaso, "Dependence, Dependency, and Power in the Global System: A Structural and Behavioral Analysis," *International Organization* 32, no. 1 (1978): 13-43.

70. For more on the distinction between sensitivity and vulnerability under conditions of interdependence see, Keohane and Nye, *Power and Interdependence*. Because this study focuses on economic dependence on Russia, it stresses the vulnerability aspects of interdependence over those related to sensitivity.

71. See, for example, Erik Gartzke, Quan Li, and Charles Boehmer, "Investing in the Peace: Economic Interdependence and International Conflict," *International Organization* 55, no. 2 (2001): 391-438; Rafael Reuveny, "Bilateral Import, Export, and Conflict/Cooperation Simultaneity," *International Studies Quarterly* 45, no. 1 (2001): 131-58; and Drezner, *The Sanctions Paradox*.

72. For an argument that stresses politics within the IMF see, Strom Cronan Thacker, "The

High Politics of IMF Lending," *World Politics* 52, no. 1 (1999): 38-75.

73. For a good statistical study that examines several factors related to donor and recipient conditions and the extension of foreign assistance see, Marijke Breuning and John T. Ishiyama, "Aiding the (Former) Enemy: Testing Explanations for Foreign Assistance to Eastern Europe and the FSU," *International Politics* 36, no. 3 (1999): 357-71.

74. These figures are drawn from International Monetary Fund, *Direction of Trade Statistics Yearbook* (Washington, D.C.: International Monetary Fund, 2000 and 2002).

75. Adapted from Karen Dawisha and Bruce Parrott, *Russia and the New States of Eurasia* (Cambridge: Cambridge University Press, 1994), 175.

76. Shock therapy was based on an equation involving macroeconomic stabilization, the initiation of more restrictive fiscal and monetary policies, the privatization of state properties and assets, and general price and trade liberalization. See David Lipton and Jeffrey Sachs, *Creating a Market Economy in Eastern Europe: The Case of Poland*, Brookings Papers on Economic Activity, no. 1 (Washington D.C.: Brookings Institution, 1990); David Lipton and Jeffrey Sachs, *Privatization in Eastern Europe: The Case of Poland*, Brookings Papers on Economic Activity, no. 2 (Washington, D.C.: Brookings Institution, 1990); Peter Murell, "What is Shock Therapy? What Did it Do in Poland and Russia?" *Post-Soviet Affairs* 9, no. 2 (1993): 111-40; and Bartlomiej Kaminiski, "Introduction," in *Economic Transition in Russia and the New States of Eurasia*, ed. Bartlomiej Kaminiski (Armonk, NY: M. E. Sharpe 1996), 8.

77. For more on the distinction between enacting and implementing reform see, Andrei Shleifer and Daniel Triesman, *Without a Map: Political Tactics and Economic Reform in Russia* (Cambridge: MIT Press, 2000).

78. Joel S. Hellman, "Winners Take All: The Politics of Partial Reform in Postcommunist Transitions," *World Politics* 50, no. 2 (January 1998): 203-34.

79. Dawisha, "Constructing and Deconstructing Empire in the Post-Soviet Space."

80. Waltz, *Theory of International Politics*, 113; Walt, *Origins of Alliances*, 29-31; and Rothstein, *Alliances and Small Powers*, 11.

81. Gary King, Robert O. Keohane, and Sidney Verba, *Designing Social Inquiry: Scientific Inference in Qualitative Research* (Princeton: Princeton University Press, 1994), 130; and Alexander L. George, "Case Studies and Theory Development: The Method of Structured, Focused Comparison," in *Diplomacy*, ed. Lauren.

82. See, for example, Hale, "Islam, State Building, and Uzbekistan Foreign Policy"; Menon and Spruyt, "Possibilities for Conflict and Conflict Resolution in Post-Soviet Central Asia"; D'Anieri, *Economic Interdependence in Ukrainian-Russian Relations*; Menon, Fedorov, and Nodia, ed., *Russia, the Caucasus, and Central Asia*; and Moroney, Kuzio, and Molchanov, ed., *Ukrainian Foreign and Security Policy*.

83. Arend Lijphart, "Comparative Politics and the Comparative Method," *American Political Science Review* 65, no. 3 (September 1971), 692.

84. Sherman Garnett, *Keystone in the Arch: Ukraine in the Emerging Security Environment in Central and Eastern Europe* (Washington: Carnegie Endowment for International Peace, 1997); and Edwin Mzoz and Oleksandr Pavliuk, "Ukraine: Europe's Lynchpin," *Foreign Affairs* 75, no. 3 (1996): 52–62.

85. For a sample of the literature that examines the centrality of Uzbekistan to the stability of Central Asia and Eurasia, see S. Frederick Starr, "Making Eurasia Stable," *Foreign Affairs* 75, no. 1 (1996): 80–92; Martha Brill Olcott, *Central Asia's New States: Independence, Foreign Policy, and Regional Security* (Washington: U.S. Institute of Peace Press, 1996); Hiro, *Between Marx and Muhammad*; Ahmed Rashid, *The*

Resurgence of Central Asia: Islam or Nationalism? (London: Zed Books, 1994); and Edward Allworth, *The Modern Uzbeks: From the Fourteenth Century to the Present* (Stanford: Hoover Institution Press, 1990).

86. For good overviews see Ilan Berman, "The New Battleground: Central Asia and the Caucasus," *Washington Quarterly* 28, no. 1 (2004-05): 59-69; Cornell, "The United States and Central Asia"; and Wishnick, *Strategic Consequences of the Iraq War.*

87. For more on the measurement of political protest in the region see, Mark R. Beissinger, *Nationalist Mobilization and the Collapse of the Soviet State* (Cambridge: Cambridge University Press, 2002).

Chapter 3

Uzbek-Russian Security Relations and Alignment Patterns

This chapter examines the security relations between Uzbekistan and Russia. This is important because before we can discuss the impact of the two independent variables of the IT/ED framework, we first must have an understanding of what it is that we are trying to explain, or more simply, what actually happened. It begins with a brief discussion of some of the factors that shaped Uzbekistan's initial alignment strategy in the wake of the Soviet Union's demise, and turns to a more explicit discussion of Uzbekistan's balancing options had it adhered to balance of power or balance of threat logic. Most likely, this would have involved strengthening security ties with either Turkey or Iran, with Russia representing the state that posed the greatest external security threat to Uzbekistan.

However, balance of power and balance of threat theories lead us astray in the discussion of Uzbek alignment patterns because they are state-centric. That is, according to traditional alignment theories, states are concerned with survival in an anarchic international system, and concerns with other more powerful or threatening states are seen as the primary determinants of alignment behavior. In this regard, realist theories tend to assume away the problem of anarchy at the state level while making it the central problem at the international level. By contrast the IT/ED framework, discussed at greater length in Chapters 4 and 5, offers a more compelling explanation of the key factors motivating Karimov's alignment towards Russia. The IT/ED framework helps us understand why Uzbekistan continued to engage in security cooperation with Russia, despite shifts in the distribution of capabilities; and it better identifies and conceptualizes the most pressing security threats in the region, which are not state-based but more transnational in character.

Two general alignment patterns are observed. These two periods span from the initial moment of independence until 1995 and from roughly 1995 until 2001. In the first phase Karimov saw aspects of security cooperation with Russia as an urgent necessity and therefore he adopted a pro-Russian alignment. This was evident in his attitudes and actions towards bilateral cooperation with Russia and his cooperation within the CIS framework. By the middle of the decade, the second phase took shape, and Karimov adopted a more independent alignment, evidenced by fiery rhetoric between Tashkent. Karimov has also been deft at shying away from more institutionalized cooperation with Russia (unlike Kazakhstan, Kyrgyzstan, and Tajikistan) in favor of a broader cooperative forum in the Shanghai Cooperation Organization (SCO), which includes China. This strategy served his pro-independence alignment well, and also enabled him to strengthen relations with the United States, coinciding with its fight against global terrorism in general and Afghanistan in particular.

Starting Points and Balancing Options

Karimov's initial pro-Russian alignment strategy was shaped by several factors related to the Soviet experience. First, the states of Central Asia never experienced true sovereignty because of Tsarist and later Soviet domination. The political map of Central Asia had long been divided into three major Khanates, each associated with an oasis and river agriculture: Kokand, Khiva, and Bukhara. But the golden days of the prosperous "Silk Road" had long since faded, as to did the mythic age of enlightened rule by benign despots. In its place, regional Emirs governed as unenlightened but all-powerful petty tyrants. Beginning in the mid nineteenth century, Russia expanded its empire into the region to ensure Russian interests vis-à-vis British interests from their colonial possessions in South Asia, and in the process it came into direct contact with these regional leaders and the vast groups of sedentary peoples, who called themselves "sarts" along the oasis valleys and nomads in hills and deserts.

This colonial relationship carried into the twentieth century and made the post-Soviet transition a difficult and obstacle-prone path. This was most evident in Central Asia's emergence to the international stage. Whereas some republics, such as the Baltic states and Ukraine, had enjoyed periods of independence during portions of the twentieth century, the Central Asian states were less ambitious about their new found independence. The nationalist element that drove much of Eastern Europe and the Baltics' drive for independence was less pronounced in Central Asia, in part, because of the presence of multiple ethnic groups within each state and as a result of the Soviet experience. As Gregory Gleason noted:

> In Central Asia, nations, and thus nationalism, did not exist. No working class existed. The political institutions that existed were subordinated to the Khanates rather than to institutions of a popularly-elected republic. The intellectuals drew most of their inspiration from Koranic teachings. The peasants tended to identify with a particular tribe, valley, or oasis rather than with some large national group....Over the years of Soviet power, because of party control, the artificiality of the borders, and the fact that most decisions, ultimately, rested on the shoulders of someone in Moscow rather than someone in the provinces, the inter-republican and inter-ethnic group borders in Central Asia had little significance.[1]

Furthermore, in the densely populated Ferghana Valley, significant ethnic minorities are found throughout regions of Uzbekistan, Kyrgyzstan, and Tajikistan. This multi-ethnic characteristic of Central Asian states is another legacy of Stalin's border demarcation policy, which served to divide and conquer the various nationalities and limit the development of pan-Turkic and pan-Islamic consciousness.[2]   From Moscow's perspective, homogeneous states could pose long-term security challenges, if nationalism grew as a dominant ideology.

Moreover, the historical ties between Uzbekistan and Russia, and for that matter the whole of Central Asia, were significantly different than relations with Eastern Europe and the Baltics, and this left these countries in an "independence limbo." As some scholars have suggested, the Central Asian states were actually "catapulted" into independence and in many ways were the recipients of an "unsolicited gift" of independence.[3] This was evident when Central Asian leaders supported Gorbachev's efforts to reform Soviet federalism, and when their populations voted overwhelmingly in favor (90 percent) of a continuation of the Soviet Union in a March 1991 referendum.[4] As we will see later in Chapter 5, this sentiment in favor of working with Russia was also a product of the economic advantages Moscow provided.

Second, the Central Asian states had only nascent independent military structures at the time of independence. Hence, without a developed and indigenously manned military, Karimov had to adopt a more pro-Russian alignment. Central Asian states faced the daunting task of reforming the armed forces to make them more representative of the various nationalities. Ethnic Russians especially at the higher levels and throughout the officer corps dominated their militaries. This Soviet legacy was readily apparent to post-Soviet leaders and warranted action.

Uzbekistan's experience with military reform is indicative of this challenge. In 1992 90 percent of the enlisted personnel were of Uzbek nationality, yet 70 percent of the officer corps were Russian speaking.[5] A variety of initiatives were designed to remedy this issue, such as Uzbek language for its officer corps and a gradual shift to making Uzbek the operational language.[6] Along with more active recruitment of ethnic Uzbeks, the military greatly reduced its reliance on non-indigenous officers. For instance, while ethnic Uzbeks made up only 6 percent of the officer corps, by 1996 the figure increased to over 80 percent.[7] In the end, Karimov's initiatives proved highly successful at strengthening the indigenous component of the Uzbek military.

Based on the logic of balance of power and balance of threat theories, this security environment would prompt Uzbekistan to align itself with states to balance the most dominant power and potentially the most threatening state in the region, Russia. The notion that Russia was the most significant security threat to Uzbekistan is also consistent with Walt's definition of threats. Despite its beleaguered military structures after the Soviet collapse, Russia still possessed the second largest nuclear stockpile in the world, and its military preeminence throughout its "near abroad" was unquestioned. While it does not share a border with Uzbekistan, Russia is still extremely close and its offensive capabilities remain impressive.

The fourth indicator for Walt's conception of threats, perceived aggressive intentions, can also be easily inferred from Russian behavior especially in the early 1990s. It was not uncommon for Yeltsin or other senior officials, let alone representatives in the Duma, to discuss the former Soviet borders as Russia's borders.[8] Karimov questioned the extent to which these types of sentiments were truly indicative of Russian policy. He challenged Yeltsin, for example, to state publicly whether the nationalistic ramblings of Vladimir Zhirinovsky were acceptable or unacceptable. As Karimov pointed out, "not once have I heard [Yeltsin] make such a statement. And this alarms me. Is Zhirinovsky perhaps voicing thoughts that certain statesmen are thinking? This is a very dangerous symptom."[9] Thus, based on traditional power assessments and Walt's definition of external security threats, Russia was the most powerful and threatening state, and the state Uzbekistan would most likely balance.

The need to find balancing partners against Russia was all the more pressing, since, as seen above, Uzbekistan lacked the necessary military capabilities to provide for its own security. Traditional balancing logic therefore would anticipate that Uzbekistan would align itself with other states to provide for its national security, presumably to balance Russia's preponderant power. However, few states had the ability or the willingness to engage Uzbekistan actively on more intensive security cooperation. The most likely candidates were Turkey and Iran.

With its similar heritage and language, Turkey was perhaps the most alluring actor for Uzbekistan. The historical connection between the two states led Uzbekistan, in the words of Karimov, to "regard Turkey as an elder brother."[10] Upon his first official visit to Ankara in December 1991, Karimov, the first Central Asian leader to visit Turkey, declared, "my country will go forward by the Turkish route. We have chosen this road and will not turn back."[11]

Yet, these words lacked substance from both sides. First, Turkey, lacking close geographic proximity, was not in a strong enough position to act as a security guarantor for Uzbekistan. Western expectations also overestimated the extent to which Turkey could "penetrate" the region. Considering that there had been a complete absence of interaction between Turkey and the Central Asian states until their independence, such expectations were largely born of ignorance about the region and Turkey's historical ties with the region. From the Central Asian perspective, there was also a sense that ties should be established with the West directly and not necessarily indirectly through Ankara, since the Turkish model was not always inspiring and tended to downplay the accomplishments of Central Asian republics under the Soviet Union.[12]

Second, cooperation between Uzbekistan and Turkey consisted primarily of economic and cultural exchanges, not security coordination.[13] Moreover, as the domestic situation became more unsettled in Turkey, the lack of Turkish resolve, especially in terms of direct economic assistance, attenuated the initial thrusts made by Ankara. Rising Islamic tendencies, ethnic and sectarian strife, and the ever-present Kurdish question occupied Turkish leaders. Indeed, as Philip Robins noted in 1993:

> Ankara may have a vision for the new republics, but it neither has a practical strategy for its realization nor the political will or diplomatic clout to implement it. Regardless of the rhetoric of Turkic brotherhood, in many respects the Central Asian republics are a mystery to the Turks of Turkey. This reflects the fact that until recently there have

been no contacts between the peoples or governments of Turkey and the Central Asian republics.[14]

In short, Turkey simply lacked the capabilities to serve as an effective balancing partner with Uzbekistan.

Iran could have served as a potential security guarantor, but these relations were also problematic. On his first diplomatic mission in November 1991, Iranian Foreign Minister Ali Akbar Velayati stressed that, while Iran respected the aspirations of Uzbek self-determination, his government would formulate its policy "within the framework of her relations with Moscow."[15] Long-enduring problems from the Iran-Iraq War left the Iranian economy in shambles, and much like Turkey, left little leeway for geopolitical gambles. Iranian caution was also prudent, since Iran was taking advantage of Russia's economic woes and its large reservoir of defense technology and scientific talent to accelerate its nuclear and ballistic missile capability. A strong Iranian alignment with Uzbekistan against Russia was the surest way to sever this coveted strategic trade. The end result is that Iran was primarily concerned with securing its strategic trade and maintaining cordial relations with Russia and was therefore a disinterested party when it came to balancing Russia.

From the Uzbek perspective, the desirability of an alignment with Iran was unsettling for other reasons. First, whereas most Uzbeks, and most Central Asians for that matter, are Turkic-speaking and followers of Sunni Islam, Iranians are Persian-speaking Shiites. This posed an internal problem for Karimov because significant Tajik minorities populated the major cities of Uzbekistan, and Tajiks are the only Persian-speakers in the region. Karimov also criticized Iran for their ideological backing of Tajikistan's Islamic democrats, which continued to fan the flame of instability in the early 1990s.[16] Thus, Iranian influence was seen as potentially detrimental to the delicate ethnic balance in Uzbekistan.

Second, political and military coordination was hampered because each state viewed cooperation differently. This divergence came to the fore when the Economic Cooperation Organization (ECO), an economic pact signed between Turkey, Iran, and Pakistan in 1964 and later expanded to include the Central Asian states began to take on a more political tone. Speaking to this growing politicization of ECO, Karimov asserted before an ECO summit:

> We cannot agree with the attempts by some countries and their leaders to foist upon us, the ECO Forum, their own vision of how to solve important international and political problems. Such a vision is absolutely unacceptable to us. In the future, if such declarations and such attempts to turn this forum into a political forum continue, I declare with total responsibility that Uzbekistan will leave the ECO.[17]

In the end, Karimov was unwilling to strengthen security cooperation with Iran.

Thus, in the initial days of independence Karimov bandwagoned with Russia because of the relative immaturity of the Uzbek military and the lack of alternative security partners willing to provide for Uzbek security. These considerations led Karimov to favor security cooperation with Russia within the CIS framework, especially during 1992 when the initial security alignment was established. As we will see later, Karimov fully understood the importance of cooperating with Russia in the short-term in order to buffer the country from the adverse consequences of the post-Soviet transition.

Uzbekistan (1991-1995): The Primacy of Stability

After the Slavic republics (Russia, Ukraine, and Belarus) dissolved the Soviet Union on 7 December 1991, Uzbekistan and the other Central Asian states joined the new CIS on 12 December 1991. The strongest provision of the new CIS agreement was the provision of equal co-founder status, which provided the former republics with *de jure* independence and sovereignty. As we will see in Chapter 5, Karimov consistently favored CIS economic integration over political and military integration.

In subsequent months, Karimov established a basic security alignment with Russia, one that would intensify in the upcoming year as civil unrest continued to destabilize Afghanistan and eventually Tajikistan. For instance, in April 1992, to ensure Uzbekistan's independence, Karimov pushed for a NATO-style CIS military in which "each state has its own army and at the same time participates in the pooling of efforts and the creation of a unified operational and strategic leadership with a unified command."[18] At the May 1992 CIS summit in Tashkent, Karimov signed the CST.[19] The Tashkent treaty stated that aggression towards one member would be interpreted as aggression towards all members and provided for a CIS peacekeeping force to be sent to areas of real or potential conflict. Thus, by the spring of 1992 the basic security arrangement between Uzbekistan and Russia was established.

Throughout the summer and fall of 1992, Karimov supported security coordination with Russia to enhance regional stability. At the eighth meeting of the CIS heads of state, held in Moscow on 6 July, Karimov was the first to initiate discussion on the idea of creating a collective peacekeeping force to serve in "hot spots" throughout the CIS, and as *Izvestiia* reported, "the discussion proved very emotional."[20] While the initial fruits of the idea resulted in the deployment of forces to Moldova, it did not take long for the Uzbek government to redirect Russian attention. Once the Oliy Majlis (Uzbek Supreme Assembly) ratified the treaty in early July, the Uzbek Foreign and Defense Ministries promptly called on Russia to provide more troops to aid in the defense of the Uzbek-Afghan border.[21] At the Tashkent meeting of the CIS foreign and defense ministries in late July, Karimov once again made an initiative to add security along the Commonwealth's southern border to the agenda.[22]

In early September Russia, Uzbekistan, Kazakhstan, and Kyrgyzstan convened to discuss possible solutions to the growing unrest in Tajikistan. On 3 September the group forwarded a warning to the Tajik government stressing how events in Tajikistan were endangering the security of the CIS. After the October 1992 summit, Uzbekistan and other Central Asian states sought to intensify the military dimension of the CIS by again calling on Russian forces to make up the core of a multilateral peacekeeping effort for Tajikistan. Beginning in November 1992, this led to a greater Russian military presence in the region (primarily by Russia's 201st Motorized Division).[23] Thus, as we will see in Chapter 4, the initial impetus for Karimov's pro-Russian alignment was the threat of religious extremism spreading into Uzbekistan and sparking greater instability.

Karimov's security cooperation with Russia focused on stabilizing the Tajik civil war, while he avoided closer CIS political and military cooperation. During the Tajik civil war, Uzbekistan and Russia played significant roles in the support of the regime of Emomali Rakhmonov. The intervention was so extensive that some referred to Tajikistan as a "Russian-Uzbek protectorate."[24] While Russia provided far more aid to Tajikistan over the years, Uzbek assistance was nevertheless indispensable and played out in a variety of ways. This aid included a cooperation treaty, which stipulated that Uzbekistan would defend Tajik airspace, the provision of weapons and military equipment (such as helicopters and armored equipment), and training for Tajikistan's internal troops.[25] Indeed, at times Uzbekistan directly controlled Tajik forces in areas of Tajikistan populated by ethnic Uzbeks, and on some occasions Karimov personally approved particular appointments to military and governmental posts in the Tajik government.

While Karimov cooperated with Russia in Tajikistan, he resisted other political and military integration with Russia that might undermine Uzbek autonomy and sovereignty. Russian statements during the early 1990s contributed to these concerns. For instance in September 1993, Yeltsin declared that the external borders of CIS states "are essentially the borders of Russia," a sentiment shared by the Russian Foreign Minister.[26] Concerns over Russian intentions, therefore, shaped the willingness of Karimov to contemplate greater coordination with Russia.

Karimov's rhetoric is indicative of his attitude towards CIS integration. He did not support efforts to make the CIS a true confederation, and he disagreed with former Soviet President Mikhail Gorbachev that the former Soviet states were "standing on the threshold of new integration processes."[27] As early as January 1993 at the Interparliamentary Assembly of the CIS, Karimov proclaimed that

> it is wrong to deceive the people by enticing them with fine talk of independence and sovereignty, while at the same time, fearing the inevitable turmoil and difficulties on the way, making advance preparations for ways of retreating to the past under various specious and seductive pretexts.[28]

Karimov also criticized the perceived dominance of Russia in the CIS, suggesting that Russia was playing the role of "dictator" in the former Soviet Union.[29] Speaking at a conference of six Turkic-speaking countries in Istanbul, Karimov charged that calls for forming various "unions and confederations smack of imperial ambitions and of a return to the previous systems."[30]

In short, concerns with regional instability motivated Karimov to adopt a pro-Russian alignment, in large part due to a lack of viable alternative security guarantors and available military capabilities. In this sense, Russia was the only state willing and able to ensure regional stability. Despite security cooperation with Russia, Karimov was unwilling to subjugate Uzbek autonomy by strengthening political and military ties with Russia, as evident in Karimov's rhetoric criticizing integration with Russia.

Uzbekistan (1995-2001): Forging Greater Independence

By the middle of the decade, security cooperation with Russia effectively calmed the situation in Tajikistan. Karimov still resisted greater security cooperation with Russia and increasingly adopted a more independent alignment away from Russia, as seen by Uzbekistan's withdrawal from the CIS Collective Security Treaty and Uzbekistan's accession into GUUAM. Karimov's pro-independence alignment has not precluded Uzbek-Russian security cooperation altogether. Yet, he continues to resist more institutionalized cooperation with Russia under the auspices of a rapid reaction force, while he is willing to work within the SCO, which includes the other regional heavyweight China.

While Russia and Uzbekistan worked to stabilize the situation in neighboring Tajikistan, there were strategic divergences between each state's agenda. Most notably, tensions arose as to how to resolve the conflict in Tajikistan. Russia supported the conservative pro-communist regime of Emomali Rakhmonov, who was elected in a race with no opposition and a state-controlled mass media and to the exclusion of other factions within the country. On the other hand, Karimov realized that a military solution was untenable, and considered the only long-term solution to be a compromise between pro-communist forces and the national opposition.[31] Karimov also played a role in conflict resolution when various factions were willing to negotiate. In April 1995, for example, Karimov met with Akbar Turajonzoda, the first deputy of the United Tajik Opposition (UTO), who had been the highest Islamic official in Tajikistan until his dismissal from the Dushanbe government in 1993. The meeting was held independent of Russian, Tajik, and UN counsel, although reportedly the substance of the meeting would be "relayed" to these participants.[32]

Also indicative of these tensions was the way in which a political compromise was eventually reached in Tajikistan. Karimov favored a coalition government that would place the most pro-Uzbek portions of Tajikistan in power. Prospects dwindled when the political alliance secured by Karimov between the Khojand region of the north, which Tashkent favored, and the Kulob region of the south began to falter by November 1994. After the Kulobis staged parliamentary and presidential elections, they began to drive the Khojandis (as well as ethnic Uzbeks) from their positions in both central and local government.

This unsettled Uzbek officials for several reasons. First, there are significant numbers of ethnic Uzbeks, which live in Tajikistan, especially in those areas contiguous to Uzbekistan. For instance, three of the principal regions in Tajikistan are heavily populated by ethnic Uzbeks. Khojand is 31 percent Uzbek; Hissar, the area west of Dushanbe, is estimated to be 45 percent Uzbek; and Kurgan Tiube, southwest of Dushanbe, is 32 percent Uzbek.[33] Second and related, the Khojand region had traditionally dominated Tajik politics (often in line with Tashkent's wishes), having provided all of the republics top leaders from the late 1930s until the outbreak of the civil war. But, the compromise did not favor this region. Indeed, when Rakhmonov met with the UTO in Moscow during the summer of 1997, the agreement reached excluded the Khojandi-based Party of National Revival from the coalition government. This weakened the position of Uzbeks in Tajik politics and eventually led to overt and covert Uzbek military interventions into Tajik territory. For instance, the Tajik leadership implicated Tashkent in sponsoring armed uprisings in Western Tajikistan in February 1996, August 1997, and October 1997. The unfavorable treatment of the Khojandis in the peace settlement also led Karimov to refuse to sign the inter-Tajik agreement as one of eight guarantor states (the others including Iran, Russia, Pakistan, Turkmenistan, Kyrgyzstan, Kazakhstan, and Afghanistan), ostensibly because there was no mechanism by which to enforce the agreement. A few months later, Karimov changed his mind, but the Tajik settlement remained unchanged.

Karimov continued to resist greater CIS political and military integration with Russia. Discussions over border protection are a case in point. During a CIS summit in May 1995 the Uzbek leadership refused to sign the Treaty for the Defense of the CIS External Borders, making it the only Central Asian state not to have Russian border troops.[34] As Uzbek officials stated, "we are capable of reliably defending our 156-kilometer border with Afghanistan with our own forces and without the intervention of border troops from other countries, first and foremost from Russia."[35] Karimov did, however, continue to maintain Uzbekistan's formal cooperation by signing the CIS Collective Security Concept in 1995.

Throughout the 1990s, Uzbek officials continued to criticize integration with Russia and the CIS. This criticism was fueled by perceptions of Russian intentions, such as when the Russian State Duma passed a resolution in March 1996 that declared the dissolution of the Soviet Union legally invalid. Such sentiments strained relations between Tashkent and Moscow, prompting considerable criticism. In responding to a question about the increasingly anti-Uzbek tone of articles in the Russian media, Karimov suggested, "individual politicians and the press that serve them in Moscow, nostalgic for the past and wishing to restore the former Union in one form of another, are haunted by the independent policy of sovereign Uzbekistan."[36] Within the parameters of CIS cooperation, Karimov challenged the development of supranational structures, suggesting that such a relationship "would not be the Commonwealth of Independent States…[but] the Community of Dependent States, in which each state would have to surrender part of its independence and sovereignty."[37] The Uzbek Foreign and Defense Ministries voiced similar concerns about security cooperation with Russia. Uzbek Foreign Minister Abdulaziz Kamilov cited the danger that "centralized control" could return through such efforts, while Defense Minister Akhmedov argued that such structures could "lead to future confrontation similar to the Cold War between the

Warsaw Treaty countries and NATO."[38] By the end of the decade, Karimov would be more capable of acting upon these sentiments and forging a more independent alignment.

By the late 1990s, the Uzbek military was restructured and greatly enhanced, and conflict in neighboring Tajikistan waned. This added sense of regional security provided Karimov with the impetus to sever Uzbekistan's formal security alignment with Russia, the CIS CST. At a January 1999 press conference in Tashkent, Karimov sharply criticized the recent developments in the CIS, charging that Russia was trying to impose its will on the CIS countries and that all matters were "dictated by Russia."[39] This sentiment led to his decision not to renew Uzbekistan's membership in the 1992 CST. As an Uzbek Foreign Ministry spokesman noted:

> In its current form, the treaty does not meet the requirements of the times and is not performing the functions it was designed to perform. [Furthermore], Tashkent objects to Russia's military activity in certain CIS states (presumably Tajikistan).[40]

Karimov has also spoken out against virtually every vital political issue for Russia including Russia's position on NATO expansion as well as Moscow's policy on Iraq and Kosovo. This did not suggest, however, that Karimov was completely unwilling to cooperate with Russia, and more recent events have prompted such renewed cooperation. This discussion of increased security cooperation aimed at combating religious extremism and terrorism is elaborated on in Chapter 4.

Karimov also resisted more institutionalized cooperation with Russia. For example, Uzbekistan did not join Russia, Kazakhstan, Tajikistan, and Kyrgyzstan in their effort to establish a 3,000 man rapid-reaction force to combat Islamic insurgency to be based in Bishkek, Kyrgyzstan.[41]

On the other hand, Karimov opted for the Shanghai Forum, now known as the SCO. The SCO, which includes Russia, China, Uzbekistan, Kazakhstan, Kyrgyzstan, and Tajikistan, originally was known as the Shanghai Treaty and was created in 1996 to ensure the sanctity of the former Soviet borders with China and to assist in the demilitarization of shared borders. The confidence-building measure agreement between Russia, China, Kazakhstan, Kyrgyzstan, and Tajikistan, signed on 24 April 1997, added additional credibility to the grouping, in its successful demilitarization of the border. More recently, Russia and China have seen the SCO as a potential counterweight to U.S. influence in the region. Nonetheless, the *raison d'etre* of the SCO is to face regional security challenges. At its founding in the summer 2001, the six countries pledged to combat the "three evil forces" of terrorism, extremism, and separatism.

While Karimov joined the SCO to address regional security threats, he once again expressed concerns that Moscow might try to use the SCO to bolster its own interests. As Karimov stated on Uzbek television on 16 June 2001:

> I have put my signature under ideas expressed in the Shanghai Cooperation Organization declaration. It says: cooperation, cooperation, cooperation. This

organization must never turn into a military political bloc…It should not be against any country, should not join certain trends, should not organize subversive activities against third countries.[42]

Karimov's pro-independent alignment strategy is strengthened by cooperation within the SCO. First, by joining the SCO and avoiding closer entanglements with the Russian led rapid reaction force, Karimov ensures diplomatic flexibility. By avoiding a security arrangement in which Russia is the dominant actor, Karimov meets his security requirements while avoiding overt and sustained integration with Russia. Second, closer cooperation with China is facilitated through the SCO, which also serves Uzbek interests. This allows Karimov to play Russia and China off one another, and it opens up a working relationship with Beijing. For instance, in September 2000 China provided military equipment to Uzbekistan such as night vision equipment, sniper rifles and bulletproof vests for its special forces, marking the first time Beijing had given military aid to a Central Asian state. Thus, in the end, the SCO enhances Karimov's more independent foreign policy from Russia, while it continues to address the overarching security concerns with religious extremism and terrorism, discussed at greater length in the next chapter.

Conclusions

This chapter sketched a basic timeline of security relations between Uzbekistan and Russia. From 1991-1995, Uzbekistan bandwagoned with Russia due to the unrest in neighboring Tajikistan and Afghanistan. From 1995-2001, Karimov adopted a more independent alignment that often times took on an anti-Russian tone.

This discussion enables us to discuss the reasons why Uzbekistan's alignment patterns have changed over the years and what the primary motivations underlying those alignment decisions were. This chapter emphasized the traditional view of security as primarily state-centric in its discussion of balance of power and balance of threat theories. That is, there was an emphasis on which state posed the greatest external threat to Uzbekistan based on power and threat intentions. However, the next two chapters examine the causal logic of the IT/ED framework to establish a more accurate picture of why Karimov chose particular alignment strategies vis-à-vis Russia. Indeed, as we will see, by 2001 with the resurgence of Islamic extremism in the region, Karimov adopted a more moderate pro-Russian alignment. Chapter 4 examines internal threats to Karimov's position in contrast to external threats to Uzbekistan, followed by an examination of Uzbek economic dependence on Russia and its influence on Karimov's alignment strategy in Chapter 5.

Notes

1. Gregory Gleason, "Uzbekistan: From Statehood to Nationhood," in *Nations & Politics in the Soviet Successor States*, ed. Ian Bremmer and Ray Taras (Cambridge: Cambridge University Press, 1993), 335-36.
2. For this and other reasons concerning border demarcation see, Robert J. Kaiser, *The Geography of Nationalism in Russia and the USSR* (Princeton: Princeton University Press, 1994), 110-12.
3. Martha Brill Olcott, "Central Asia's Catapult to Independence," *Foreign Affairs* 71, no. 3 (1992): 108-30; and Anthony Hyman, "Moving Out of Moscow's Orbit: The Outlook for Central Asia," *International Affairs* 69, no. 2 (1993): 295.
4. Webber, *CIS Integration Trends*, 25.
5. Susan Clark, "The Central Asian States: Defining Security Priorities and Developing Military Forces," in *Central Asia and the World*, ed. Michael Mandelbaum (New York: Council of Foreign Relations Press, 1994), 196.
6. For more on military reform see the interview with Colonel Arslan Khalmatov, deputy chief of staff of the CIS Joint Armed Forces and representative of the Uzbekistan Armed Forces, in A. Dokuchaev, "Pod krylom ptitsy khumo" (Under the wing of the khumo bird), *Krasnaia Zvezda*, 20 May 1993, 2; and U. Mirzaiarov, "Armeiskuiu sluzhbu na rodnoi zemle" (Army service in the homeland), *Pravda Vostoka*, 7 May 1992, 1.
7. Annette Bohr, *Uzbekistan: Politics and Foreign Policy* (London: Royal Institute of International Affairs, 1998), 58.
8. For more on this neoimperial sentiment and its impact on Russian foreign policy see, Menon, "In the Shadow of the Bear."
9. V. Portnikov, "Ia uzhe mnogo raz prigovoren" (I have already been sentenced many times), *Nezavisimaia Gazeta*, 21 June 1994, 3.
10. "President Karimov Interviewed on Turkish Ties," *Foreign Broadcast and Information Service-Soviet Union-91-249* (hereafter cited as *FBIS-SOV*), 27 December 1991, 72. In a later statement, Karimov stated, "the people of Turkey, the Turkic peoples are very close to us. Their language and their heart but primarily their religion and their destiny are very close to us." "Karimov Cited on Relations with Turkey," *FBIS-SOV-94-122*, 22 June 1994, 65.
11. Hiro, *Between Marx and Muhammad*, 176-77; and S. Novoprudskii, "Informatsionnoe nastupleniia Turtsii" (Turkey's Information Offensive), *Nezavisimaia Gazeta*, 22 July 1992, 1.
12. Writing about the Turkish model, Patrick Clawson argued: "The 'Turkish model' looks rather uninviting to those who see Turkey as at best a second-class economy, with profound problems – a foreign debt that has had to be rescheduled several times in recent decades, a growth record well below that in East Asia, continuing macroeconomic imbalances (budget deficits and inflation), etc." Suggesting that there is a different balance of accomplishments that exists, Azimbay Ghaliyev, a Kazakh demographer, wrote: "Turkey is a developing country. Internal conditions and internal stability are inadequate; religious and nationalist fundamentalism and powerful Kurd and Arab nationalities are increasingly important factors. The light and food industries and tourism are well developed in Turkey. On the other hand, non-ferrous metallurgy, chemistry, and machinery construction technology are just now becoming established. Sectors such as space research, astrophysics, nuclear physics, mathematical physics, and chemical medicine are mostly nonexistent. They are striving to learn these from

us. Likewise, it would be more suitable for us to learn the banking system from the United States, Germany, and Japan. In this area, we must look at the Turkish example with critical eyes." Both authors cited in Daniel Pipes, "The Event of Our Era: Former Soviet Muslim Republics Change the Middle East," in *Central Asia and the World*, 52, 55.

13. V. Volodin, "My priekhali k krovnym brat'iam, zaiavil prem'er-ministr Turtsii v Uzbekistane" (We visited our blood brothers, the Turkish Prime Minister announced in Uzbekistan), *Izvestiia*, 28 April 1992, 5; "Foreign Minister on Relations with Turkey and Iran," *FBIS-SOV-92-246*, 22 December 1992, 49; and Hale, "Islam, State-Building, and Uzbekistan Foreign Policy," 156-57.

14. For an analysis of the growing disillusionment between Turkey and Uzbekistan see, Philip Robins, "Between Sentiment and Self-Interest: Turkey's Policy Toward Azerbaijan and the Central Asian States," *Middle East Journal* 47, no. 4 (1993): 593-610.

15. "Further on Karimov Talks," *FBIS-SOV-91-233*, 4 December 1991, 86.

16. S. Novoprudskii, "Druzhba s druz'iami, mir s sosediami" (Friendship with friends, peace with neighbors), *Nezavisimaia Gazeta*, 2 December 1992, 3.

17. Ch. Annamuradov and G. Kolodin, "Opredeleny prioritety na budushchee" (Defined priorities for the future), *Nezavisimaia Gazeta*, 22 May 1996, 3.

18. *Krasnaia Zvezda*, 25 April 1992, 1, in *Current Digest of the Post-Soviet Press* (hereafter cited as *CDPSP*) 44, no. 17 (1992): 20.

19. Besides Uzbekistan and Russia, Kazakhstan, Tajikistan, Turkmenistan, and Armenia signed the Tashkent Treaty.

20. V. Kononenko, "Itogi moskovskoi vstrechi glav gosudarstv SNG vnushaiut umerennyi optimizm" (Result of Moscow meeting of CIS heads of state inspires moderate optimism), *Izvestiia*, 7 July 1992, 1-2.

21. "CIS Peacekeepers To Be Used in Hot Spots," *FBIS-SOV-92-137*, 16 July 1992, 3.

22. *Moskovskie Novosti*, July 26, 1992, 3, in *CDPSP* 44, no. 29 (1992): 17-18.

23. The official provision for the Tajik operation was issued at the April 1994 CIS summit, although a general agreement reached the previous September provided for the deployment of collective peacekeeping forces, with no specific reference to Tajikistan. This underscores the fact that peacekeeping action was often taken by the most interested regional actors and had less to do with the overarching cooperation of the entire CIS. The formal agreement attracted only six signatures including Russia, the Central Asian states (excluding Turkmenistan), and Georgia. Foreign Ministry of the Russian Federation, *Diplomaticheskii vestnik* (Diplomatic bulletin), no. 9-10 (1994): 46-47.

24. Rubin, "Tajikistan," 207-224.

25. Susan Clark, "The Central Asian States," 191-92; and Olcott, *Central Asia's New States*, 120, 128.

26. Therese Raphael, Claudia Rosett, and Suzanne Crow, "An Interview with Russian Foreign Minister Andrei Kozyrev," *Radio Free Europe/Radio Liberty Research Report*, no. 28 (1994): 38.

27. "Karimov News Conference Previews Summit," *FBIS-SOV-92-095*, 15 May 1992, 7-8; and "Karimov Praises CIS, Criticizes Confederation," *FBIS-SOV-92-252*, 31 December 1992, 65.

28. G. Melikiants, "Piat' byvshikh respublik sovetskogo soiuza idut k novomu soiuzu. Chto by eto znachilo?" (Five republics of the former Soviet Union are entering a new union. What would this mean?) *Izvestiia*, 5 January 1993, 1.

29. "President Says Future 'Inconceivable' Without Russia," *FBIS-SOV-94-017*, 26 January 1994, 57.

30. "Calls To Restore Soviet Union Concern Karimov," *FBIS-SOV-94-203*, 20 October 1994, 30.

31. Rubin, "Tajikistan," 220.

32. "Karimov Holds Talks With Tajik Opposition," *FBIS-SOV-95-065*, 5 April 1995, 70; and "Unprecedented Meeting of Uzbek Leaders, Tajik Opposition," *FBIS-SOV-95-078*, 24 April 1995, 87.

33. Rubin, "Tajikistan," 211.

34. Foreign Ministry of the Russian Federation, *Diplomaticheskii vestnik* (Diplomatic Bulletin), no. 7 (1995): 43-46.

35. N. Musienko, "Boiatsia dazhe nameka na SSSR" (They fear even a hint of the USSR), *Pravda*, 22 February 1996, 2.

36. "My verim v nashi sily i vozmozhnosti" (We trust in our strength and opportunities), *Pravda Vostoka*, 17 October 1996, 1.

37. "Karimov Criticizes Integration Accords," *FBIS-SOV-96-073*, 15 April 1996, 66.

38. "Foreign Minister in India; Opposes CIS Military Bloc," *FBIS-SOV-96-168*, 24 August 1996, 24; and "Defense Minister on Opposition to CIS Military Bloc," *FBIS-SOV-96-177*, 10 September 1996, 35. Accordingly, the Uzbek government passed legislation in December 1996 that outlawed Uzbek participation in any political-military blocs. "Participation in Military-Political Blocs Ruled Out," *FBIS-SOV-96-252*, 31 December 1996, 45.

39. V. Kuznechevskii, "Karimov khlopnul dver'iu?" (Did Karimov slam the door?) *Rossiiskaia gazeta*, 5 February 1999, 4.

40. V. Georgiev, "Uzbekistan zanial osobuiu pozitsiiu" (Uzbekistan has taken a special position), *Nezavisimaia Gazeta*, 4 February 1999, 1.

41. Douglas Frantz, "Central Asia: Force to Fight Muslim Rebels," *New York Times*, 26 May 2001, A5.

42. "Russia has Misgivings about Shanghai Cooperation Organization," *Eurasianet*, 20 June 2001, 2.

Chapter 4

Islam Karimov and Internal Threats

Whereas in the previous chapter we discussed the pattern of security cooperation between Uzbekistan and Russia and found that Uzbekistan aligned both towards and away from Russia during the decade, this chapter examines more specifically the relationship between internal threats to Karimov's regime and Uzbek alignment patterns. The IT/ED framework suggests that the more CIS leaders are threatened by internal threats, the more likely a leader is to adopt a strong pro-Russian alignment. That is, when threatened CIS leaders turn to Moscow for both direct and indirect assistance. However, if leaders face few internal threats or are able to eliminate them over time, then the necessity of a strong pro-Russian alignment is significantly lower. Based on the IT/ED framework, a leader would then be constrained only by the extent of their economic dependence on Russia, which if high could limit a leader's ability to adopt a more independent alignment.

This chapter reveals that both types of internal threats – traditional internal threats outlined by David and domestic political opposition – existed during Karimov's tenure in office. It examines more critically Karimov's perception of Islamic extremism and domestic political opposition and how these factors shaped his alignment towards Russia. More to the point, what becomes evident is that Karimov was concerned primarily with his political position – a central thesis of this book. And, internal threats to his position were the primary threats warranting balancing behavior. This logic runs counter to balance of power and balance of threats theories that focus on the state as the main actor in world affairs and the importance of balancing external threats to a state's survival in an anarchic international system. Based on the discussion provided in Chapter 3 about limited security cooperation between Uzbekistan and Russia, primarily dealing with extremism and terrorism, it becomes clearer that internal threats were the major determinant of Karimov's alignment strategies towards Russia.

The next section discusses the political ascendancy of Karimov before independence and offers a brief overview of his initial political consolidation. The chapter then moves to a more explicit discussion of the two types of internal political threats – traditional internal treats and domestic political opposition – that Karimov perceived throughout the decade and how he dealt with these internal threats. As we will see, he was much more effective at preventing the rise of any galvanizing opposition leaders or parties than the more intense internal threats outlined by David, given the resurgence of Islamic extremism in the latter part of the decade.

Karimov's Political Ascendancy

Karimov's unconventional political rise began before the collapse of the Soviet Union. Traditionally, Communist leaders were groomed early and rose through the political ranks over time, thereby learning the intricacies of bureaucratic maneuvering and building bases of political support. Unlike most senior party leaders, Karimov was seen as a rising economic technocrat, and not a significant political figure. Before his appointment to the head of the republic, he had not held any party post or been a member of a party bureau at any level. He had not even attended a republic Communist Party congress until 1986, but circumstances would make his outsider status more appealing. After riots broke out in the Ferghana Valley, the Soviet leadership was looking for a fresh face and appointed Karimov to be the new Communist leader of the republic in June 1989. Karimov's lack of political experience worked in his favor. Because he was not a major figure in the Uzbek Communist Party he avoided the purges of the 1980s, which occurred after the scandals surrounding the previous Sharaf Rashidov regime (1959-1983) and ended after a major cotton scandal revealed extensive corruption throughout the regime.

Due to his unconventional rise, Karimov lacked the political base most senior party leaders possessed. Accordingly, he relied on local politicians for support, but these individuals saw him as their puppet. They naively assumed that because he needed their support and patronage, he would be malleable. During this transition, Karimov relied heavily on his old friend, Shukurulla Mirsaidov, who he shared power with informally.[1] Mirsaidov was instrumental in Karimov's political rise because of his own influence within the republic, based on his previous positions in planning agencies and as mayor of Tashkent for several years. But, once the necessity of working with Mirsaidov waned, Karimov was in a stronger relative position to outmaneuver him, thereby solidifying his position as the eventual president of independent Uzbekistan.

In subsequent years, Karimov implemented a variety of political reforms, which gradually shifted power in his favor. Karimov's power rested in his official capacity as the head of the Communist Party in Uzbekistan, and secondarily in his election as chairman of the local Supreme Soviet. After Supreme Soviet elections in the spring of 1990, the body was seen as more legitimate, which paralleled the general power shift from the Communist Party to the state organs themselves. Shortly thereafter, Karimov strengthened his position relative to Mirsaidov, by drawing on the example of Mikhail Gorbachev and creating the office of the presidency, which would be beholden to a legislature and have the power to issue decrees under the rule of law. The Supreme Soviet subsequently elected Mirsaidov as chairman of the Council of Ministers, in essence a prime minister.

The next step in Karimov's power consolidation occurred in October 1990, when the Supreme Soviet eliminated the Council of Ministers (headed by Mirsaidov), in favor of a Cabinet of Ministers subordinate to the president. With Mirsaidov's former post abolished and the president as the new chairman of the Cabinet, the Supreme Soviet created the post of vice-president, to which Mirsaidov was appointed. Thus, through a variety of legal and political reforms, Karimov was able to solidify his legitimate position as head of state, even before the Soviet collapse. The power struggle between Karimov and Mirsaidov continued and resembled a struggle "between two bears that could not continue unresolved much longer."[2] The struggle ended in Karimov's favor, but the final blow came from events in Moscow.

After the failed August 1991 putsch in Moscow, Karimov strengthened his grip on Uzbekistan, since Mirsaidov appears to have backed the coup-plotters.[3] Sensing his precarious and desperate situation, Mirsaidov called for a no confidence vote on Karimov in the republic Supreme Soviet in October 1991. While secrecy surrounded the "October mutiny," Karimov survived the vote, and Mirsaidov's political ouster was only a matter of time.[4] After the failed putsch, Karimov called for presidential elections and a referendum on Uzbekistan's independence to take place on 29 December 1991. Karimov won this election, although they were only partially competitive, and the populace voted resoundingly in favor of independence.

This chapter now turns to an examination of the two basic types of internal threats leaders face – traditional internal threats and political opposition. As we will see, Karimov has been successful at thwarting internal threats. However, his early successes through overt repression have also contributed to an even stronger backlash of political violence in recent years. In this regard, the persistence of internal threats prompted the Uzbek president to increase security cooperation with Russia, which as Chapter 3 pointed out began in 2000.

Traditional Internal Threats

The IT/ED framework suggests that leaders tend to focus on internal threats to their regime because of concerns with their political survival. This consideration is intensified when these threats come in the more extreme form outlined by David's omnibalancing theory. This section examines internal threats to Karimov's regime and finds that Islamic extremism in the region was a major factor in shaping his alignment with Russia. In recent years the threat posed by Islamic extremists, and more specifically the Islamic Movement of Uzbekistan (IMU), resurfaced and prompted renewed security cooperation with Russia. A February 1999 assassination attempt in Tashkent, allegedly masterminded by domestic political opponents and religious extremists, and a series of more recent bombings in 2004 were indicators that Karimov's concerns with internal threats were unlikely to change, and if anything would only intensify.

Violent political unrest in Uzbekistan was not without precedent, although in the past it was closely linked to socio-economic conditions. When the economic climate declined and there were fewer resources, jobs, and living space available, tensions were inevitable and at times violence erupted. For instance, shortly before the Soviet demise, Uzbekistan experienced violent domestic unrest. In June 1989 some Uzbek youths turned on local Meshketian Turks, who were forced to move to the region by Stalin during World War II. More than one hundred deaths occurred over several days. A year later an even bloodier clash between Uzbeks and Kyrgyz over housing in the Kyrgyz border city of Osh led to over one thousand deaths. Despite this ethnic dimension, these clashes, as one regional observer noted, were rooted in the internal social and political conditions of Soviet rule, where the underlying causes of conflict were more complex than simple interethnic hostility.[5]

In January 1992 a similar shock was felt when Russia engaged in economic shock therapy with little concern for its impact on other CIS states. Russia's unilateral economic action undermined other members of the Ruble Zone, causing a short-term economic crisis. In Uzbekistan students took to the streets to protest, and Karimov subsequently cracked down on these demonstrations in Tashkent. These events were fresh in his mind, with the first in 1989 sparking his political rise. Coupled with religious extremism in neighboring Tajikistan and Afghanistan, these experiences shaped Karimov's perceptions of his internal threats and what measures were necessary to ensure his political position.

By the spring of 1992, security cooperation between Russia and Uzbekistan grew, as we saw in Chapter 3. Regional instability, closely linked to Islamic extremism in Afghanistan and its penetration into Tajikistan, was the primary catalyst. As Karimov suggested,

> the political and military crisis in Afghanistan and the instability in Tajikistan cannot avoid having a negative impact on both the regional stability of Central Asia as a whole and the national security of Uzbekistan in particular.[6]

From a security perspective, the most serious concern was that the porous nature of the Tajik-Afghan border allowed individuals to pass with relative ease, which complicated efforts to stabilize the situation. The crises were "sobering" to Uzbek officials and underscored the importance of Russia as a guarantor of regional security and border defense.[7]

Indeed, Karimov demonstrated great interest in the events in Tajikistan, primarily because of his understanding of the threat environment in Central Asia. He did not fear that Tajikistan would invade Uzbekistan, but rather that the local intercommunal conflict there could spread into Uzbekistan itself. In a recent book he elaborates on the dynamics of regional conflict:

> So what is the real threat of regional conflicts to the well being and the progress of Uzbekistan? At first glance, it may seem that the conflicts taking place close to our borders have no direct impact on the political, economic, and social stability of our state. But that view is short-sighted. A similar political myopia leads to the opinion that the alarming developments nearby will avoid our country, that our stability will be

preserved of itself, and that the future of the country will be secured automatically. These myopically "optimistic" views do not see the huge efforts it costs the state to secure peace and order and to prevent adverse developments from spilling over onto our soil. If acute problems, like those surrounding us, are ignored, they lead to crisis, and an unmanageable crisis sooner or later grows into a destructive cataclysm indifferent to state borders and to other political, economic, and ethnic realities.[8]

Karimov feared that religious extremism could flourish in such an unstable environment and spread from neighboring Afghanistan and Tajikistan. On Tashkent Television in 1992, for instance, he stated, "I assure you that tomorrow, when they declare Tajikistan an Islamic state, they won't stop at that. An Islamic state with its ideology will come to us for sure through the Ferghana Valley. While I'm president, we won't allow any Islamic order in Uzbekistan."[9] As Karimov has stated, the fundamentalist threat "to the security of Uzbekistan is not hypothetical, but its existence is obvious."[10]

Karimov's depiction of Islamic extremism in the region does warrant qualification. The Islamic fundamentalism typically associated with the creation of politics embodying the strict tenets of the *Koran* and the *shari'a* (e.g. post-1979 Iran, post-1991 Afghanistan) does not accurately reflect Islam in post-Soviet Central Asia. Because of the nomadic and merchant ways of life that flourished during the height of the Silk Road, Islam became more of a way of life than a strict code of religious piety and order. Indeed, Islam in Uzbekistan has been tolerant to other religions and not radical, as for instance, Wahhabism. Much of the radical Islam that exists in the region today, thus, has been exported there from other states, such as Saudi Arabia, and accordingly it lacks the deep-seated roots necessary for its spread throughout the region. Moreover, political Islam is further weakened by diversity and competing allegiances to clan, tribe, and region.[11] Therefore, while Islam does provide a deep-rooted sense of identity and community in Uzbekistan, and Central Asia for that matter, it has not translated into widespread political extremism. As we will see, though, Karimov's repressive tactics and inability to promote economic growth and opportunity in Uzbekistan fueled this animosity of late.

In many ways, Karimov has been instrumental in his use of the term "fundamentalism." As one Russian editorial charged, "the Uzbek leadership is not simply afraid of fundamentalism, seeing it as a real and dangerous rival, but is also using it to try to scare Uzbekistan's neighbors (Russia and the West), which is particularly sensitive to fundamentalism."[12] Moreover, by latching onto it as a bogeyman, he has attempted to keep Western governments (especially the United States) from isolating his regime, which in the post 9/11 international system translated into even greater engagement with the United States in the military campaign against the Taliban and al Qaeda in Afghanistan. In this regard, Karimov's efforts to prevent regional instability have been received warmly, despite the extent to which he maintains authoritarian control in Uzbekistan. Even the United States praised Uzbekistan for being an "island of stability" during Secretary of Defense William Perry's visit to Tashkent in the mid 1990s. This is important to keep in mind when discussing Karimov's rhetoric, as it provides a more accurate depiction of his fundamentalist bogeyman.

The murder of seventeen policemen in the Ferghana Valley in December 1997 by alleged Islamic extremists, though, served as a catalyst for a renewed crackdown. Eight men were eventually tried and sentenced for the acts of violence, while hundreds more were detained and imprisoned.[13] In January 1998 Karimov provided journalists with an official account that claimed the "Islamists" came from neighboring Tajikistan.[14] Later in February, Uzbek Foreign Minister Abdulaziz Kamilov held a news conference in Tashkent in which he suggested that Islamic groups in Pakistan and Afghanistan were training young Central Asians in terrorism in order to destabilize the region and bring about Islamic governments throughout the region. According to Kamilov, it was these groups that were responsible for the December attacks in Namangan.[15]

In response to these actions, Karimov turned to vitriolic rhetoric. In a speech to parliament in May 1998 broadcast on Uzbek radio, he stated that Islamic guerillas "must be shot in the head" or else "Tajikistan will come to Uzbekistan tomorrow." He went on to say, "if necessary I'll shoot them myself, if you lack the resolve."[16] This rhetoric was also backed up by an increase in security cooperation with Russia. Accordingly, to enhance regional security, Uzbekistan signed an agreement in May 1998 with Russia and Tajikistan to counter Islamic extremism in the region, although the agreement remained ambiguous as to what such cooperation would entail.[17]

As part of the continued crackdown, parliament also enacted tougher laws on religious freedom. The amendment to the country's law "On Freedom of Conscience and Religious Organizations" of 1991 forced all mosques, churches, and synagogues and other places of worship to register with the state, and re-register in many cases. Thus, any non-registered organizations became subject to criminal prosecution. Moreover, the previous law held that organizations only need ten adult members to register with the state, but the more stringent version raised that figure to 100, thereby criminalizing previously recognized organizations with fewer members. Some estimated that 80 percent of all mosques in the country were closed in late 1997-1998.[18]

Despite Karimov's repressive tactics, and perhaps directly because of them, political violence resurfaced. On 16 February 1999 car bombs exploded in Tashkent killing over a dozen people, injuring 120 people, and destroying government buildings. Karimov accused exiled opposition leader Mohammad Solih, who had run against him in the first presidential election, with plotting the president's assassination along with the leader of the IMU, Tahir Yuldash, and other Islamic radicals from Uzbekistan, Tajikistan, and Afghanistan. However, many domestic political opponents living in exile asserted that the bombings were organized by Karimov to legitimate his repressive tactics. As Abdurahim Polat stated, Tashkent organized the attacks because many leaders of the democratic opposition were seriously considering returning to Uzbekistan prior to the upcoming elections.[19]

Karimov's actions only fueled the IMU. The IMU emerged after a number of Islamists fled Uzbekistan into neighboring Tajikistan as a result of Karimov's domestic crackdown. There they were better able to launch raids into southern Kyrgyzstan and Uzbekistan. The IMU leader, Yuldash, stated publicly his aspirations to continue the armed struggle against the Uzbek government in a BBC interview in September 1999. Thus, with the IMU publicly stating its intentions to undermine and potentially destroy the present regime, Karimov focused on the threat of political violence posed by Islamic extremists. In early 2001, Kyrgyz General Askar Mameev estimated that there were still between 1,500 and 2,000 IMU militants operating from Tajikistan.[20]

Beyond the more radical and violent IMU, another secretive organization, Hizb-ut-Tahrir (HuT), rose from the political and economic stagnation common throughout the region. HuT shares the IMU's goal of establishing Islamic states across Central Asia, although its methods vary considerably. Whereas the IMU has taken up arms against the Karimov regime, HuT pursues its objectives by propagating its tenets at the grassroots level with leaflets and fliers.[21] Active members of HuT tend to be the relatively educated, urban youth, but tremendous effort is spent on spreading their message to more rural areas, which are some the poorest segments of society. While HuT remains a largely non-violent movement, cracks in the group have appeared more recently. That is, some splinter segments of the movement have become increasingly frustrated with the lack of action on the group's part, and are beginning to call for more action in line with the more violent methods proposed by the IMU.[22] Thus, Karimov's perception of this group is no less threatening than the IMU, and one which warrants his attention.

Regional security services have arrested hundreds if not thousands of suspected members of HuT, yet its membership continues to grow. In southern Kyrgyzstan it was estimated at one time that 10 percent of the population were active members.[23] HuT has also played on the perceptions of ethnic minorities as second class citizens to further swell its ranks, most notably disenfranchised ethnic Uzbeks living in southern Kyrgyzstan, Uzbeks in Tajikistan, and Tajiks in Uzbekistan.[24]

The rise of HuT underscores the importance of economic conditions and how they can influence the political stability of a region, and more specifically the political security of a particular leader. As long as the economic picture remains bleak, such organizations will continue to gain support. Karimov himself has acknowledged the connection between poverty and Islamic extremism, suggesting militants are able to find recruits because of the "disastrous socioeconomic status of people, demographic problems in some regions, mass unemployment, and economic insecurity, especially among young people."[25]

The IT/ED framework suggests that when internal threats to leaders rise, a more pro-Russian alignment is likely to emerge. This became evident in Karimov's case as the threat from Islamic extremists grew by the end of the decade. For instance, in 1999 and 2000, the IMU launched raids from Tajikistan into Kyrgyzstan and Uzbekistan proper once mountain passes thawed after winter, demonstrating the increasing viability of this group to cause instability and provoke fear.

To address this ever-expanding threat, Karimov, as he had in the early 1990s, turned to Moscow for assistance. During talks between the deputy foreign ministers of Russia and Uzbekistan on 28 August 2000, Russian officials stated they were ready "to provide the necessary assistance to Uzbekistan and other members of the Commonwealth in their struggle against subversive activities of extremists."[26] Similarly, in February 2001 Colonel General Leonid Ivashov, head of the Russian Defense Ministry's Department for International Military Cooperation, and Uzbek Defense Minister Kadyr Gulyamov concluded three days of talks in Tashkent. Those discussions focused on military-technical cooperation and regional security, including the threat posed by IMU guerrillas, counterterrorism measures, the situation in the districts of Uzbekistan that border on Afghanistan, and the possibility of training Uzbek servicemen at Russia military colleges.[27] In late April 2001, General Anatolii Kvashnin, the chief of the Russian Staff, also visited Tashkent to help Uzbekistan plan for its defense against an expected onslaught of Islamic fighters in the summer.[28]

As the extremist threats rose, security cooperation between Uzbekistan and Russia entered a qualitatively new phase. During Karimov's official visit to Moscow in May 2001, Russian President Vladimir Putin stressed the importance of military cooperation in dealing with regional security, and stated that Russia "is doing much" to provide Uzbekistan with up-to-date arms to combat extremist threats.[29] At an informal CIS summit in Sochi on 1 August, Putin and Karimov again met on the side to discuss military cooperation as well as measures to combat drug trafficking and terrorism.[30] Thus, the rise of Islamic extremism in the region prompted Karimov to adopt a more moderate alignment towards Russia.

The type of actions taken against the Uzbek government cannot be seen in isolation. That is, by the very actions taken against not only Islam but also political opposition in general, Karimov's extremism has produced a counter-reaction. As Vitality Ponomarev, Director of the Information Center for Human Rights in Central Asia, pointed out, "total persecution and a crackdown on secular opposition in the early 1990s created the vacuum inside Uzbekistan that is now being filled by radical ideology. Karimov himself is responsible for this."[31] By denying individuals legitimate outlets within the political process, groups turn to less legitimate methods of political change such as the use of political violence. In this sense, the rise of political violence is a byproduct of Karimov's actions, and as we have seen in neighboring Afghanistan most recently, such extremism is difficult to root out.

Moreover, the threat from Islamic extremism hardly waned in Uzbekistan over time and reached unprecedented levels in 2004. In the first major incident, for instance, a series of suicide bombings and shootings at the main bazaar in Tashkent in March 2004, according to official figures, claimed the lived of 47 individuals, including 33 militants and 10 police officers. Uzbek officials were quick to link these attacks with the larger specter of international terrorism. Uzbek Prosecutor-General Rashid Kadyrov noted that the use of suicide bombers in the attacks "indicated foreign involvement." Meanwhile, Foreign Minister Sadiq Safayev stated that the "hands of international terror" were behind the violence, adding that such "attempts are being made to split the international anti-terror coalition." For his part, in a March 29 television address, Karimov alleged, it should be noted without producing concrete data, that "terrorists had been planning the attacks for six to eight months." He added, "From all that we know, the goal of these crimes was the destruction of popular peace, in order to sow disorder in society and subvert the political course of the country."[32]

Critics have questioned the validity of claims pointing to international terrorists as the main culprits, but there can be little doubt that the attacks were well-planned and coordinated. Human rights groups, along with many Western and Russian media outlets, instead contend that the violence was connected primarily to popular frustration generated by government policies that have stifled political freedom and economic opportunity. Others speculate that while the attacks could have been in the planning stages for a while, the attacks may have been triggered by the police beating of an elderly man at the bazaar on 28 March. Or perhaps, they constitute a reprisal against the rapacious police force, which has been known for its brutality. Fueling this view is the fact that most of the attacks targeted police officers, while avoiding strikes at government buildings and other strategic installations.

Then only a few short months later in July 2004, a cluster of coordinated suicide bombings at the U.S. and Israeli embassies and the Uzbek Prosecutor General's Office left five dead. Amid uncertainty over what Islamic extremist group carried out these attacks, Uzbek authorities arrested at least 85 individuals. Despite the militant nature of the IMU, Karimov instead indicted HuT as the culprit not only for the July bombing, but the March incident as well. During a nationally broadcast address on 31 July, Karimov indicated that evidence from both incidents suggest "that they were organized by members of the same group, that they acted in accordance with one plan and that they were pursuing the same aim." Challenging the non-violent position of HuT, Karimov added, "If [HuT] intends to set up a caliphate in Uzbekistan, overthrow the current system, give up the modern style of life and create a state based on Islamic law, then how will they be able to do this in a peaceful way."[33] Regardless of the motivation or the actual group behind the attacks, Karimov's perception of the threat from more extreme internal threats to his position has only grown of late, despite his measures to curb them. But the bloodiest incident during Karimov's reign was yet to come.

In May 2005, a peaceful protest in support of 23 businessmen accused of Islamic militancy in the Uzbek city of Andijon turned unexpectedly violent when some protesters seized weapons from a military barracks and occupied the regional administrative headquarters.[34] In an effort to stamp out such opposition, Uzbek special forces opened fire without warning on thousands of unarmed civilians who had gathered to support, or merely observe, the protests. Accurate death toll figures were obscured by Uzbek authorities, but range from hundreds of dead to thousands. As he had in the past, Karimov depicted the protesters as Islamic extremists bent on destabilizing the country and region. He told a news conference on 14 May that an offshoot of HuT was responsible for the Andijon violence, adding that the rebels made phone calls to "masters" in Afghanistan and Kyrgyzstan.[35]

While Washington was relatively silent and only later called for an independent investigation into the events, Moscow was quick to support Karimov. Russian officials supported his arguments that the violence was planned in advance and orchestrated by Islamic extremists with ties to the Taliban in Afghanistan. This perception was reiterated during Karimov's June 2005 official visit to Moscow.[36] This was welcome support because, as the IT/ED framework would predict, Karimov was primarily concerned with which outside power was most willing to ensure his political survival and help combat his perceived internal threats. His heavy-handed tactics could not be overlooked by Washington, but Moscow was under no such moral restraints. Thus, given increased U.S. pressure on Karimov, the Uzbek leader turned back towards Russia for international recognition and cover from international condemnation. Nonetheless, as the IT/ED framework suggests, beyond traditional internal threats, leaders also perceive domestic opponents as viable threats to their positions. The next section discusses the role and evolution of domestic political opposition in Uzbekistan and how Karimov greeted it.

Political Opposition

Given Karimov's concerns with religious extremism and his desire to stay in power, domestic political opposition faced a difficult uphill battle. However, before independence, some domestic political opposition existed. Yet, Karimov limited it because of his concern that political parties, such as Birlik (Unity), Erk (Freedom Democratic Party), and the Islamic Renaissance Party (IRP), could mobilize popular support against him through demonstrations or open elections, such as on the issue of Uzbek independence. Birlik leaders, for instance, tended to demand Uzbek independence from Russia much stronger than Karimov. Erk, which splintered off from Birlik in early 1990, was often seen as a more moderate version of Birlik, but they too sought greater autonomy for Uzbekistan within the Soviet system. These parties placed political pressure on Karimov to embrace independence, if he was to win popular support – an issue he willingly and wisely adopted in his political program. The IRP was the greatest concern for Karimov because of its religious orientation, although its political influence was limited. For instance, the party enjoyed meager support outside of the traditionally devout Ferghana Valley.[37] Furthermore, popular support for the IRP stemmed more from a revival of local Islamic culture, than any desire to establish a strict theocratic state similar to Iran.[38] Nonetheless, as Karimov would witness in Tajikistan a few years later, such Islamic groups could pose considerable problems to the political stability of the country.

At first, Karimov tolerated domestic opposition. For instance, Birlik and Erk elected members to the republic Supreme Soviet in the 1990 elections, providing

them with a legitimate political outlet. Karimov was not without reservations
though. In commenting about this burgeoning opposition in a March 1991
interview, he stated:

> Were it a healthy opposition which had its own ideas, understanding, and view of the
> future, I would welcome it. But if we are talking of those I have run into and had to
> debate with, it is absolutely clear: The majority of them are straining for power. Give
> them a place in the sun, and they'll relax and forget the people. And they'll turn into
> conservatives who are worse than the present ones.[39]

More generally, Uzbek leaders questioned democratic principles on cultural
grounds. In a June 1991 interview, Karimov remarked, "before talking about
comprehensive democracy; one should think about whether this democracy is
governable, whether you can control the processes, or the processes will control
you."[40] As Karimov is quick to point out, "in other parts of the Soviet Union, like
the Baltics and Moscow, people are able to conduct themselves peacefully for
hours at a demonstration. But here people quickly get excited and violence
begins."[41] In September 1991, the Presidium of the Supreme Soviet and the
Cabinet of Ministers issued the following joint statement:

> At this difficult time, there are destructive elements that want and are striving to disrupt
> people's tranquility, introduce disorganization and disorder, pit some groups against
> others, sow distrust in their bodies of power, and instill suspicion, fear, and panic
> among the population.[42]

Opening the political system would presumably only strengthen such destructive
forces. In the words of one senior Uzbek official, "diplomats try to teach us
lessons, but our traditions are different. Uzbek people are very kind, but it is
dangerous to give [them] things like democracy. We have to practice how to be a
democratic state [first]."[43] Similarly, Akmal Saidov, the head of the National
Center for Human Rights, suggested that "Western norms and social structure are
not appropriate to the Uzbekistan mentality and the tradition of the East as a whole,
and therefore it is necessary to develop one's own understanding of civil rights and
liberties, adequate to local conditions."[44] Thus, many in the Uzbek leadership
questioned the practicality of an open political process, where various interests
could voice their direct opposition to the president.

Shortly after independence, Karimov developed the perception that domestic
political opposition, both religious and secular, was a threat to his political
position. In the December 1991 elections, Karimov blocked the entrance of the
other political heavyweight in Uzbekistan, Abdurahim Polat of Birlik, leaving only
one minor candidate to run against him.[45] Karimov monopolized public
communication and held the support of former communists throughout the country
that had joined his People's Democratic Party (PDP). Prior to the election, he was
featured on daily news bulletins televised nationwide by state-run television
stations, while his opponent, Mohammad Solih of Erk, received only fifteen
minutes of airtime one week before the polling day. Out of those fifteen minutes,

three minutes were officially censored. Karimov received 86 percent of the vote with Solih a distant second with 13 percent. With victory in hand, he ensured his political survival both in the short and long term.

The first targets of political repression were religious organizations. In December 1991 some residents of the regional center of Namangan, in the heart of the densely populated Ferghana Valley, seized the local administrative building.[46] They demanded that Karimov swear on the Koran that their concerns be met. This incident set the tone for Karimov's relationship with Islamic groups to come. He struck first at the IRP and Adolat (Justice Party), who drew their strongest support from Muslims in the Ferghana Valley. Shortly after his meeting with U.S. Secretary of State James Baker concerning democratic reform in February 1992, Karimov arranged for seventy-one opposition figures to be arrested.[47] The Islamic center in Namangan was ransacked, and its property thrown into the streets.

Violence against secular political opponents also started in the summer of 1992. As the Birlik leadership struggled to gain political recognition, they also found themselves under physical attack. When Polat refused to cancel a political rally, for which he had already gained government approval, four unknown assailants attacked him.[48] Shukhart Ismatullaev and Pulat Akhunov, co-chairmen of Birlik, also reported being severely beaten during incarceration.[49] Polat and Ismatullaev were forced to leave the country, while Akhunov was jailed on a fabricated charge of petty hooliganism.[50] By December 1992, the Uzbek Supreme Soviet ordered the Supreme Court to consider the legal status of Birlik.[51] Once Erk began to assert its claim for more political freedom, their leader, Solih, who had run against Karimov in 1991, was brought in for questioning, after which he fled the country in the spring of 1993.[52]

With the ratification of a new constitution in December 1992, Karimov's eradication of opposition continued unfettered. Article 57 prohibited political parties based on national and religious principles. In January 1993 this meant that the government would no longer recognize Birlik. Upon appeal, the Justice Ministry claimed the abolition of the movement was "legal and expedient," citing the arrests of 166 Birlik members between 1991 and 1993, and upheld the ban for an interim period ending on 15 April 1993.[53] Re-registration attempts in 1993 again proved futile because Birlik lacked an official address after the government confiscated their headquarters shortly before the registration deadline.

Erk also came under fire when plans for a "long-term" coup were discovered. In September 1994 the Uzbek Security Service began a thorough investigation of Erk plans to recruit young Uzbeks and send them to Turkey for political and military training.[54] The hope was that ties with Turkey would help ensure the survival of the opposition movement. The trial was held several months after September to avoid darkening the mood of citizens before the parliamentary elections to be held in December.[55] Several defendants were arrested for possession of the banned Erk publication and illegal weapons. Murad Dzhuraev, the editor of the banned publication, was arrested by the Uzbek secret service in Kazakhstan. All told by April 1995 severe sentences were administered ranging from four to twelve years for Dzhuraev. In light of Erk allegations, Uzbek spokesman, Fakhritdin Parpiev, responded that "anyone who is in jail belongs there for seeking to publish underground newspapers or for other illegal activities. No one has the right to agitate against power, against the regime, against nationalism."[56] The weight of evidence against these individuals sealed Erk's political fate.

The new constitution retained its democratic façade. The Oliy Majlis was intended to be a legislative body of elected officials on a "multi-party basis." There was also a renewed commitment to a "free mass media with no censorship." Yet, according to public opinion research performed in 1996, Uzbeks seriously doubted whether any uncensored material is obtainable. Indeed, 60 percent of the people polled stated that there were no forms of media, readily accessible, free of government control.[57] These phrases again highlight the gap between what is said and what is practiced in Uzbek politics. Even on the day of ratification, political repression could not be resisted. Abdumannov Polat, chairman of the Uzbekistan Society for Human Rights and brother of Birlik leader, Abdurahim Polat, was abducted by the Uzbek secret police after addressing a human rights conference in neighboring Kyrgyzstan.[58] He was rushed to Tashkent and charged with insulting the honor of the president.[59] The charge stemmed from a 1992 photograph taken of Polat with two students who had a portrait of Karimov bearing the slogan "some animals eat their young." International outcry led to his release eight days later, but such a demonstration reinforces the control that Karimov has within and outside his country.[60]

The effectiveness of Karimov's domestic repression is evidenced by the first post-Soviet "multi-party" elections held in December 1994.[61] While these elections were truly multi-candidate (634 candidates stood for 250 legislative seats), there were only two registered political parties that participated. Karimov's PDP dominated the new legislature: 69 deputies were directly elected from the PDP, 167 deputies came from local administrative bodies, which favor Karimov,[62] and 14 were elected from Vatan Tarakkiyeti (Progress of the Homeland Party).[63] This latter party emerged on the coattails of the PDP in 1992 and served the same function as Erk had back in the 1991 elections. It upheld the democratic façade and gave the illusion that political opposition existed.[64] The inability of the independent political opposition (Birlik and Erk) to field a candidate then left three groups in the Oliy Majlis all beholden to Karimov. Citing the results of the elections, Karimov urged the world to accept Uzbekistan "as a society that is being transformed into a democracy."[65]

Despite Karimov's take on Uzbek democracy, he apparently was aware that the democratic façade needed strengthening, and the state sponsored the creation of another political party. In late February 1995, five days before the opening session of the Oliy Majlis, Adolat was created.[66] Once the government recognized Adolat, 47 deputies elected from the regional bloc, who had become members of the newly formed party, were officially registered as another parliamentary faction. In May 1995 two other political groups emerged. The political party, Mili Tiklanish (the National Revival Party), was founded supposedly at the initiative of a group of artists; and the Birlik Social Movement was permitted, although it was not a political party and therefore could not nominate candidates for elected office.

The official programs of these pro-government groups varied little, as all were dedicated "to the development of an independent and democratic state."[67] The dominant PDP officially endorses "a gradual, evolutionary development of the economy and the preservation of social peace and interethnic harmony." In contrast to its former Communist ideology, the PDP claims to support the interests of all citizens and not just the proletariat. Other recognized groups have comparable goals, but differ in the interest groups they supposedly represent. For instance, Vatan Tarakkiyeti supports the interests of businessmen and entrepreneurs; Mili Tiklanish defends the interests of the intelligentsia; and Adolat professes that its primary goal is "to facilitate the development of a law-based state and the strengthening of social justice." Finally, the Birlik Social Movement advocates "the construction of a just civil society on the basis of socio-political stability, cultural dialogue, and openness." Despite this appearance of pluralism in Uzbekistan, the purpose of these groups is not to defend the interests of their respective constituents per se, but rather to contribute to the democratic façade within Uzbekistan and provide Karimov with a compliant national parliament willing to support his initiatives. This became clear when the newly elected legislature came to office.

In its first session, the pro-Karimov legislature voted to hold a referendum in March 1995 on extending the president's term until the year 2000. As in Soviet times, official returns recorded that 99.3 percent of the eligible voters turned out to vote, with 99.6 percent of them voting in favor of extending Karimov's presidency. Thus, Karimov successfully secured his political position for another five years without holding another presidential election scheduled for 1996. By this extension of his first presidential term, Karimov also remained eligible to run in the 2000 election, thereby bypassing the provision in the constitution that limits a president from holding office for more than two consecutive terms. In response to the vote, he stated,

> I regard the referendum results as a mandate of confidence, a mandate of confidence in the president and the government, and in the course that is being pursued in the republic. I regard the referendum results as being the faith and confidence of our society and people in their own future.[68]

Independent political opposition fared little better in subsequent years. In December 1998, another political party, Fidokorlar (Altruistic People), was formed, in response to Karimov's call for a political movement to bring honest people to office. The birth of this party brought the total number of political parties to five that could participate in the December 1999 parliamentary elections. In these elections, the PDP won 48 seats, Fidokorlar 34 seats, Vatan Tarakkyeti 20 seats, Adolat 11 seats, Mili Tiklanish 10 seats, while local and regional groups that support Karimov won 110 seats. There was one vacancy and independent initiative groups claimed 16 seats. Yet, once again political parties were less a tool to channel and lobby for the interests of the Uzbek people, and more a manipulation by Karimov to support some semblance of political pluralism.

Karimov's political position was solidified after the most recent presidential elections. On 9 January 2000 Karimov retained the presidency with 92 percent of the vote against nominal opposition, which attests to the success of his domestic tactics.[69] His opponent, Abdulhafez Jalalov, First Secretary of the Central Council of the People's Democratic Party (which Karimov headed until he left the party in 1996), received 4 percent of the vote but was rarely seen during the election. Ironically, among those that voted for Karimov were Jalalov himself, who told reporters that he had done so in the interests of "stability, peace, our nation's independence [and] the development of Uzbekistan." When asked why he ran in the first place, he stated: "So that democracy would win."[70] Karimov's final coup de grace came on 6 December 2001, when Uzbekistan's parliament endorsed a proposal to extend his current term from 5 to 7 years.

Throughout the decade, Karimov embarked upon the systematic and calculated elimination of internal political threats to his political position. He focused primary attention on balancing the most extreme threats posed by Islamic extremists, which as we saw in the previous chapter, prompted security cooperation with Russia shortly after independence and more recently in 2000 as well as with the United States after 11 September. But he also took measures to prevent the rise of any galvanizing opposition leader or party, which could threaten his political security. He did so through outright repression at times, and more generally, by manipulating and controlling the political process and those that participated in it.

Conclusions

This chapter examined the domestic political setting within Uzbekistan and highlighted the role internal threats played in Karimov's alignment calculations. The principal assumption of the IT/ED framework – that leaders focus on their political survival – was clearly demonstrated by Karimov over the past decade, as he consolidated his political position. While much of the previous discussion demonstrated the extent to which Karimov thwarted any domestic political opposition, the fear of Islamic extremism was the primary motivation for his alignment towards Russia. This prompted Karimov to adopt a rather strong pro-Russian alignment early in the 1990s because of his fear of domestic religious and secular opponents, the rising intensity of regional instability, and the need for Russian military assistance to secure the Tajik-Afghan border and provide a stabilizing force during the Tajik civil war. This falls in line with the logic of the IT/ED framework, which suggests that the more internal threats to leaders exist, the more likely a pro-Russian alignment will be adopted.

The necessity of this alignment changed once Karimov secured his political position with the 1995 referendum (as well as lessen Uzbek economic dependence on Russia discussed in Chapter 5). With his political security in hand and a decline in the number of internal threats challenging his regime, Karimov was in a stronger position to adopt a more independent alignment, which led to Uzbekistan's withdrawal from the CIS CST. The lingering specter of religious extremism, however, prompted Karimov to cooperate with Russia to combat this common foe shortly thereafter.

Karimov's actions against extremism have also shaped the changing geopolitical landscape and made Uzbekistan a welcomed partner of the United States in the Bush administration's war on terrorism. The inherent difficulty is that Karimov's actions towards religious groups in Uzbekistan have directly contributed to the resurgence of extremism in the region. After 11 September, the United States was willing to lend political and military assistance to Uzbekistan, especially given Uzbek willingness to use its airspace and the military base at Karshi Khanabad to support operations in Afghanistan. Perhaps, more importantly, the U.S. military went along way to ridding Karimov of the IMU threat, when IMU guerillas went to Afghanistan to fight along side the Taliban and al Qaeda. However, as one Uzbek official stated, while much of the IMU was defeated in the war, the group lies "dormant" and remains a potential threat to regional stability.[71]

Karimov's stock rose after 11 September, but the United States must keep in mind the regional peculiarities of the extremist threat and the underlying motives of leaders in this international struggle. In the short-term, Karimov's attempts to balance his internal threats have greatly been enhanced through overt security cooperation with Russia and the United States. This is also interesting because it suggests that the United States, and perhaps only in this limited capacity in the fight against global terrorism, is willing to assist Karimov in his struggle against internal threats. Previously, this was a role that was almost exclusively held by Russia. Given the shifting priorities of the Bush administration, however, the United States sees Karimov's political security as a vital security interest, especially insofar as Uzbekistan is a critical regional power neighboring Afghanistan. However, the massacre in Andijon in May 2005 made it more difficult for Washington to accept Karimov's repressive tactics, which led to a cooling of relations with the United States, especially after Karimov gave the U.S. military 180 days to withdraw from its base at Karshi Khanabad. Moscow was quick to fill this vacuum offering diplomatic assistance in support of Karimov's actions, while the leader faced increased international pressure. Yet, beyond this political dimension, there were also considerable developments on the economic front that influenced Karimov's political security and shaped his alignment strategies towards Russia.

Notes

1. Donald S. Carlisle, "Islam Karimov and Uzbekistan: Back to the Future?" in *Patterns in Post-Soviet Leadership*, ed. Timothy J. Colton and Robert C. Tucker (Boulder, CO: Westview, 1995), 196.
2. Ibid., 198.

3. "Soobshchenie press-sluzhb prokuratury i MID respubliki Uzbekistan" (Press announcement of the prosecutor office and the Interior Ministry of the republic of Uzbekistan), *Pravda Vostoka*, 8 March 1997, 3.

4. D. Sabov and I. Cherniak, "Golobnyi bunt v khlebnom gorode" (Hunger riot in a grain-rich city), *Komsomol'skaia Pravda* 30 January 1992, 2.

5. Anara Tabyshalieva, *The Challenges of Regional Cooperation in Central Asia: Preventing Ethnic Conflict in the Ferghana Valley*, U.S. Institute of Peace Peaceworks, no. 28 (Washington, D.C.: U.S. Institute of Peace Press, 1999), vi.

6. Islam Karimov, *Uzbekistan on the Threshold of the Twenty-First Century* (Cambridge, Mass., 1998), 14; and "Karimov Assesses Situation in Tajikistan," *Foreign Broadcast and Information Service-Central Eurasia-94-151* (hereafter cited as *FBIS-SOV*), 5 August 1994, 39.

7. V. Portnikov, "Govorit' o granitsakh—znachit razorvat' sredniuiu aziiu" (To speak of borders means to tear up Central Asia), *Nezavisimaia Gazeta*, 15 May 1992, 2.

8. Karimov, *Uzbekistan on the Threshold*, 13.

9. Bess Brown, "Whither Tajikistan?" *Radio Free Europe/Radio Liberty (RFE/RL) Research Report*, no. 24 (1992): 1-6; "Karimov Views Regional Security Issues," *FBIS-SOV-92-180*, 16 September 1992, 49; Bess Brown, "Tajik Civil War Prompts Crackdown in Uzbekistan," *RFE/RL Research Report*, no. 11 (1993): 1-6; and "Karimov Speaks About Regional Security at UN," *FBIS-SOV-95-205*, 24 October 1995, 63-64.

10. Karimov, *Uzbekistan on the Threshold*, 13.

11. Mehrdad Haghayeghi, *Islam and Politics in Central Asia* (New York: St. Martin's Press, 1995); and Pauline Jones Luong, *Institutional Change and Political Continuity in Post-Soviet Central Asia: Power, Perceptions, and Pacts* (Cambridge: Cambridge University Press, 2002).

12. A. Malashenko, "Kem prigovoren Islam Karimov?" (Who sentenced Islam Karimov?) *Nezavisimaia Gazeta*, 22 July 1994, 3.

13. Commission on Security and Cooperation in Europe, *Democratization and Human Rights in Uzbekistan: Hearing before the Commission on Security and Cooperation in Europe*, 106th Cong., 1st sess., 18 October 1999, 26.

14. "Dushanbe prisoedinitsia k 'soiuzu trek'" (Dushanbe will join the 'union track'), *Rossiiskaia Gazeta*, 6 January 1998, 3.

15. G. Zhukova, "Protest Tashkenta Islamabadu" (Tashkent's protest to Islamabad), *Nezavisimaia Gazeta*, 19 February 1998, 5; and G. Chernogaeva and Iu. Chernogaev, "Uzbekistan obviniaet Pakistan v podgotovke boevikov" (Uzbekistan charges Pakistan with training militants), *Kommersant'-daily*, 18 February 1998, 5.

16. Paul Goble, "Reading Fundamentalism Right," *RFE/RL Newsline*, 7 May 1998.

17. "More on Karimov Visit to Moscow," *RFE/RL Newsline*, 7 May 1998.

18. Commission on Security and Cooperation in Europe, *Democratization and Human Rights in Uzbekistan*, 26.

19. Ibid., 41.

20. "'Shanghai Forum' Participants Anticipate New Incursions By Islamic Militants," *RFE/RL Newsline*, 15 February 2001.

21. For more on HuT see, Uran Botobekov, "Spreading the Ideas of the Hizb-ut-Tahrir in South Kyrgyzstan," and Bakhtiyar Babadzhanov, "On the Activities of Hizb-ut-Tahrir in Uzbekistan," in *Islam in the Post-Soviet Newly Independent States: The View from Within*, ed. Alexei Malashenko and Martha Brill Olcott (Moscow: Carnegie Moscow

Center, 2001), 129-69.

22. Alisher Khamidov and Alisher Saipov, "Islamic Radical Group Bides Time on the Sidelines of Kyrgyzstan's Revolution," *Eurasianet*, 14 April 2005.

23. Svante E. Cornell and Regine A. Spector, "Central Asia: More than Islamic Extremists," *Washington Quarterly* 25, no. 1 (2002): 200.

24. Alisher Khamidov, "Frustration Builds among Uzbeks in Southern Kyrgyzstan," *Eurasianet*, 26 March 2001.

25. "Government Response to IMU Threat Fuels Radicalism in Uzbekistan," *Eurasianet*, 24 July 2001.

26. "Uzbekistan Denies Requesting Russian Military Help," *RFE/RL Newsline*, 30 August 2000.

27. "Uzbek, Russian Defense Officials Conclude Talks," *RFE/RL Newsline*, 1 March 2001.

28. "Russian General in Tashkent for Defense Planning," *RFE/RL Newsline*, 30 April 2001.

29. "Uzbekistan, Russia Discuss Economic, Military Cooperation," *RFE/RL Newsline*, 7 May 2001. Russia provided Uzbekistan with a variety of military equipment, such as Russian-manufactured armoured personnel carriers, mortars, and multiple-launch rocket systems. See "U.S. Holds Talks in Kyrgyzstan, Uzbekistan on Regional Security Threats," *RFE/RL Newsline*, 21 May 2001; and Ariel Cohen, "The Arms Trade Flourishes in Central Asia," *Eurasianet*, 5 September 2001.

30. "Putin, CIS Leaders Meet Without Ties to Form New Ties," *RFE/RL Newsline*, 2 August 2001.

31. "Government Response to IMU Threat Fuels Radicalism in Uzbekistan," *Eurasianet*, 24 July 2001, 1.

32. Esmer Islamov, "Fighting Rages for Third Straight Day in Uzbekistan," *Eurasianet*, 30 March 2004; and Esmer Islamov, "Bombings and Shootings Rock Uzbekistan," *Eurasianet*, 29 March 2004.

33. "Karimov Believes Hizb-Ut-Tahrir Behind Most Recent Tashkent Bombings," *Eurasianet*, 2 August 2004; and Igor Rotar, "Popular Frustration with Karimov Fuels Terrorist Attacks in Uzbekistan," *Jamestown Eurasia Daily Monitor*, 2 August 2004.

34. "Uzbekistan Heads Towards Violent Regime Change," *Jane's Intelligence Review* (July 2005): 12-19.

35. "Uzbek President Blames Extremists," *RFE/RL Newsline*, 16 May 2005.

36. Roger McDermott, "Russia Blames Taliban for Uprising in Uzbekistan," *Jamestown Eurasia Daily Monitor*, 17 May 2005; and Claire Bigg, "Uzbekistan: Karimov, Putin Say Andijon Violence was Planned Abroad," *RFE/RL Report*, 29 June 2005.

37. James Rupert, "Dateline Tashkent: Post-Soviet Central Asia," *Foreign Policy*, no. 87 (1992): 188.

38. Robin Wright, "Islam, Democracy, and the West," *Foreign Affairs* 71, no. 3 (1992): 141.

39. A. Alimov and A. Mursaliev, "Nas uchili prygat' cherez kapitalizm" (We have been taught to leapfrog capitalism), *Komsomol'skaia Pravda*, 7 March 1991, 1.

40. "Uzbek President Karimov Interviewed," *FBIS-SOV-91-106*, 3 June 1991, 101.

41. "Prezident schitaet, chto ego respublika ne gotova k demokratii" (President believes his republic is not ready for democracy), *Izvestiia*, 17 September 1991, 1.

42. V. Vyzhutovich, "Ottseplennyi vagon: Uzbekistan posle provozglasheniia nezavisimosti" (Uncoupled train car: Uzbekistan after the proclamation of independence), *Izvestiia*, 13 September 1991, 3.

43. Hiro, *Between Marx and Muhammad*, 187.
44. A. Musin, "Vyrabatyvaetsia natsional'naia kontseptsiia prav cheloveka" (A national concept of human rights is being developed), *Nezavisimaia Gazeta*, 22 November 1996, 3.
45. In late November the electoral commission required that all opposition groups present 100,000 voter signatures within three days to make a candidate eligible for election. Birlik reportedly obtained the appropriate number of signatures. However, when they arrived at the commission's office during the afternoon of the deadline day, a Friday, they found the office closed. Hiro, *Between Marx and Muhammad*, 176-88.
46. *Nezavisimaia Gazeta*, 1 February 1992, 3.
47. *Nezavisimaia Gazeta*, 21 March 1992, 3.
48. "Prosecutor Investigates 'Birlik' Leaders Attack," *FBIS-SOV-92-128*, 2 July 1992, 72.
49. Knight, *Spies Without Cloaks*, 188. After a similar attack, Polat and fellow Birlik leader, Muralim Adylov, were denied treatment and refused as inpatients. The hospital called the police, and a senior police officer informed the two that they would have to leave, or else they would be removed by force. "Police Evict Opposition Leaders From Hospital," *FBIS-SOV-92-139*, 20 July 1992, 64. Adylov was also assaulted in late May, while Ravshan Dzhuraev, leader of Birlik's youth organization, was attacked on the streets a week earlier. *Nezavisimaia Gazeta*, 28 May 1992, 3.
50. I. Rotar', "'Demrossiia' i 'Birlik' obviniaiut Uzbekskoe rukovodstvo" ("Democratic Russia" and "Birlik" accuse Uzbek leadership), *Nezavisimaia Gazeta*, 26 September 1992, 3.
51. *Nezavisimaia Gazeta*, 12 December 1992, 3.
52. O. Panfilov, "Khel'sinki Voch o Situatsii v Srednei Azii" (Helsinki Watch on the situation in Central Asia), *Nezavisimaia Gazeta*, 7 May 1993, 3.
53. "Government Suspends Activities of Birlik Opposition Group," *FBIS-SOV-93-012*, 21 January 1993, 73-74.
54. "Sentenced Erk Leaders' Activities Profiled," *FBIS-SOV-95-100*, 24 May 1995, 66-67.
55. A. Musin, "V Tashkente gotovitsia krupnyi sudebnyi protsess nad oppozitsiei" (Tashkent is preparing a big trial of opposition), *Nezavisimaia Gazeta*, 23 September 1994, 3; and "Erk Party Trial Resumes," *FBIS-SOV-95-029*, 13 February 1995, 76-77.
56. Fred Hiatt, "Uzbekistan Cracks Down on Dissidents," *Washington Post*, 24 September 1994, A24.
57. Steven Wagner, *Public Opinion in Uzbekistan, 1996* (Washington, D.C.: IFES, 1997), 69.
58. I. Rotar', "Vlasti provotsiruiut Tadzhikskii variant" (The authorities provoke the Tajik variant), *Nezavisimaia Gazeta*, 12 January 1993, 3; and M. Lebedeva, "V Tashkente novii raund davleniia na oppozitsiiu. V Bishkeke—otstavka zamministra VD" (A new round of pressure on the opposition in Tashkent. In Bishkek, the resignation of the Interior Minister), *Izvestiia*, 12 February 1993, 2.
59. For more on the trial see, M. Lebedeva, "Uzbekskogo pravozashchitnika Abdumannoba Pulatova khotiat upriatat' v tiurmu na 6 let, khotia vina ego ne dokazana" (They want to imprison Uzbek human rights leader Abdumannob Pulatov for six years, although guilt has not been proven), *Izvestiia*, 27 January 1993, 2; and idem, "Abdumannob Pulatov otpushchen na svobodu" (Abdumannob Pulatov set free), *Izvestiia*, 28 January 1993, 1. Similarly, Vasiliia Inoiatova, a well-known Uzbek human rights activist and secretary of Birlik, was charged with insulting the dignity of Karimov in a poem that depicted a ruler issuing orders to execute people by firing

squad. The depictions closely resembled events that occurred during unrest in January 1992, and supposedly warranted her charge disrespecting the head of state. O. Panfilov, "Sud nad poetessoi-pravozashchitnitsei" (Trial of poetess-human rights activist), *Nezavisimaia Gazeta*, 27 February 1993, 3.

60. In his trial Polat's lawyer was not able to see any materials pertaining to the case until shortly before the trial began. Ironically, the court released Polat, even though he had been convicted of the crime. Earlier that year another attempt was made to abduct Polat from a similar conference in Kazakhstan. This attempt was unsuccessful because of the intervention of Kazakh authorities. Olcott, *Central Asia's New States*, 107. In September 1993 Uzbek secret police also tried to arrest Abdurashid Sharif, Yadigar Abit, and Abdurahim Polat while the three dissidents were in Baku, Azerbaijan. "Uzbek Secret Service Tries to Seize Dissidents," *FBIS-SOV-93-185*, 27 September 1993, 29.

61. On face value the elections appeared completely democratic, but the parties themselves conducted the nominations for deputy seats. The old conservatives nominated themselves for various positions and limited outside nominees except for the occasional non-party members. A. Pulatov, "Uzbekistan vstupaet v polosu sotsial'nykh potriasenii" (Uzbekistan enters a period of social upheaval), *Nezavisimaia Gazeta*, 15 February 1995, 2.

62. Out of the unaffiliated block of candidates sponsored by regional legislative councils, 124 members were also members of the PDP, giving that party a much higher *de facto* count. Roger Kangas, "The Heirs of Tamerlane," in *Building Democracy: The OMRI Annual Survey of Eastern Europe and the Former Soviet Union* (Armonk, NY: M. E. Sharpe, 1996), 278.

63. "Pervaia sessiia Olii Mazhlisa respubliki Uzbekistan pervogo sozyva" (Convening of the first session of the Oliy Majlis of the republic of Uzbekistan), *Pravda Vostoka*, 25 February 1995, 1.

64. Vatan Tarakkiyeti began under the leadership of Uzman Azim, who left Birlik to join Karimov's Presidential Council, the body charged with carrying out governmental policy.

65. "Uzbekistan Elects a New Legislature," *New York Times*, 26 December 1994, A10.

66. "Novaia politicheskaia partiia" (New political party), *Pravda Vostoka*, 21 February 1995, 1.

67. For more on these platforms see, Bohr, *Uzbekistan*, 12.

68. "Referendum Results Reflect Confidence in Reform," *FBIS-SOV-95-062*, 21 March 1995, 74. Karimov also stated, "the initiative to hold it came from the parliament elected by the people, and it based its decision on the Constitution. Therefore, the legitimacy of the arrangement cannot be doubted in the slightest." "Put' Uzbekistana – integratsiia v mirovoe soobshchestvo" (Uzbekistan's path is integration into the world community), *Pravda Vostoka*, 30 March 1995, 2.

69. Abdumannob Polat, "Karimov Will Stay in Office, But Recent Elections Send Mixed Messages," *RFE/RL Newsline*, 7 January 2000; and "Uzbekistan's President Re-Elected," *RFE/RL Newsline*, 10 January 2000.

70. Commission on Security and Cooperation in Europe, *Human Rights and Democratization in Uzbekistan and Turkmenistan*, 106th Cong., 2nd sess., 2000, 8.

71. Author's interview with senior Uzbek official, Washington, D.C., 15 October 2002.

Chapter 5

Uzbekistan and Economic Dependence on Russia

This chapter examines Uzbek economic dependence on Russia and assesses its influence on Karimov's alignment calculations towards Russia. The IT/ED framework suggests that the more economically dependent a country is on Russia, the more likely a pro-Russian alignment will be adopted. However, when leaders can mitigate or sever this dependence, then they are less constrained in their relations towards Russia, allowing for a more independent alignment strategy. As we will see, Karimov looked to Moscow for economic assistance in the days after independence. But becoming aware of the asymmetrical nature of these relations, he developed a self-sufficiency strategy to lessen Uzbek dependence on Russia by the middle of the decade.

The first section of this chapter examines Karimov's perceptions of Uzbek dependence on Russia and strategies envisioned by the president to address the dependence. The initial phase of Uzbek-Russian economic relations (1991-93) is assessed in light of Karimov's stated economic objectives (drawn from a series of booklets and pamphlets written by him). This period is chosen purposefully because it also relates to the lifespan of the Ruble Zone, the post-Soviet monetary system most former Soviet republics adopted. The collapse of the Ruble Zone is thus a defining moment in the economic independence of CIS states since thereafter they were forced to introduce their own currencies. During this period, Karimov became increasingly aware of the inherent asymmetries in Uzbek-Russian economic relations, and, accordingly, sought to develop a self-sufficiency strategy that increased domestic production, namely in the field of energy production.

After setting the context, the chapter turns to a more explicit discussion of Uzbekistan's dependence on Russian trade and energy, while also examining the availability of alternative Western economic resources. As the chapter reveals, Karimov has been highly successful at first understanding the economic needs of Uzbekistan, and then developing an economic strategy that lessened Uzbek dependence on Russia. The success of Karimov's self-sufficiency strategy made an independent alignment possible. This was critical because Karimov failed to obtain significant Western economic resources necessary to adopt a more independent foreign policy. The lack of economic reform and consistent state intervention into the economy were the main factors that undermined Western assistance. In the end, while Karimov was unsuccessful at promoting the economic growth and development of the Uzbek economy, he was at a minimum able to enhance the self-sufficiency of the country, thereby broadening his foreign policy options vis-à-vis Russia.

Karimov's Economic Approach

Several factors shaped Karimov's understanding of Uzbekistan's economic dependence on Russia, and most were the result of years of Russian and Soviet domination. First, Uzbekistan was a relatively poor republic within the former Soviet Union at the time of independence, a consideration true for all Central Asian states. Just 41 percent of its population lived in urban areas, and 13 percent of its employed population possessed a higher education as of 1989, compared with 15 percent for Russia, Estonia, and Latvia, and 20 percent for Georgia (the republic with the highest ranking in this category). Uzbekistan's retail commodity turnover in 1988 was only 760 rubles per capita, far below Ukraine at 1,210 rubles, Russia at 1,400 and Estonia at 1,970. Moreover, the country produced far fewer consumer goods per capita than most other states; its 1988 output was valued at 490 rubles per capita, whereas Russia's was worth 1,190 rubles, Ukraine's 1,230 and Latvia's 2,570. Based on indices of development and standards of living, Uzbekistan also scored lower than any other Soviet republic.[1]

Second and related, the Uzbek economy traditionally focused on the extraction of raw materials. Uzbekistan's main export is cotton, dominating exports at roughly 80 percent. Other resources exist such as vast mineral deposits including gold, silver, copper, lead, zinc, wolfram, tungsten, uranium and other minerals. Natural gas and oil deposits also exist in sizable quantities. However, under the Soviet system, only 10 percent of these raw materials were processed within Uzbekistan, with the lion's share being sent to Russia. Thus, while Uzbekistan was endowed with vast natural resources, it lacked the ability to process these goods and deliver them to the world market directly. Third, as we will discuss at greater length below, the structure of trade was tilted strongly towards Russia, with Russia making up about 53 percent of both imports and exports in 1992.[2] Karimov recognized these factors, which led to several conclusions: 1) Uzbekistan needed to reorient its trade balance away from Russia; 2) Uzbekistan needed to restructure its domestic production of goods; and 3) given the difficulties of these transitions, economic cooperation with Russia would be necessary in the short-term.

Karimov's assessment of Uzbek economic dependence on Russia fundamentally shaped his economic strategy. In a March 1991 interview, Karimov highlighted the many challenges that justified cooperation with Russia:

> After sober analysis of the situation in Uzbekistan, however, we have come to the view that our republic's best prospects lie in a renewed federation. I would like to give you just two figures. The per-capita national income in Uzbekistan is not only three times lower than in the Baltic states, but it is also only half of the Union average. The republic has a completely underdeveloped, one-sided economy. We are mainly deliverers of raw material, and even the existing processing industry provides mostly

only intermediate products. A total of 92 percent of all Uzbek cotton fibers are not processed in our country. On the other hand, we have to import more than half of the goods needed by the population.[3]

The country's concentration on raw material exports hampered the development of the Uzbek economy. Even before the Soviet collapse, the Communist Party of Uzbekistan acknowledged that despite the benefits from Uzbekistan's membership in the Soviet Union, its economy was heavily skewed towards raw material exports and its main social and economic indicators were low in comparison to other Soviet republics.[4] At times, Karimov even suggested that this was a result of Moscow's exploitation of Uzbekistan natural resources, where, he noted, profits were taken out of the country.[5] Uzbek leaders agreed that the country needed to focus less on the exportation of raw materials, but economic reform did not appear to be the answer either.[6]

Unlike other former Soviet countries that adopted "shock therapy," Karimov preferred gradual economic reform, and heavily state-guided reform at that. The experiences of shock therapy in Eastern Europe, the Baltic states, and Ukraine were unsettling, where reform brought with it severe short-term costs, such as unemployment, inflation, and general economic uncertainty. These short-term costs would presumably threaten Karimov's political security and place added pressure on his regime. Thus, while it was widely accepted that Uzbekistan needed to reorient its economy and address its dependence, cooperation with Russia was needed in the short-term. Shock therapy was seen as just too costly in political terms.

Based on these factors, Karimov's initial economic strategy outlined a gradual path to economic reform and focused on several related principles. First, the economic realm has priority over politics. Second, the state is to serve as the main agent of reform, in essence controlling the economy during the transition. Third, priority is given to law and legal obedience. Fourth, the state must adhere to a strong social policy that takes into account the demographic structure of the country. And fifth, the transition to a market economy must come through evolutionary means, thereby buffering the country from the instability associated with shock therapy.[7] Karimov's strategy placed a tremendous amount of power in the hands of the state, and more specifically the president, to ensure that the transition and the distribution of economic resources would occur in the most favorable manner to Karimov. This also placed Karimov in the position to maintain, and support when necessary, the social safety net that would provide for Uzbeks hit hard by the economic conditions.

The next section discusses how Karimov went about implementing this strategy in his relations with Russia. After establishing the pattern of cooperation or lack thereof with Russia, the chapter returns to the key economic indicators of the IT/ED framework – trade, access to energy, and economic reform – to suggest ways in which they influenced relations with Russia and the West.

Economic Relations with Russia and the CIS: The Early Years

Before independence, Karimov supported a renewed relationship between Russia and the former Soviet republics, although he stressed Uzbek sovereignty and independence. To this end, he added a second question to the March 1991 referendum ballot on the Soviet Union: "Do you agree that Uzbekistan should remain within the renewed Union (federation) as a sovereign, equal republic?"[8] The Uzbek people widely supported the March 1991 referendum, with over 90 percent of the voters in every region voting to preserve the Soviet federation.[9] This was a clear mandate that Uzbeks wanted to continue cooperating with Russia.

After the failed 1991 August putsch, Karimov continued to support a renewed Economic Community Treaty, which would maintain links between Russia and other Soviet republics. However, he was skeptical of a rekindling of the old Soviet hierarchy. For instance, in October 1991, he drew attention to the proposed executive bodies: "Coordination is needed. But when they write 'executive managerial organs,' this means that they are again creating new structures over us. I would pose the question thus: 'coordinative-managerial,' but 'executive,' not in any instance."[10] The new Economic Community Treaty, which was signed by Uzbekistan on 18 October 1991, contained an executive body, the Interstate Economic Committee, but the emphasis was on coordination and not top-down approaches. The new treaty was short-lived as the three Slavic states disbanded the Soviet Union in December 1991. Uzbekistan, as did the other Central Asian states, agreed to join the new CIS, which would presumably serve many of the same functions as the Soviet system.

Karimov joined the CIS based on Uzbekistan's immediate economic needs. He realized that economic cooperation with Russia at least in the short-run was necessary to achieve "genuine independence" faster, since inter-republic cooperation could presumably address the most difficult economic problems the countries would face.[11] As Henry Hale found through interviews with Uzbek officials and presidential advisors, while there was some disagreement over the scope and nature of cooperation with Russia and the CIS, there was consensus that such coordination was necessary.[12] Indeed, Karimov continued to speak of the utility of CIS cooperation, as opposed to Ukrainian President Leonid Kravchuk who believed that the CIS was not really a viable institution.[13] There were limits however.

Given Russia's preponderance within the CIS, economic policies initiated by Moscow tended to have far ranging consequences and because of Russia's relative economic position it was not constrained by other CIS states. By January 1992, for example, it became clear that Russia intended to engage in economic liberalization despite its impact on other CIS states. These decisions had a direct impact on the political stability of Uzbekistan, as price hikes sparked student riots in Tashkent. Karimov consistently voiced his concerns with Russian policies throughout 1992. Shortly after the student riots he argued:

> Economic reform, price liberalization, and privatization should take place in a coordinated manner. And not like this: One president, to put it crudely, releases prices on a whim. We are not living on the other side of the fence, so we too are forced to hurry, even if our situation is different. Then you get the campus demonstrations and inflamed passions. I am basically now a hostage to decisions made in Moscow… The main point is that the Commonwealth should make decisions collectively, collegially, after careful consideration, in an atmosphere of tolerance.[14]

As Karimov pointed out in the spring of 1992:

> Moscow is not taking us into consideration in formulating its next measures. This is a cause of great concern for us. What will the reforms produce tomorrow? What will the Russian government reconsider next? And in what kind of situation will these developments put us?[15]

This sentiment and a growing awareness of Russia's unwillingness to work with other CIS members prompted Karimov to suggest in April 1992 that each republic should conduct its own pricing policy. Individual strategies would take into account demographic and cultural factors since comparable price adjustments "could cause the situation to explode" in Uzbekistan.[16] Tensions also rose as Russia pressured other members of the Ruble Zone to adopt specific policies, and by November 1993 Uzbekistan announced its own currency and left the Ruble-zone altogether, therein ending the first phase of Uzbek-Russian cooperation.

Perhaps even more significant in these initial years of independence, Uzbekistan looked to Russia for a continuation of direct and indirect subsidies. After independence, however, these subsidies became increasingly scarce. In 1992, for example, Uzbekistan effectively received subsidies equal to 69 percent of its Gross Domestic Product in the form of printed rubles.[17] But, as Russia looked inward, these much-needed subsidies dried up, and without these highly coveted subsidies, one of the major *raison d'etre* of Uzbek economic cooperation with Russia ended as well. Thus, Karimov focused on ways in which Uzbekistan's economic dependence could be addressed. As we will see, tremendous inroads were made in the trade and energy sectors, while the lack of economic reform limited Uzbekistan's access to alternative Western economic resources.

Structure of Trade with Russia

The inherent economic dependence that existed between Russia and Uzbekistan prompted Karimov to adopt an economic strategy that sought to limit the import of industrial and finished products from other countries of the CIS (notably Russia) while increasing the domestic production of critical supplies often imported. As seen above, there was also an awareness of the need to orient the Uzbek economy away from the exportation of raw materials.[18] To this extent, Karimov's strategy was one of self-sufficiency and adjusting the structure of trade with Russia was of paramount concern. By the end of the decade, the trade balance with Russia would be drastically restructured. In the early 1990s, when the trade balance favored Russia, Uzbekistan adopted a pro-Russian alignment, but once Uzbek trade dependence on Russia was lessened by the mid 1990s, a more independent alignment was possible.

The structure of trade between Russia and Uzbekistan gradually improved in terms favorable to Uzbekistan. For instance, between 1994-95, Uzbek exports to Russia declined as a percentage of Uzbekistan's total trade from 38.9 percent to 29.7 percent, while total Uzbek exports increased over the same period of time by about 40 percent (see Table 5.1). After 1995, in which Uzbek foreign policy became more independent, Uzbek exports to Russia as a percentage of total trade averaged around 20 percent annually.

This shifting trade balance was also offset by an increase in Uzbek exports to Organization for Economic Cooperation and Development (OECD) countries. Between 1994-1996, for example, exports to OECD countries averaged 31.7 percent of total exports, while exports to Russia averaged 30.4 percent over the same period of time. Despite these optimistic figures, exports to OECD countries declined between 1997-2001, averaging 20 percent of total exports, although they remained slightly higher than exports to Russia at 19 percent of total exports.

Despite the stated intentions of Uzbek leaders, raw material exports, like cotton and gold, remained central to Uzbek exports. The rationale behind this policy was two-fold. First, it allowed Uzbekistan to mitigate its existing dependence on Russian markets, and second, it increased Uzbekistan's access to hard currency. For example, between January and August 1992, $411 million in hard currency was obtained through cotton fiber, while the second highest export (copper and copper products) secured only $31 million.[19] This was inconsistent with Karimov's long-term goals of reorienting the Uzbek export market, but cotton remained the primary source of hard currency and this could not be ignored. Cotton production and its share of Uzbek exports remained strikingly high. Based on exports to countries outside the CIS (which is a more accurate measure of competitiveness in world markets), cotton exports continued to account for roughly 70 to 80 percent of exports followed by nonferrous and ferrous metals between 4 to 6 percent.[20]

Beyond reorienting exports towards OECD countries, there was also an additional effort to improve Uzbekistan's import structure. Uzbek imports from Russia continued to decline throughout the decade (see Table 5.2). In 1994, Russia represented 36.4 percent of total Uzbek imports, while this figure declined to 29.9 percent in 1995. Much like export values, imports from Russia continued to decline to 21.2 percent of total imports in 1997, 13.2 percent in 1998, with this figure averaging 11 percent between 1999-2001. The decline in Russian imports was primarily the result of an increase in the domestic production of goods typically imported from Russia, especially energy, fuel, and cereal grains. Prior to independence, Uzbekistan received the vast majority of its oil from Russia, approximately 4.5 million tons each year. As we will see in the next section, the increased domestic production of oil within Uzbekistan enabled the country to sever this dependence on Russian supplies.

Table 5.1 Uzbek Foreign Export Trade, 1994-2001[21]
(millions of US dollars)

	1994	1995	1996	1997	1998	1999	2000	2001
Total (world)	1,991	2,718	2,620	2,896	3,309	2,888	3,309	3,121
Russia	774	808	593	923	474	423	602	527
	(38.9)	(29.7)	(22.6)	(31.9)	(14.3)	(14.6)	(18.2)	(16.9)
OECD Countries	693	724	886	731	663	497	617	593
	(34.8)	(26.6)	(33.8)	(25.2)	(20.0)	(17.2)	(18.6)	(19.0)
Intra-Region Trade	134	564	387	495	442	410	336	306
	(6.7)	(20.7)	(14.8)	(17.1)	(13.4)	(14.2)	(10.2)	(9.8)

Table 5.2 Uzbek Foreign Import Trade, 1994-2001[22]
(millions of US dollars)

	1994	1995	1996	1997	1998	1999	2000	2001
Total (world)	2,522	3,030	4,854	4,538	4,032	3,245	2,596	3,283
Russia	917 (36.4)	907 (29.9)	1,191 (24.5)	962 (21.2)	533 (13.2)	264 (8.1)	302 (11.6)	400 (12.2)
OECD Countries	782 (31.0)	833 (27.7)	1,736 (35.8)	1,524 (33.6)	1,156 (28.7)	1,194 (36.8)	809 (31.2)	835 (25.4)
Intra-Region Trade	377 (14.9)	434 (14.3)	563 (11.6)	470 (10.3)	319 (8.0)	330 (10.2)	366 (14.1)	320 (9.7)

Part of Karimov's economic strategy also entailed diversifying the country's sources of imports, especially in finding alternative trading partners. Preference was given to the OECD countries that could provide the largest source of economic resources. For instance, Russian imports as a percentage of total Uzbek imports declined by 25 percent from 1994 to 2001. This was balanced with a reciprocal increase in the amount of imports received from OECD countries. Throughout the decade, imports from OECD countries averaged 32 percent of total Uzbek imports.

This shift towards Western imports resulted from Uzbekistan's desire to import new machinery and equipment. These imported goods represent roughly one third of all Uzbek imports, with over 70 percent of them coming from the countries of the OECD.[23] This fell in line with Karimov's state industrial strategy that emphasized a need to upgrade and modernize the industrial base through state investment. This top-down strategy focused on importing technology to increase domestic production, and resembled import-substitution strategies, but the results have not been spectacular in the economic development of Uzbekistan.

Perhaps the most significant economic factor that allowed Karimov to adopt a more independent alignment from Russia was his ability to restructure the balance of trade, by eliminating the import of Russian energy supplies in favor of heightened domestic production. This issue is discussed below.

Strategic Goods

The IT/ED framework suggests that the availability of domestic energy supplies is a crucial if not determining factor in a country's ability to forge more independent relations from Russia. Uzbekistan was fortunate in this regard because it possessed natural gas and oil deposits that enabled it to sever its energy dependence on Russia, unlike other states of the CIS like Ukraine, as we will see in Chapter 8. Under the Soviet system, Uzbekistan's role as an energy producer was limited in favor of the production of cotton and gold. But, this underdevelopment of energy resources would not last long.

A fundamental element in Uzbekistan's self-sufficiency strategy was domestic energy production. Uzbekistan relied heavily on oil deliveries from Russia, and as of 1991, the republic imported almost three-quarters of its oil needs, approximately 4.5 million tons of oil each year. After independence, Karimov embarked on a more ambitious plan for the development of indigenous oil and gas supplies. Indeed, Uzbekistan holds a rare distinction among the energy producers of the CIS, in that it is the only state in which oil and gas production increased (or at least equaled) every year from 1991-1999 (see Table 5.3). Domestic production started off slowly, but by the middle of the decade Uzbekistan severed its dependence on Russian energy imports. Whereas in 1991, the republic produced 2.8 million tons of oil, this figure increased to 5.5 million tons in 1994, 7.6 million tons in 1995 and 1996, and 8.1 million tons in 1999. Thus, these figures exceeded what Uzbekistan produced as well as what it imported from Russia before independence.

Table 5.3 CIS Oil Production, 1991-2000[24] (*millions of tons*)

	1991	1992	1993	1994	1995	1996	1997	1998	1999	2000
Ukraine	4.9	4.5	4.2	4.2	4.1	4.1	4.1	3.9	3.8	3.7
Uzbekistan	2.8	3.3	3.9	5.5	7.6	7.6	7.9	8.1	8.1	-
Russia	462.0	399.0	354.0	318.0	307.0	301.0	306.0	303.0	305.0	324.0
Kazakhstan	26.6	25.8	23.0	20.3	20.5	23.0	25.8	25.9	30.1	35.3
Azerbaijan	11.7	11.1	10.3	9.6	9.2	9.1	9.1	11.4	13.8	14.1
Turkmenistan	5.4	5.2	4.8	4.4	4.5	4.4	-	-	-	-

Table 5.4 CIS Natural Gas Production, 1991-2000[25] (*billion cubic meters*)

	1991	1992	1993	1994	1995	1996	1997	1998	1999	2000
Ukraine	24.3	20.9	19.2	18.3	18.2	18.4	18.1	18.0	18.1	17.8
Uzbekistan	41.9	42.8	45.0	47.2	48.6	49.0	51.2	54.8	55.6	-
Russia	643.0	641.0	618.0	607.0	595.0	601.0	571.0	591.0	592.0	584.0
Turkmenistan	84.3	60.1	65.3	35.7	32.3	35.2	-	-	-	-
Kazakhstan	7.9	8.1	6.7	4.5	5.9	6.5	8.1	7.9	9.9	11.5
Azerbaijan	8.6	7.9	6.8	6.4	6.6	6.3	6.0	5.6	5.0	5.6

Similarly, gas production, which Uzbekistan is even more endowed with, increased steadily over the decade (see Table 5.4). In 1991 41.9 billion cubic meters were produced, which increased to 45.0 billion cubic meters in 1993, 48.6 billion in 1995, 51.2 billion in 1997, and 55.6 billion in 1999. Programs that capitalized on Uzbekistan's vast natural gas reserves complemented the increased production. For example, Karimov initiated programs, such as the conversion of 250,000 state-owned vehicles from gasoline to compressed natural gas, which capitalized on Uzbekistan's vast gas reserves.[26]

While it is seen as secondary importance to energy supplies, another strategic good that Karimov highlighted was grain production and overcoming Uzbek reliance on grain imports. This strategy called for a reallocation of arable lands for agricultural purposes. To complement this gradual reduction of land used for cotton production, more advanced technologies were introduced that made production more efficient. Land that was once used to produce cotton was now used to produce cereals and grains. More specifically, the government from 1990-1996 reduced the areas sown to cotton (from 44 to 35 percent), while increasing the arable land used for cereal production (from 24 to 41 percent).[27] Accordingly, the gross output of cereals grew by 1.6 times, which enabled domestic producers to meet almost half of the republic's demand for cereals. Although cereal imports remain high (almost half of grain and cereals are still imported), Karimov's initiatives provided some additional level of security. While this strategy proved effective in the short-term, long-term issues need to be addressed to more sincerely alter Uzbek dependence on grain imports. For instance, this policy does not increase hard currency earnings; it will be increasingly difficult to maintain in the event of privatization once state intervention is curtailed; and its yields significantly less value than cotton production.[28]

Karimov addressed the dependence on imported goods, especially energy supplies, through a consistent policy of domestic self-sufficiency and increased production. This proved the decisive factor in alleviating Uzbek dependence on Russia, since Karimov had difficulty obtaining Western economic resources. As we will see, this was a direct result of his unwillingness to engage in economic reform and restrict state intervention in the economy.

Alternative Resources from the West

Uzbekistan has been somewhat successful at reorienting its trade balance to gain greater access to Western markets and hard currency. But despite Karimov's previous inclinations, this reorientation merely capitalized on the export of raw materials. This strategy allowed Uzbekistan to mitigate its economic dependence on Russia, but more sincere economic reorientation towards the West has been less forthcoming. The IT/ED framework suggests that the main factor determining the extent to which CIS leaders can obtain Western economic resources rests on a leader's willingness to enact and implement economic reform. In this regard, Uzbekistan's limited and inconsistent path of economic reform undermined efforts to obtain Western economic resources. This section surveys the extent to which economic reform was implemented, and its influence on Karimov's ability to obtain alternative Western economic resources (or lack thereof).

The initial interaction between Uzbekistan and the IMF was difficult. By 1994 Karimov appeared to be willing to implement economic reform as evidenced by his 21 January decree. The decree, "On Measures for Further Deepening Economic Reforms, Providing for the Protection of Private Property and for the Development of Entrepreneurship," was seen at the time as a major turning point and bolstered the power of the state to promote economic reform. Among the most important aspects of this initiative were the establishment of an inter-ministerial committee on economic reform, entrepreneurship, and foreign investment and the expansion of powers of the privatization committee to include aspects of private sector development. However, by increasing the role of the state in the reform process, a consideration largely consistent with Karimov's objectives, the policy ran counter to that articulated by the IMF and other international financial institutions.

Support of the fledgling Uzbek currency was the first pressing issue. Negotiations began in February 1994 but broke off in May. Uzbekistan independently introduced its new currency and provided for a transfer of the sum-coupon to the sum on 1 July at a rate of seven to the dollar. The Uzbek government and the Central Bank of Uzbekistan believed this was possible without IMF assistance because Uzbek foreign exchange reserves ($700 million) and gold ($440 million) could allow the currency to be floated.[29] This proved shortsighted, however, as inflation and the anticipated currency risk undermined the stability of the new currency, which depreciated to 20 to the dollar by October. By the end of 1994, Uzbek officials sought IMF economic assistance, and the first agreement with the IMF was signed in January 1995. Uzbekistan received $74 million under the systemic transformation facility to support the government's program of macroeconomic stabilization and systemic reform. These funds were negotiated against the Uzbek government's program of reducing the fiscal deficit to 3.5 percent of GDP (of which 2 percent was funded by domestic banks), and other reforms including the further liberalization of prices, the phasing out of budgetary subsidies, and the increased privatization of medium and large-scale enterprises.[30]

The IMF apparently was pleased by the progress of the Uzbek government on these measures since it continued to extend assistance in December 1995 (see Table 5.5). The IMF approved a package totaling $259 million to support the government's 1995-96 economic reform program. Of this total, $185 million was made available under a 15-month stand-by credit, while a second drawing under the systemic transformation facility was made for $74 million. As per the negotiated agreement, the program sought to cut the rate of inflation to 21-25 percent, while keeping the overall deficit at about 4 percent of GDP. The IMF also established clear expectations for the Uzbek government with respect to structural reform. The government was required:

to add momentum to its structural reform efforts, with particular emphasis on the privatization of medium and large-scale enterprise, enterprise reform, continued liberalization of foreign trade, and further disengagement of the government in economic activity.[31]

This interaction underscores how Western assistance could be obtained when economic reform was initiated. But, initial reform successes did not last long, especially when the IMF continued to criticize administrative interventions into the economy. This was consistent with Karimov's strategy to make the state the main agent in the reform process. Government intervention was also necessary to capitalize on the most valuable raw materials Uzbekistan had to offer, including cotton and gold for exportation and oil and gas production for domestic consumption. Karimov's top-down strategy was not well received in international financial institutions, but it stemmed in part from his unwillingness to relinquish control over economic decisions fearing economic decline and the resultant political consequences.

Table 5.5 IMF Disbursements and Repayments to Uzbekistan[32] (*in SDRs*)

	Disbursements	Repayments
1995	105,950,000	0
1996	59,250,000	0
1997	0	0
1998	0	0
1999	0	18,365,625
2000	0	49,350,000
2001	0	35,140,625
2002	0	16,625,000
2003	0	4,156,250

As reform slowed, so to did Western assistance. Many problems identified during 1995 became apparent as Uzbekistan fell into economic crisis. The most serious problems related to the production of cotton, which remained a major source of hard currency. First, the 1995 domestic cotton harvest proved disastrous; and second, world prices for cotton remained low. These realities compelled the government to disregard IMF advice and increase its intervention into the economy, most notably through the imposition of foreign exchange controls and an increase in the printing of money that stoked inflation. These decisions ran counter to the conditions of the December 1995 stand-by credit, and the IMF suspended it on 19 December 1996. Officially, the IMF suspended the funds because the government missed its inflation targets, and the imposition of tighter state control over currency transactions further limited foreign direct investment. Apparently, Karimov was unwilling to weather the short-term adjustment costs associated with economic reform, as seen in the Baltic states, Russia, and Ukraine.

During 1997 and 1998 Karimov continued to resist economic reform. He was unwilling to restructure and privatize enterprises and postponed the privatization of the oil and gas sectors, which as we have seen, were critical in Uzbekistan's drive for energy self-sufficiency. In this regard, Karimov preferred a more mercantilist approach, which protected vital industries in Uzbekistan, in contrast to greater integration into the world economy.

By 1998, the possibility of obtaining Western economic resources remained bleak. Negotiations with the IMF stalled over currency convertibility. This issue remains a significant obstacle in IMF negotiations because it has become increasingly difficult to promote and attract foreign direct investment. The main stumbling bloc is over multiple currency exchanges. In essence, there are three types of exchange rates in Uzbekistan: 1) the official rate established by the Republican Hard Currency Exchange through a complex system of administrative transactions; 2) the commercial rate which differs from the official rate in that a surcharge of up to 15 percent is levied for bank services; and 3) the black market rate which differs from the official rate by a factor of two or more.[33] This multiple exchange rate system allows the government to control vital aspects of the country's economy. This is consistent with Karimov's objectives because it ensures state purchases of imports, especially investment goods and allows the government to improve the balance of payments by establishing control over import transactions. However, such practices run counter to the more laissez-faire attitude of the IMF and other international financial institutions, and continue to inhibit Uzbek access to Western economic resources. The lack of reform even prompted the IMF to remove their representative in Tashkent.

Conclusions

This chapter examined the extent of Uzbek economic dependence on Russia and determined how this shaped Karimov's patterns of cooperation with Russia. Karimov's pursuit of economic resources did not propel the leader strongly towards Russia (i.e. Belarus) or the West (i.e. the Baltic states). Rather, he pursued a different path; one of economic self-sufficiency. There were two overarching economic considerations that shaped his relations with Russia: 1) the need to cooperate with Russia in the short-term to assist the country's transition and prevent economic collapse; and 2) the need to increase domestic energy production to sever Uzbek economic dependence on Russian energy imports.

Shortly after the collapse of the Soviet Union, it became apparent that economic cooperation with Russia came at great cost. In the early years Uzbekistan sought to reorient its structure of trade to limit its dependence on Russian markets and increase access to Western markets and goods. This strategy proved relatively successful although it relied on the export of raw materials, notably cotton. By the middle of the decade Uzbekistan severed its energy dependence on Russia. The balance of trade became less skewed towards Russia, and domestic energy production proved highly successful. This left Karimov less economically constrained, and coupled with a decline in his internal threats as we saw in Chapter 4, enabled the leader to adopt a more independent alignment by the mid to late 1990s.

Western economic resources have been less forthcoming because of Karimov's unwillingness to implement economic reform. There were initial signs that Uzbekistan may work with the IMF, but this faded by the middle of the decade. Karimov continued to intervene in the economy in order to buffer the country from the economic consequences of reform. The rationale is simple and closely linked to his pursuit of political survival. By embracing radical economic restructuring, the likelihood of economic dislocation within Uzbekistan would increase dramatically. This decline in the country's economy ultimately would have political consequences and further jeopardize Karimov's political position (a fact most evident in the relatively frequent executive turnover in the Baltic states).[34] Concerns over rapid economic decline and its potential impact of political stability were not without precedent having occurred in the Ferghana valley in 1989, 1990, and again in Tashkent in January 1992. Thus, the safer political path for Karimov was one of gradualism, whereby the president could distribute economic benefits to Uzbek citizens. By consistently bringing home the bacon and weathering any economic vicissitudes, Karimov ensured his political position, since the average Uzbek citizen feels they are better off with the more conservative strategy that provides some sense of economic stability. According to public opinion data from 1996, 56 percent of the people polled felt that life had improved since independence, whereas only 32 percent felt it got worse, although this has changed more recently.[35] Long-term growth and development remains elusive, but Karimov remains surely entrenched in his political position, which as this book explains is the primary goal of CIS leaders.

In the end, Uzbekistan has adopted a more independent alignment from Russia, but the long-term question remains as to how long such a path can persist. This is evident in Karimov's stated goals of the need to reorient the Uzbek economy away from simple raw material extraction, yet the short-term necessities for the country have forced it to continue its exportation of raw materials.

Notes

1.   For more on these indicators see, Hale, "Statehood at Stake," 447.
2.   International Monetary Fund, *Uzbekistan: IMF Economic Reviews*, no. 4 (1994): 73.
3.   "Uzbek President on Nationality Conflicts," *FBIS-SOV-91-051*, 15 March 1991, 85.
4.   "Kompartiia Uzbekistana: pozitsiia v perestroike" (Communist party of Uzbekistan: position on perestroika), *Pravda Vostoka*, 9 June 1990, 1.
5.   Islam Karimov, *Uzbekistan: Sobstvennaia model' perekhoda na rynochnye otnosheniia* (Uzbekistan: Its own model for transition to a market economy) (Tashkent: Uzbekiston Publishers, 1993), 13-14.
6.   Islam Karimov, *Uzbekistan: Svoi put' obnovlenniia i progressa* (Uzbekistan: The road of renewal and progress) (Tashkent: Uzbekiston, 1992), 57.
7.   Karimov, *Uzbekistan: Sobstvennaia model' perekhoda*, 37-38.

8. A. Orlov, "Vtoroi biulleten' dlia referenduma v Uzbekistane" (Second ballot for referendum in Uzbekistan), *Izvestiia* 21 February 1991, 1.

9. The only exception was in Tashkent, where the referendum received 87 percent of the vote.

10. V. Kuznetsova and V. Desiatov, "V Alma-Ate v mukakh rozhden dogovor ob ekonomicheskom soobshchestve byvshikh soiuznykh respublik" (An agreement on economic community of the former soviet republics is partially born in Alma-Ata), *Nezavisimaia Gazeta*, 2 October 1991, 1.

11. Karimov, *Uzbekistan: Svoi put' obnovlenniia i progressa*, 25.

12. Hale, "Statehood at Stake," 54-55.

13. "Karimov News Conference Previews Summit," *FBIS-SOV-92-095*, 15 May 1992, 7-8.

14. "Kak zhit' v sodruzhestve" (How to live in the Commonwealth), *Sovetskaia Rossiia* 23 January 1992, 2.

15. V. Portnikov, "Govorit o granitsakh—znachit razorvat sredniuiu aziiu" (To speak of borders means to tear up Central Asia), *Nezavisimaia Gazeta*, 15 May 1992, 2.

16. "Presidents Hold News Conference," *FBIS-SOV-92-080*, 24 April 1992, 9.

17. Hale, "Statehood at Stake," 167.

18. Karimov, *Uzbekistan: Sobstvenniia model' perekhoda*, 108.

19. Internal government document cited in Hale, "Statehood at Stake," 31.

20. This structure does not factor in the export of uranium or gold, however. Eshref F. Trushin, "Uzbekistan: Foreign Economic Activity," in *Central Asia: The Challenges of Independence*, ed. Boris Rumer and Stanislav Zhukov (Armonk, NY: M. E. Sharpe, 1998), 215.

21. International Monetary Fund, *Direction of Trade Statistics Yearbook* (Washington, D.C.: International Monetary Fund, 2000), 479; and International Monetary Fund, *Direction of Trade Statistics Yearbook* (Washington, D.C.: International Monetary Fund, 2002), 485.

22. IMF, *Direction of Trade Statistics Yearbook* (2000), 479; and IMF, *Direction of Trade Statistics Yearbook* (2002), 485.

23. Ibid., 214.

24. Total oil production includes crude petroleum and gas condensate. CIS Interstate Statistical Committee, *Sodruzhestvo Nezavisimykh Gosudartsv v 2001 godu: Statisticheskii Spravochnik* (Commonwealth of Independent States in 2001: Statistical Abstract) (Moscow: CIS Interstate Statistical Committee, 2002), 146-47; and CIS Interstate Statistical Committee, *Deciat' Let Sodruzhestva Nezavisimykh Gosudartsv (1991-2000): Statisticheskii Sbornik* (Ten Years of the Commonwealth of Independent States, 1991-2000: Statistical Abstract) (Moscow: CIS Interstate Statistical Committee, 2001), 46-47.

25. CIS Interstate Statistical Committee, *Sodruzhestvo Nezavisimykh Gosudartsv v 2001 godu*, 146-47; and CIS Interstate Statistical Committee, *Deciat' Let Sodruzhestva Nezavisimykh Gosudarstv*, 46-47.

26. Akira Miyamoto, *Natural Gas in Central Asia: Industries, Markets and Export Options of Kazakstan, Turkmenistan, and Uzbekistan* (London: Royal Institute of International Affairs, 1997), 56-57.

27. Eskender Trushin, "Uzbekistan: Problems of Development and Reform in the Agrarian Sector," in *Central Asia: The Challenges of Independence*, ed. Boris Rumer and Stanislav Zhukov (Armonk, NY: M. E. Sharpe, 1998), 272.

28. For more on these long-term problems see, ibid., 272-73.

29. Michael Kaser, *The Economies of Kazakhstan and Uzbekistan* (London: Royal Institute of International Affairs, 1997), 29.
30. International Monetary Fund Press Release no. 95/7 of 25 January 1995, www.imf.org/external/np/sec/pr/1995/pr9507.htm.
31. International Monetary Fund Press Release no. 95/67 of 18 December 1995, www.imf.org/external/np/sec/pr/1995/pr9567.htm.
32. "Republic of Uzbekistan: Transactions with the Fund to May 31, 2003," www.imf.org/external/country/UZB/index.htm.
33. For more on the multiple exchange rate system and its consequences see, Trushin, "Uzbekistan: Foreign Economic Activity," 216-19.
34. Hellman, "Winners Take All."
35. Wagner, *Public Opinion in Uzbekistan*, 57.

Chapter 6

Ukrainian-Russian Security Relations and Alignment Patterns

This chapter examines Ukrainian-Russian security relations and offers a basic timeline for the understanding of how and when policy shifts occurred. It begins with a discussion of the basic differences between the security environment of Ukraine and Uzbekistan. Three factors stand out, namely geographic location, military position after the Soviet collapse, and historical ties with Russia.

Balance of power and balance of threat theories are then used in a similar way as in Chapter 3. That is, if we assume that Russia posed the greatest external threat to Ukraine, both in terms of capabilities and perceived aggressiveness, then it would be the state Ukraine would most likely balance. Indeed, because of its vast military and nuclear resources, realists would suggest that Ukrainian balancing efforts should be easier since Kyiv could deter Russia with nuclear weapons and its conventional forces.

Traditional alignment theories lead us astray, however, and the case of Ukraine is puzzling for several reasons. First, why would Ukraine be willing to give up nuclear weapons, when they could be used to ensure their security from a potentially neo-imperial Russia; second, why did Ukraine not balance Russia as strongly as some would predict; and third, why would Ukraine choose to return back to Russia after a decade of establishing its independence from Moscow in the first place? While these are all contradictory outcomes for traditional alignment theories, the IT/ED framework sheds light on these actions. It provides us with a better understanding of why alignment strategies unfolded as they did and what the underlying motivations for leaders' alignment calculations were. As we will see in Chapters 7 and 8, respectively, the best answers are found by examining the way in which leaders ensured their political positions in the face of internal threats and the extent of economic dependence on Russia.

Ukrainian-Russian security relations are presented in two general phases. The first phase runs from 1991 until 1997 when relations with Russia were normalized and many of the outstanding disagreements between Ukraine and Russia, such as the political status of the Crimea and the Black Sea Fleet (BSF), were resolved. Much of the initial security focus for Western policy makers was on ensuring that Russia would emerge from the Soviet collapse as the only nuclear power, which meant that Ukraine would have to join the NPT to win the approval of Western countries. The second phase runs from 1997 to present where Ukraine worked with both Russia and the West, making sure that Ukrainian sovereignty and territorial integrity were not compromised. More recently, there has been an even greater willingness of Kyiv to cooperate with Russia along a variety of security lines, although there has not been a tremendous shift in the overall military capabilities of the two states. This timeline chronicles security cooperation between Russia and Ukraine based on a traditional alignment discussion, although as we will in subsequent chapters, the alignment patterns observed based on the IT/ED framework differ.

Starting Points and Balancing Options

This section begins by highlighting the fundamental differences – namely geographic location, military preparedness, and historical ties – between the initial security environments Ukraine and Uzbekistan faced after independence, before turning to a more explicit discussion of balance of power and balance of threat logic. These differences are rooted in geographic location, the military inheritance after the Soviet collapse, and historical ties between Ukraine and Russia. First, Uzbekistan is a land-locked state in Central Asia with little direct contact with Western security institutions, although it is strategically placed because it borders every country in the region. On the other hand, Ukraine was the second largest republic within the Soviet Union and located strategically between Russia and other European states, and geographically proximate to European security and economic institutions, like the NATO and European Union (EU). This made discussion of eventual Ukrainian integration into European institutions possible, although highly problematic.

The second major difference between Ukraine and Uzbekistan is in military preparedness immediately after the Soviet disintegration.[1] Uzbekistan did not possess nuclear weapons, unlike Russia, Ukraine, Belarus and Kazakhstan. As we will see, the issue of nuclear disarmament shaped the discourse between Ukraine and Western policy makers in the early 1990s, almost to the exclusion of other issues, although it did provide Ukraine with some degree of leverage in arms control negotiations. Ukraine possessed 1,512 warheads, 212 strategic carriers of which 176 were intercontinental ballistic missiles and 36 heavy bombers, and in fact, Ukraine held the third largest nuclear arsenal in the world behind only the United States and Russia.[2] Moreover, the sheer size of Ukraine's armed forces totaling 700,000 made it the second largest military power on the European continent. Uzbekistan lacked such military capabilities.

A third factor stemmed from the historical connection between Ukraine and Russia. One of the greatest obstacles for Ukraine was overcoming the stigma of being considered the "younger brothers" of the Russians. Thus, there is an immense historical legacy shared between Russia and Ukraine that is not present between Uzbekistan. Indeed, as Leonid Kuchma has pointed out, "in Russia they pretend that Ukraine as a sovereign, independent state does not exist…the stereotype of viewing Ukraine as its constituent part or, at any rate, as the sphere of its prevailing influence has not yet been eliminated."[3] In another instance, Kuchma identified what he called a "divorce syndrome," characterizing it as a "complicated political-psychological problem that casts an ominous shadow on the entire complex of Ukrainian-Russian relations."[4] Similarly, Kuchma's top national security advisor, Volodymyr Horbulin, stated in a 1997 interview that he could not provide a rational explanation for why differences remain within the Ukrainian-Russian relationship. Providing one impression, he went on to quote Henry Kissinger: "I often recall what former U.S. Secretary of State Henry Kissinger told me: 'I never met a single Russian who thought that Ukraine could be independent.'"[5] Commenting on the importance of Ukraine to Russia and its status as a great power (an underlying factor in Russian-Ukrainian relations), Zbigniew Brzezinski suggested that "It cannot be stressed strongly enough that without Ukraine, Russia ceases to be an empire, but with Ukraine suborned and then subordinated, Russia automatically becomes an empire."[6] This sentiment clearly complicated relations between Kyiv and Moscow, and as we will see, it often led to bouts of inflamed rhetoric that only exacerbated tensions.

A related issue involves Russians living abroad. This was less an issue in Uzbekistan, where Russians only made up a fraction of the population, approximately 8 percent. The same was not true in Ukraine, where there was a clear distinction between Western Ukraine and Eastern Ukraine, which had many Russians and Russian-speaking Ukrainians residents. For instance, throughout eastern and southern Ukraine, the percentage of Ukrainian speakers as a share of total population is less than one-third.[7] Samuel Huntington described Ukraine as a "torn" country in his clash of civilizations thesis, in large part because Russians made up 22 percent and native Russian speakers 31 percent of the total population.[8] With these preliminary differences outlined, we can now turn to a more explicit discussion of possible alignment outcomes based on traditional alignment theories.

From the perspective of balance of power and balance of threat theories, Ukraine was in a much stronger position to balance Russia based on its own military capabilities than Uzbekistan. This is an important factor for realist scholars because it suggests that the need to find balancing partners may not have been as great given the status of Ukraine's military, notably its possession of nuclear weapons. The nuclear deterrent gave Kyiv an advantage that Tashkent did not enjoy. Accordingly, some prominent realists, such as John Mearsheimer, suggested that Ukraine should hold onto them to ensure the country's security, noting, "nuclear proliferation sometimes promotes peace."[9]

If balance of power were employed in purely Waltzian terms, then we might anticipate that Ukraine would align with Russia against the U.S.-led NATO alliance. This prediction would stem from the overwhelming capability of NATO, as it would be seen as the strongest pole, and as Waltz would predict, the likely result would be that a state would want to balance such power. However, this is a prediction that Ukraine seems to be resisting at all costs. Much of the problem with balance of power is that it ignores the perception of threat that stems from the perceived aggressiveness of other states. In this light, balance of threat theory is far more compelling because it factors in the concern of Ukraine as to Russia's potential hostility and neoimperial impulses. Given the power disparity between Ukraine and Russia and these concerns over Russian intentions, balance of threat theory would predict that Ukraine would increase its security cooperation with the West, and inevitably NATO.[10] Hence, the best way to deal with a Russian threat would be to join the principle Western alliance that at one time stood toe to toe with the Soviet Union and Warsaw Pact. The Baltic states adopted this approach, although few other CIS states embraced such cooperative relations with NATO. Thus in the end, traditional alignment theories, especially balance of threat theory, would suggest that 1) Ukraine would keep its nuclear arsenal as the best security guarantee from a Russian invasion; and 2) they would work to join the NATO alliance. As we will see in Chapters 7 and 8, traditional alignment logic did not hold true for reasons associated with domestic political and economic factors.

The rest of this chapter identifies the general patterns of security relations between Ukraine and Russia, with the United States and other NATO countries playing a significant counterveiling force to Russia. Throughout negotiations with Russia, the overarching concern for both Kravchuk and Kuchma was ensuring Ukraine's sovereignty and territorial integrity, realized eventually by the signing of the Friendship Treaty in 1997, which also brought about a new partnership with NATO.

Ukraine (1991-1997): Looking West and Struggling with the East

This section examines the first phase of Ukrainian security relations with Russia that stretches from independence until the signing of the Treaty of Friendship in May 1997. The treaty solved a number of long-standing issues with respect to Crimea and the BSF and Russia's recognition of Ukraine's territorial integrity. It therefore serves as a defining moment for Ukrainian-Russian relations, although as we will see, it did not imply that Ukraine's foreign policy would be any more or less pro-Russian.

The principal objective for the Kravchuk administration in the wake of the Soviet collapse was ensuring that Ukraine's territorial integrity would be respected and that independence could be assured free of Russian domination. This was in fact a main current throughout the early and mid 1990s, as both Ukrainian presidents Kravchuk and later in 1994 Kuchma agreed on this larger principle, although this did not always coincide with Washington's approach in the early 1990s. Indeed, in the initial days of independence U.S. policy makers were uncertain about a more independent strategy for a nuclear Ukraine. Yet, once Ukraine agreed to relinquish its nuclear weapons and once Kuchma came into power in the summer of 1994, there was more active discussion of working both with Russia and the West.

The Kravchuk Years (1991-1994)

This section discusses the initial phase of Ukrainian foreign policy, which was largely defined by the initial collapse of the Soviet Union and Ukraine's attempt to solidify independence from Russia. As a bold measure, Kravchuk attempted to sever ties with Moscow in favor of working with the West. He tried to assert Ukrainian independence by demonstrating an unwillingness to settle a wide range of issues on Russian terms, including the ownership of former Soviet foreign assets and the fate of nuclear weapons located in Ukraine. His pro-independence sentiment was coupled with a pro-Western orientation, aimed at garnering Western security guarantees. This was a strategy that, as we will see, proved difficult in the initial years of independence largely because U.S. interests favored a strong Russia.

As part of Kravchuk's initial policy of looking away from Russia, he remained critical of CIS integration suggesting that the organization facilitated a "civilized divorce." In February 1992 Kravchuk described the CIS in starker terms as "a committee to liquidate the old structures."[11] Indeed, the Ukrainian parliament ratified the initial CIS agreement only after adding twelve reservations, including the affirmation of the inviolability of state borders, the right to independent military forces, and the downgrading of joint foreign policy activities from "coordination" to "consultation." During the initial years of independence, Kravchuk consistently criticized the development of centralized structures within the CIS, stating that Ukraine would go no further than a loose form of economic cooperation. He emphasized that CIS structures should base their activities on the principles promoted by the United Nations and Organization for Security and Cooperation in Europe, and that the CIS should not be viewed as a supra-national structure, but rather as an international organization for facilitating the resolution of problems and tensions among member-states.[12]

In this view, CIS political and military integration was not a priority for Ukrainian leaders. For instance, Ukraine did not join the collective security agreement signed in Tashkent in May 1992 by representatives of six CIS governments, as Kravchuk feared that this agreement could have been used to legitimate Russian military intervention. In so doing, Kravchuk passed on one of the strongest indicators of a pro-Russian alignment.

While Kravchuk sought to distance Ukraine from Russia, he also pursued security cooperation with the West. The difficulty for Ukraine was that while he wanted to strengthen relations with Western countries and institutions, Western countries themselves, especially the United States, were unsure if a strong and independent Ukraine was a good idea. Moreover, U.S. policy makers focused narrowly on the nuclear arsenal of Ukraine and its dismantling, which tended to limit discussions between Ukraine and Western countries to these issues. To U.S. policy makers supporting reform was secondary, especially for the first George Bush administration, what was most important was ensuring that Russia emerged as the only nuclear power from the Soviet Union. Bush's now infamous speech to the Ukrainian Parliament in August 1991 is illustrative of this sentiment. In his

"Chicken Kyiv" speech, Bush in effect warned Ukraine "...freedom is not the same as independence...[Americans] will not aid those who promote suicidal nationalism based on ethnic hatred."[13] This clearly demonstrated that the outgoing Bush administration was not in touch with the interests and concerns of Kyiv, as much as they were with how Ukraine should fit into a collapsing Soviet organization.

In the early 1990s Western interaction with Ukraine focused on these larger security concerns for geopolitical reasons. Washington preferred to deal with one single de facto power on security and economic issues, rather than having to deal with a multiplicity of new and relatively unpredictable independent former Soviet republics, and U.S. policy remained Russo-centric.[14] Therefore, during the first year and a half of Ukraine's independence, U.S.-Ukrainian relations were, to a large degree, one side of a triangular relationship involving Russia as well.[15]

Ukraine's nuclear arsenal provided Kravchuk with a compelling bargaining chip, and one that would eventually be used to "blackmail" the United States into meeting, or at the minimum addressing, the legitimate security concerns of Ukraine. Since Western and U.S. policy makers focused on the fate of Ukraine's nuclear weapons, Kravchuk's policies initially tried to attract Western attention by questioning the right of Russia to ratify START on behalf of Ukraine. In response to this issue, U.S. Secretary of State James Baker and the foreign ministers of Belarus, Kazakhstan, Russia, and Ukraine signed the Lisbon Protocol on 23 May 1992. The protocol recognized all four states as parties to START and provided for the adherence of the non-Russian republics to the NPT. The Lisbon Protocol did not resolve the nuclear weapons issue completely, and some problems remained, such as the sale of enriched uranium extracted from warheads located on Ukrainian territory. Nonetheless, Ukraine demonstrated its willingness to work with the United States on the nuclear question, but the road to ratification was anything but simple.[16]

Kravchuk's approach to START and the NPT was multifaceted. He made ratification conditional on compensation for nuclear weapons materials, security guarantees from the nuclear powers, as well as generous economic assistance for its disarmament program. Much to the dismay of U.S. policy makers, ratification was also difficult. In January 1993 the Ukrainian parliament made no movement on the Lisbon Protocol, and by February the speaker of the parliament stated that START ratification was not a priority.[17] On 8 April the Ukrainian government emphasized that the timing of nuclear weapons removal from Ukraine would depend on a wide range of factors, such as the progress in Russian-Ukrainian talks over the liquidation of these weapons including the issue of compensation for nuclear fuel.[18] These sentiments were shared in an open letter "on Ukraine's nuclear status" signed by 162 deputies of the parliament made public in the same month. Citing similar considerations about the necessity of financial compensation, the letter warned:

> at the same time it would be a mistake to agree to promises of insignificant monetary compensations in exchange for Ukraine's immediate nuclear disarmament. The

question of nuclear disarmament, state independence, national security, and territorial integrity cannot become an object for bargaining or "monetary compensations."[19]

Thus, underscoring the importance for U.S. policy makers of dealing with both Ukraine's security and economic needs during the disarmament process.

By the end of 1993, U.S. policy makers were more attuned to the interests of Ukraine and willing to address its legitimate security concerns. Early on in the Clinton administration there was a general policy review of the post-Soviet situation and especially Ukraine's nuclear arsenal. The review led to a more balanced policy approach. For instance, in May 1993 then U.S. Ambassador-at-Large Strobe Talbott visited Ukraine to discuss ways in which a "turning of the page" could occur between Kyiv and Washington. Discussions moved beyond nuclear issues to include economic assistance, expanded defense and security ties, and a renewed political relationship between Washington and Kyiv. This was followed by a June visit by Secretary of Defense Les Aspin, who was returning from a trip to Russia where nuclear disarmament discussions took place. So by October when Secretary of State Warren Christopher traveled to Kyiv tensions between Kyiv and Washington subsided, and a genuine trilateral negotiating process emerged between Washington, Kyiv, and Moscow. This led to the signing the next January of the Trilateral Agreement in Moscow between the presidents of the United States, Russia, and Ukraine.

The Trilateral Agreement was important and proved to be a defining moment in the disarmament process. The agreement and its provisions finally addressed Ukraine's basic security requirements. For the first time in both theory and practice, a trilateral process had brought about resolution of the nuclear issue, which not only legitimated U.S. involvement in the eventual dismantling but also brought much-needed technical assistance to the negotiating process.

Furthermore, the United States, Russia, and the United Kingdom extended basic security assurances to Ukraine upon Ukraine's signing of the NPT. President Clinton also promised to expand the assistance to Ukraine beyond the minimum of $175 million already agreed to. Kravchuk was rewarded for securing his country's accession to the treaty upon his trip to Washington in March 1994, where U.S. aid to Ukraine was doubled to $700 million (half of which was provided for nuclear disarmament). While Ukrainian officials cited security guarantees as the major reason for joining the NPT, the timing of this decision clearly indicates that economic factors were of considerable importance. As Sherman Garnett noted, "the key to success in the U.S. policy toward Ukraine was the marriage of U.S. nuclear non-proliferation policy with a broad-based policy that supported economic and political reform and addressed Kyiv's security concerns."[20]

Throughout this period of negotiations over nuclear disarmament, Kyiv and Moscow were also at odds over the contested Crimea, a region dominated by ethnic Russians, and ownership of the BSF. As we will see, this was a heated issue that sparked some of the most vehement rhetoric between the two countries. In 1991 Ukraine recognized the autonomous status of Crimea and allowed the republic to enact laws that did not conflict with Ukrainian laws. Although Russian leaders assured their Ukrainian counterparts that they fully respected the independence of Ukraine and had no intention of reclaiming parts of the country, tensions remained high. In May 1992, for instance, the Russian parliament declared that the transfer of Crimea from Russia to Ukraine in 1954, a gesture of Russia's "eternal friendship," was illegal. Despite threats by some Russian politicians to renegotiate its border with Ukraine, Moscow accepted the inviolability of Ukrainian borders by June 1992, although in July 1993 Russia's parliament declared that Sevastopol, home to the BSF, was and remained part of the Russian Federation. The Ukrainian response to this latter action was understandable. Kravchuk characterized it as "blatant interference in the internal affairs of Ukraine, an encroachment on her territorial integrity and the inviolability of her border." He added:

> By this Resolution the Russian Parliament is attempting to provoke conflict on the territory of Crimea, and to create tension and enmity in relations between Russia and Ukraine.[21]

The Ukrainian Parliament responded by denouncing the Russian Supreme Soviet's resolution on the ownership of Sevastopol as an act of political aggression against Ukraine.[22] Dmytro Pavlychko, head of the Ukrainian Parliament's Foreign Affairs Commission, described the claim on Sevastopol as "similar to a declaration of war."[23] At a press conference, the Deputy Minister of Foreign Affairs, Boris Tarasyuk, argued that the Russian action was irresponsible, illegal, and dangerous. In his testimony to the UN Security Council, which had been asked by Ukraine to consider the deteriorating situation, Tarasyuk highlighted the significance of this claim:

> I should like, in particular, to draw the Council's attention to the fact that in this case we are dealing with a decision of the highest legislative organ of a neighboring nuclear power whose international commitments extend equally to the legislative and executive branches. It is quite clear that this decision by the Supreme Soviet of the Russian Federation is in essence an overt territorial claim by one state against another.[24]

He went on to add that the claim "is a timebomb, and the one who wields it cannot imagine its full destructive force."[25] Linking the resolution to the ratification of START, Tarasyuk suggested how

> Certain Ukrainian members of parliament have begun to come out firmly against ratification of the treaty, quite rightly seeing in the action of their Russian colleagues a threat not only to national, but international peace and security. It is not difficult to guess where such a pattern of action and reaction could lead.[26]

While Yeltsin never enforced this resolution, it clearly aggravated relations and heightened tension between Moscow and Kyiv, raising concerns over Russian intentions.

Ukrainian fears about Russia's intentions were further exacerbated by the publication of the new Russian military doctrine. The doctrine, which was approved by the Russian Security Council in November 1993, was similar to its earlier 1992 draft, in that it could be interpreted as making explicit Russian claims to the right to intervene in Ukraine's internal affairs.[27] The new doctrine identified "the suppression of the rights, freedoms, and legitimate interests of citizens of the Russian Federation in foreign states" as a source of external military danger to Russia. This suggested that the Russian government was the violation of ethnic Russian rights in neighboring republics as a direct threat to Russia's security. As Raymond Garthoff suggested, while this was not given as a justification for intervention, intervention does seem to be implied in the doctrine.[28] Similarly, Stephen Blank argued that the doctrine spells out "Russia's self-proclaimed role of protector of Russian minorities abroad" and that it describes any threat to the civil rights of Russians in the CIS as a potential cause for military action.[29] Clearly negotiations over Crimea were destined to be tense, given this overarching context.

Within the larger Crimean question, the most complicated issue was over the ownership of the BSF and its base in Sevastopol. While the Minsk agreement of December 1991 clearly stated that the former Soviet navy was under CIS High Command, Kyiv viewed strategic forces as only those that carried nuclear weapons, and since the BSF did not carry them, it belonged to Ukraine. Major General Georgy Zhivitsa, Chief of the General Staff of the Ukrainian Armed Forces, argued:

> Ukraine is laying claim to all large and small units and all equipment and weapons of the three military districts on its territory, with the exception of the strategic missile force and long-range aircraft units, and to the entire Black Sea Fleet, which, as it is known has no strategic units of ships.[30]

Russia disagreed with this approach, and asserted control over the fleet. The Black Sea commander, Admiral Igor Kastanov, outlined the Russian position, which drew no distinction between strategic and non-strategic weapons:

> The leadership of the Defense Ministry and the navy consider that the fleet cannot be divided into strategic and non-strategic forces, even if only because any fleet is an operational-strategic formation and resolves the corresponding tasks.[31]

Following the spring 1992 war of decrees between Kravchuk and Yeltsin, attempts were made to settle this issue during meetings at Dagomys in 1992 and Moscow in 1993. At Dagomys the two leaders postponed discussion of the Crimea to the indefinite future and agreed in principle on a division of the BSF, and that the two states would refrain from unilateral actions until the conclusion of future negotiations. In August 1992 Kravchuk and Yeltsin agreed to put an end to the CIS joint command and to consider the BSF a Ukrainian-Russian fleet under joint command until 1995.[32] As we will see, the issue was finally resolved in 1997 under Kuchma.

During his years as president, Kravchuk attempted to sever ties with Russia and forge new ones with the West. As we have seen, much attention during his term focused solely on the nuclear question. Ultimately, given the concerns of Washington little constructive dialogue could be pursued until this larger security question was addressed. Once this occurred, a new era of U.S.-Ukrainian relations emerged. Kravchuk ushered in this new era and began Ukraine's trajectory towards the West, as for instance, when Ukraine joined the Partnership for Peace (PfP) program with NATO in February 1994 or when Ukraine signed a partnership agreement with the European Union in June 1994. This was all the more provocative since Ukraine was the first CIS country to establish such ties with European institutions. Yet, Kravchuk would play little role in this new era, since his political leadership ended with Kuchma's victory in the July 1994 presidential elections.

The Kuchma Years (1994-1997)

Kuchma came to power suggesting that Kravchuk's approach to dealing with Russia proved wholly unsuccessful, as evidenced by the staggering energy debt (examined in greater detail in Chapter 8). At times, Kuchma also based this reorientation towards Moscow on loftier ideas of Ukraine's place on the continent. For instance, during his presidential inauguration address in July 1994, he suggested: "Ukraine is historically a part of the Eurasian economic and cultural space. Today, the vitally important national interests of Ukraine are focused precisely on this territory of the former Soviet Union."[33] As we will see, this more pro-Russian orientation led to a softening of policies in both the CIS and over the contested Crimea and BSF, although in neither case was Ukrainian sovereignty or territorial integrity compromised.[34]

After the initial pro-Russian honeymoon was over, however, Kuchma began to look more actively to the West as part of his "multi-vectored" foreign policy. 1997 proved a watershed year because of NATO's enlargement into Central Europe, which culminated in NATO's creation of a "distinctive partnership" with Ukraine in May. Days later Ukraine and Russia finalized the much debated Treaty of Friendship, Cooperation, and Partnership. Thus, the security picture for Ukraine was largely secured and many of the problematic issues that caused tension with Russia were resolved in 1997.

On the issue of nuclear disarmament, Kuchma continued Kravchuk's policies. Domestic politics slowed the decision over the NPT until November 1994, when the parliament ratified the treaty on the eve of Kuchma's trip to the United States. While in Washington, Kuchma received an additional $200 million in gratitude for his efforts in implementing economic reform and achieving Ukraine's nuclear disarmament, both of which he supported in the parliament. After Ukraine's accession to the NPT, the Conference on Security and Cooperation in Europe provided Ukraine with a document during its December 1994 meeting in Budapest. The document was a memorandum on security assurances (although not a formal security guarantee) that essentially promised to respect Ukraine's borders in accordance with the principles of the Helsinki Final Act, refrain from the threat or use of force against the territorial integrity or political independence of Ukraine, refrain from economic coercion, and seek UN Security Council action in the event of nuclear aggression or the threat of nuclear aggression.[35] Interestingly, Ukrainian sources published the memorandum suggesting the document represented security guarantees, which it did not.[36] Ultimately, Ukraine's nuclear disarmament allowed it to avoid pariah status, and become a welcome member of the international community.[37] Accordingly, Ukrainian relations wit the West could grow with this lingering impediment removed.

Ukraine also took steps to resolve the outstanding issues over the Crimea and the BSF with Russia. In June 1995 Yeltsin and Kuchma signed an agreement that resolved in principle the dispute over the BSF fleet. Russia argued that for strategic reasons it needed the full use of the Sevastopol naval base and insisted on having a long-term lease on the bulk of Crimean naval bases and exclusive rights over Sevastopol, while Ukraine insisted that the base be used jointly. Under this agreement the port where Ukraine would base its navy was not specified, leaving open the opportunity that two navies could share Sevastopol.[38] The two countries agreed in principle to split the fleet, with Russia purchasing most of the Ukrainian share, ending up with 82 per cent of the vessels.[39]

The question of dividing the BSF for all practical purposes was resolved on 31 May 1997, when Yeltsin and Kuchma signed the bilateral Treaty of Friendship, Cooperation, and Partnership. At long last, Russia formally recognized Ukraine's independence and territorial integrity. Ukrainian officials agreed to give Russia 32 percent of its half-share of the BSF as compensation for its outstanding debt, while the remaining 18 percent would be used either to enhance its own navy or be sold for scrap.[40] It was also agreed that the Russian fleet would be based in three bays in Sevastopol on a 20-year lease; that Ukraine could not enter into any agreements with third parties aimed against Russia; and that Ukraine could not allow the stationing of NATO troops and nuclear weapons on its territory. As these developments between Kyiv and Moscow unfolded, Kuchma simultaneously pursued security cooperation with the West, notably NATO.

As we saw earlier, Ukrainian relations with the West improved dramatically after the signing of the Trilateral Agreement in January 1994, which addressed the issue of Ukraine's nuclear disarmament and potential for security assurances. Since February 1994, when Ukraine became the first CIS country to join NATO's PfP program, which provides 27 countries with associative membership, and the first to sign the agreement on Partnership and Cooperation with the EU, it has extensively participated in alliance activities, particularly in military exercises. Ukraine intensified its participation in NATO's PfP program, and, according to the Individual Partnership Program, agreed to cooperate in all 19 spheres of activities envisaged by PfP, which included preparation for joint activities in cases of civil emergencies.[41]

Kuchma's foreign minister also suggested in 1995 that Ukraine desired to participate "in several organs of NATO whose sphere of activity represents a particular interest for Ukraine."[42] Clinton's visit to Ukraine in May 1995 highlighted the improvement in U.S.-Ukrainian relations with the proclamation of the "strategic partnership" between the United States and Ukraine. Ukraine took part in NATO-PfP field training exercises such as Peaceshield 96, Cooperative Neighbor 97, and Peaceshield 99, which were conducted on Ukrainian territory. This strengthening of ties between Ukraine and the West was extremely positive for Ukraine, but not surprising to Kuchma, since as he suggested, "Ukraine's return to Europe is a completely natural process," a far cry from his 1994 campaign rhetoric.[43] Thus, shortly after a year of promising a more pro-Russian orientation, Kuchma made sure that his avenues to the West remained open.

By the spring and summer of 1996, Ukraine's more balanced security policy between East and West took form. Kuchma and his advisors had set a course for a return to Europe, which was expressed clearly in the president's address at a meeting with top foreign policy officials in July. For Kuchma, Kyiv's most strategic path was to "integrate" with European and transatlantic organizations while "cooperating" within the CIS framework:

> I would also like to note that our foreign policy terminology should reflect the principled political line of the state. Along with the strategic choice of adhering to the processes of European integration, Ukraine's firm and consistent line is the line of maximum broadening and deepening of bilateral and multilateral forms of cooperation both within and outside the framework of the CIS while safeguarding the principles of mutual benefit and respect for each other's interests and abiding by the generally recognized norms of international law.[44]

As Ukrainian Foreign Minister Hennadyi Udovenko stated repeatedly, "Our strategic goal is to fully integrate into European and transatlantic structures and to play an important role in the economic of East and Central Europe."[45]

NATO expansion into Eastern Europe brought much of this debate to the fore. Kuchma's perception of NATO expansion was that it is "no menace to Ukraine," but he did caution that the alliance should take Russia into consideration when expanding, since "a nation like Russia cannot be left out of processes currently under way."[46] Nevertheless, Kuchma was not deterred from cooperating with NATO and in fact cooperation under the PfP auspices was common. In 1997, for example, 228 joint exercises were conducted under the PfP program, 200 with NATO, 70 with the United Kingdom, and only 10 were held jointly with Russia over the same span of time.[47]

Moreover, as NATO expanded to the east, it opened up a greater dialogue with Kyiv, which enabled Ukraine to improve relations with both the West and Russia. Two days after the agreement was signed between NATO and Russia on 27 May, Ukraine and NATO signed a cooperation agreement that provided for a special partnership with NATO, which would be officially signed on 8 July 1997 at the Madrid meeting. The document outlined practical areas of cooperation between NATO and Ukraine and established a standing mechanism for consultation.

The heightened Western interest in Ukraine also prompted Russian leaders to complete the Friendship Treaty and after the NATO-Ukraine accord was signed,

Russia finally signed the treaty on 31 May that recognized the unconditional borders of Ukraine. At long last Ukrainian leaders had been able to ensure the legitimacy of Ukraine's borders irrespective of Russian interests. With this assurance that Russia could no longer contest Ukrainian territory, Ukrainian security relations could continue along the dual path of working both with NATO and Russia. This balanced approach enabled Kuchma to maximize his security relations, however, as we will see in Chapter 7, changes in his domestic standing greatly increased the necessity of fostering ties with Moscow.

This discussion of security relations appears to fall in line with aspects of balance of power and balance of threat logic. That is, Ukrainian leaders strengthened security cooperation with the West and NATO, although it fell short of full membership into NATO. However, what is most puzzling is that once normalization occurred and Ukrainian inroads to European institutions were laid, Ukrainian foreign policy began to shift back to a more pro-Russian alignment. So why did Ukrainian security policy take this unexpected path and reverse its original trajectory? The answer rests in domestic political and economic factors discussed in Chapters 7 and 8. The following section, though, draws attention to some of the primary indicators that highlight Ukraine's slow drift back East.

Ukraine (1997-2001): The Slow Drift Back East

What became apparent in this second phase of Ukrainian foreign policy is that the "multi-vectored" approach was not without problems. Increasingly, the Western nations, who Kuchma had warmed to after his election in 1994, slowly lost patience with the reform process, or lack thereof, in Ukraine. As we will see in Chapter 8, this was most evident in Ukraine's failure to implement economic reform, and in the process undermined Kyiv's ability to receive Western economic assistance. This was a gradual shift, but one that became visible by the end of the decade.

While relations with NATO warmed in 1997, the extent to which Ukraine would become an active member remained in limbo. Kyiv embraced cooperation and joint exercises, as this strengthened the regional security while facilitating a greater dialogue with Western nations. In 2001 Ukraine continued to cooperate with NATO, including 120 joint-participation events with NATO, more than 70 with Poland, more than 60 with the United States, and more still with other NATO members.[48]

Yet, while cooperation continued, actual membership was fraught with difficulties. As Volodymyr Horbulin admitted, "We recognize that we are not yet ready to become a NATO member both in terms of meeting the necessary criteria and in terms of public opinion in Ukraine."[49] This latter consideration raised questions within Ukraine about the desirability of membership. Based on 1997 opinion polls, attitudes towards NATO membership varied considerably: 42 percent of the people polled could not answer the question saying it is difficult to say, 19 percent said yes as soon as possible, 18 percent favored the idea but that it should be done later, while 21 percent opposed the idea altogether.[50] Similarly, according to Deputy Head of National Security and Defense Council of Ukraine, Oleksandr Razumkov, almost 60 percent of the population of Ukraine opposes integration of Ukraine into NATO.[51] Thus, the reality was that Ukrainian cooperation with NATO and formal entrance into the organization were two separate issues. Ukraine remained stuck in the middle, but as the years progressed, the limits of security cooperation with the West became clearer, and Kyiv began to drift back to the East.

Several indicators suggest that Ukraine was more willing to cooperate with Russia by the end of the decade. In 2000 alone Putin and Kuchma held eight meetings with one another, a clear indicator of a burgeoning relationship.[52] Indeed, as Kuchma proclaimed on several occasions, Russia is a strategic partner of Ukraine aside from which "there is no alternative."[53] In January 2001 Ukrainian and Russian officials also signed a 52-point military cooperation plan that foresaw the creation of a joint command post in Sevastopol and a joint rescue detachment of the Russian and Ukrainian BSF.[54] After a 12 February 2001 meeting in Dnipropetrovsk, Ukraine and Russia signed a series of agreements culminating in 16 documents on economic cooperation aimed at strengthening cooperation in the areas of high technology, industry and energy. Additionally, Ukrainian and Russian space agencies signed a memorandum on cooperation with rocket and aerospace equipment. The most compelling development, however, surrounded the decision to reconnect the Ukrainian and Russian electricity power grids with subsequent exportation of Russian electricity through Ukrainian territory. The delivery of Russian electricity to Ukraine significantly weakens Ukrainian power generating companies, and reduces Ukraine's long-term capacity to meet its own electricity requirements. Such energy exports increase Russia's ability to influence Ukraine in more indirect ways, as we will see later. Furthermore, on 13 June 2001 the Russian and Ukrainian prime ministers met in St. Petersburg and agreed to restart the work of a permanent intergovernmental commission that will deal with outstanding issues, with Kinakh suggesting that the two sides should be more serious in the implementation of agreements already signed.[55] Kuchma also chose to join the Eurasian Economic Community in March 2002, a community that consists of the remaining core of the CIS including Russia, Kazakhstan, Kyrgyzstan, Tajikistan, and Belarus. His rationale stems from his growing awareness that there are fewer alternatives in the world for Ukraine. Kuchma explained Ukrainian needs, stating: "We can see that the world isn't becoming a kinder place, and new trade barriers are emerging over time. These barriers have to be overcome."[56]

While Kuchma strengthened his alignment with Russia in the past few years, the real impetus came not from a shift in the military balance or the rise of a newly threatening state, but rather the rising political insecurity he felt by late 2000 and the lingering effects of Ukrainian economic dependence on Russia. Chapter 7 argues that the increasing intensity of internal threats to Kuchma made him fear his political security, which as the IT/ED framework suggests, typically leads CIS leaders to adopt strong pro-Russian alignments. Chapter 8 then examines the constraining effect economic dependence on Russia has had on Ukraine's alignment vis-à-vis Russia.

Conclusions

This chapter has provided a timeline for understanding Ukrainian-Russian security relations based on two security cooperation periods. The first spanned from 1991 to 1997 and ended with the signing of the Friendship Treaty that resolved several outstanding disputes. This was a period of normalization that led to a series of agreements signed with the United States and NATO that also placed Ukraine in its respective geopolitical light. The second phase highlights a gradual return back to Russia, although there were few changes in the immediate security environment that could be used to explain this alignment strategy. Indeed, why would Ukraine reverse its trajectory towards the West in the late 1990s, when it had proven successful during the mid 1990s?

More recently, Ukraine has sought to maintain its position of cooperating with Russia, while at the same time outlining more concrete steps toward greater integration into European security and economic institutions. For instance, in the wake of 11 September 2001, Ukraine did not want to be overshadowed by the rapprochement between the United States and Russia, and for the first time openly stated its desire to enter the EU and NATO. In February 2002, Kuchma presented a schedule for Kyiv to meet EU accession criteria by 2011, and on May 23, the Security and Defense Council of Ukraine noted the necessity for Ukraine to "start practical implementation of the course to join NATO," although an official application has not been submitted. In support of these initiatives, on 19 June 2003, a constitutional majority of the Ukrainian parliament voted overwhelmingly (319 of 450 deputies voted "yes", with only 3 "no" votes) for the new Law on the Foundations of Ukraine's National Security, which proclaims the goal of joining NATO.[57]

However, Kuchma's balancing act faced some significant challenges that called his westward orientation into question. Indeed, under Kuchma, Ukraine's international image significantly deteriorated as the former president drifted towards authoritarianism, corruption, and a propensity for approving nefarious arms deals. As we will see in the next chapter, Kuchma's alleged involvement in the murder of the journalist Georgiy Gongadze – the so-called "Kuchmagate" scandal – was the first prominent sign of his shift away from Euro-Atlantic political ideals. Moreover, scandalous arms deals only added to the unsavory character of the Kuchma regime.[58] The alleged sale of the Kolchuga radar system to Iraq was a harbinger to the West and prompted NATO to advise Kuchma not to attend the November 2002 NATO summit in Prague. In June 2004, Turkish officials found a Ukrainian ship en route to Egypt containing numerous items not listed on its manifest, including sophisticated weapons, such as a radio-controlled missile and launcher. And in 2001, Ukraine sold 18 unarmed nuclear-capable X-55 cruise missiles to Iran and China. Not even Kuchma's willingness to send 1,600 troops to Iraq as part of the Bush administration's "coalition of the willing" could repair the country's image. More importantly, the political fallout from these various scandals led Kuchma to alter his previously stated objective of Euro-Atlantic integration. Indeed, in July 2004, presumably at the behest of Moscow, he amended the country's military doctrine, deleting Kiev's goal of attaining NATO membership. Returning to the central argument of this book, it could be argued that Kuchma was more forthcoming about Ukrainian intentions to become full fledged members in the Euro-Atlantic community at precisely a time when the leader's personal image and the country's international image were tarnished. But as it became more apparent that this international image could not be shaken, Kuchma had few places to turn but back to Russia. In the end, though, to better understand the motivations of Ukrainian leaders throughout the 1990s, we must examine not what was happening outside of Ukraine, but rather what was occurring within the country.

Notes

1. For good overviews of the Ukrainian armed forces and its adaptation after independence see, Paul D'Anieri, Robert Kravchuk, and Taras Kuzio, *Politics and Society in Ukraine* (Boulder, CO: Westview Press, 1999); and John Jaworsky, "Ukraine's Armed Forces and Military Policy," in *Ukraine in the World: Studies in the International Relations and Security Structure of a New Independent State*, ed. Lubomyr A. Hajda (Cambridge: Harvard University Press, 1998).

2. Marta Dyczok, *Ukraine: Movement without Change, Change without Movement* (Singapore: Harwood Academic Publishers, 2000), 113.

3. V. Timoshenko, "Leonid Kuchma gotov postupit'sia mnogim radi podpisaniia dogovora s Rossiei" (Leonid Kuchma is ready to give up a lot for the sake of signing an agreement with Russia), *Nezavisimaia Gazeta*, 20 February 1997, 1-3.

4. A. Bovina, "Chto stoit za 'chetverkoi' Kuchmy?" (Why does Kuchma grade Russian-Ukrainian relations a B minus?) *Izvestiia*, 24 February 1998, 4.

5. V. Timoshenko, "Vladimir Gorbulin: Sodruzhestvo Nezavisimykh Gosudarstv perspektivy ne imeet" (Volodymyr Horbulin: The Commonwealth of Independent States does not have a future), *Nezavisimaia Gazeta*, 5 February 1997, 3.

6. Zbigniew Brzezinski, "The Premature Partnership," *Foreign Affairs* 73, no. 2 (1994): 80.

7. Valeri Khmelko and Andrew Wilson, "Regionalism and Ethnic and Linguistic Cleavages in Ukraine," in *Contemporary Ukraine: Dynamics of Post-Soviet Transformation*, ed. Taras Kuzio (Armonk, NY: M. E. Sharpe, 1998), 73.

8. Samuel P. Huntington, *The Clash of Civilizations and the Remaking of World Order* (New York: Simon & Schuster, 1996), 165-68.

9. John J. Mearsheimer, "The Case for a Ukrainian Nuclear Deterrent," *Foreign Affairs* 72, no. 3 (1993): 51.

10. Victor Chudowsky, "The Limits of Realism: Ukrainian Policy toward the CIS," 12-14.

11. B. Grushin and V. Tret'iakov, "Chelovek Ianvaria v Rossii – Leonid Kravchuk" (Leonid Kravchuk is the man of January in Russia), *Nezavisimaia Gazeta*, 12 February 1992, 1.

12. "Chy Viryte Vy u Perspektyvy SND?" (Do you believe in the future of the CIS?) *Uriadovyi Kur'ier*, 1 January 1994, 2.
13. George Bush, *Public Papers of the Presidents of the United States: 1991*, vol. 2 (Washington, D.C.: U.S. Government Printing Office, 1992), 1007.
14. Yaroslav Bilinsky, "Basic Factors in the Foreign Policy of Ukraine," in *The Legacy of History in Russia and the New States of Eurasia*, ed. S. Frederick Starr (Armonk, NY: M. E. Sharpe 1994), 173.
15. James A. Baker, III with Thomas M. DeFrank, *The Politics of Diplomacy: Revolution, War & Peace, 1989-1992* (New York: G. P. Putnam's Sons 1995), 560; and Atlantic Council of the United States, *The Future of Ukrainian-American Relations: Joint Policy Statement with Joint Policy Recommendations* (Washington, D.C.: Atlantic Council of the United States, 1995), 10.
16. For a good overview see, Deborah Sanders, *Security Co-operation between Russia and Ukraine in the Post-Soviet Era* (London: Palgrave, 2001).
17. "Supreme Soviet Chairman on START I Ratification Delay, Further Plyushch Comment," *FBIS-SOV-93-027*, 11 February 1993, 33.
18. "Zaiava Press-Sluzhby Kabinetu Ministriv Ukrainy" (Statement of the press office of the Cabinet of Ministers of Ukraine), *Uriadovyi Kur'ier*, 8 April 1993, 2.
19. "People's Deputies Advocate Country's Nuclear Status," *FBIS-SOV-93-082*, 30 April 1993, 51.
20. Sherman W. Garnett, "Ukraine's Decision to Join the NPT," *Arms Control Today* 25, no. 1 (1995): 7.
21. "President Kravchuk Repudiates Russian's Claims to the City of Sevastopol," *In Ukraine* (July 1993), 16.
22. "Chronology of Events in Crimea," in *Crimea Dynamics, Challenges and Prospects*, ed. Maria Drohobycky (London: Rowman & Littlefield, 1995), xxxvii.
23. "Russia Claims City of Sevastopol," *In Ukraine* (July 1993), 10.
24. "Security Council Sides With Ukraine on Sevastopol," *In Ukraine* (July 1993), 13.
25. Ibid.
26. Ibid.
27. For details of the draft Military Doctrine and the latter accepted copy see, Raymond L. Garthoff, "Russian Military Doctrine and Deployment," in *State Building and Military Power in Russia and the New States of Eurasia*, ed. Bruce Parrott (London: M.E. Sharpe, 1995), 44-64.
28. Ibid., 57.
29. Stephen J. Blank, *Proliferation and Non-Proliferation in Ukraine, Implications for European and U.S. Security* (Carlisle, PA: Strategic Studies Institute, U.S. Army War College, 1 July 1994), 13.
30. Sanders, *Security Co-operation between Russia and Ukraine*, 106.
31. Ibid.
32. "Ialtyns'kyi Kompromiss" (Yalta's compromise), *Uriadovyi Kur'ier*, 7 August 1992, 1.
33. Roman Solchanyk, *Ukraine and Russia: The Post-Soviet Transition* (Lanham: Rowman & Littlefield Publishers, 2001), 92.
34. Taras Kuzio argues that Kuchma's "pro-Russianism" was "always highly exaggerated, as was Ukraine's division into two foreign policy camps neatly divided along linguistic lines." Kuzio, "European, Eastern Slavic, and Eurasian: National Identity, Transformation, and Ukrainian Foreign Policy," in *Ukrainian Foreign and Security Policy*, 218.

35. For the text of this document see, Garnett, "Ukraine's Decision to Join the NPT," 11.
36. Solchanyk, *Ukraine and Russia*, 92.
37. Scott D. Sagan, "Why Do States Build Nuclear Weapons? Three Models in Search of a Bomb," *International Security* 21, no. 3 (1996/97): 54-86.
38. Ustina Markus, "Black Sea Fleet Dispute Apparently Over," *Transition*, 28 July 1995, 31-34.
39. Steven Erlanger, "Russia and Ukraine Settle Dispute over Black Sea Fleet," *New York Times*, 10 June 1995, A3.
40. Stephen D. Olynyk, "The State of Ukrainian Armed Forces: ROA National Security Report," *The Officer* (November 1997): 27.
41. Serhiy Tolstov, "Ukrainian Foreign Policy Formation in the Context of NATO Enlargement," *The Ukrainian Review* 44, no. 2 (1997): 9.
42. Hale, "Statehood at Stake," 328.
43. Solchanyk, *Ukraine and Russia*, 90.
44. Roman Solchanyk, "Ukraine, Russia, and the CIS," in *Ukraine in the World: Studies in the International Relations and Security Structure of a New Independent State*, ed. Ludomyr A. Hajda (Cambridge: Harvard University Press, 1998), 32.
45. Dyczok, *Ukraine*, 120. Several bureaucratic changes were made to reflect Ukraine's interest in strengthening ties with the EU. For example, in the fall of 1997, a European Union Department was created in the Ukrainian Ministry of Foreign Affairs. Similarly, the National Agency of Ukraine for Reconstruction and Development was renamed the National Agency of Ukraine Development and European Integration.
46. Marta Kolomayets, "Ukraine to Seek Special Partnership with NATO," *The Ukrainian Weekly*, no. 26 (1996): 1.
47. Dyczok, *Ukraine*, 121.
48. Carlos Pascual and Steven Pifer, "Ukraine's Bid for a Decisive Place in History," *Washington Quarterly* 25, no. 1 (2002): 185.
49. Volodymyr Horbulin, "Ukraine's Contribution to Security and Stability in Europe," *NATO Review* 46, no. 3 (1998): 12.
50. Solchanyk, *Ukraine and Russia*, 97; and Maria Kopylenko, "Ukraine: Between NATO and Russia," in *Enlarging NATO: The National Debates*, ed. Gale A. Mattox and Arthur R. Rachwald (Boulder, CO: Lynne Rienner, 2001), 196.
51. T. Ivzhenko, "Ukraina ne vstupit v NATO v blizhaishie 10 let" (Ukraine will not join NATO within the next 10 Years), *Nezavisimaia Gazeta*, 11 February 1999, 1-2.
52. "Politicheskie Itogi—2000" (Political summary—2000), *Zerkalo Nedeli*, 30 December 2000, 1-4.
53. "Naveki s Russkim Narodom" (Forever with the Russian people), *Zerkalo Nedeli*, 21-27 October 2000.
54. "Ukraine, Russia Agree on BSF, But Differ on NATO," *RFE/RL Newsline*, 19 January 2001.
55. "Kasyanov, Ukrainian Counterpart Agree to Expand Cooperation," *RFE/RL Newsline*, 14 June 2001.
56. *Nezavisimaia Gazeta*, 19 March 2002, 6, in *Current Digest of the Post-Soviet Press* 54, no. 12 (2002): 14.
57. Olexiy Haran and Rostyslav Pavlenko, "The Paradoxes of Kuchma's Russian Policy," PONARS Policy Memo No. 291 (September 2003), 5.
58. Eric Miller and Victor Zaborsky, "Curbing Arms Industry is Vital for Ukraine's NATO Ambitions," *Jane's Intelligence Review* (July 2005): 51-53.

Chapter 7

Ukrainian Leaders and Internal Threats

Whereas Chapter 6 focused on security cooperation between Ukraine and Russia, this chapter analyzes how internal threats to Ukrainian leaders shaped relations with Russia. The IT/ED framework suggests that when leaders feel their political positions are threatened, they are more likely to align with Russia. Based on the conceptualization of internal threats used in this book, there were two moments in which internal threats to Kravchuk and Kuchma were most evident, and in both instances leaders survived by adopting strong pro-Russian alignments. Kravchuk met his political fate in the 1994 presidential elections, with Kuchma winning the election primarily on the political support of the eastern and southern regions of the country and promising a more pro-Russian alignment.

Kuchma's experience in office is a bit more puzzling. After his re-election in the 1999 presidential elections, he faced a political scandal surrounding the mysterious death of opposition journalist Georgii Gongadze in the fall of 2000, when allegations linked Kuchma and some of his advisors to the killing. This prompted an unprecedented level of political protest in Ukraine's political system. While no galvanizing opposition group emerged in earnest, the rise of political opposition to Kuchma in general and the subsequent international isolation that occurred as a result of the scandal prompted Kuchma to strengthen ties with Moscow to secure his political position at home. As the IT/ED framework would predict, when internal political threats are high, a leader is likely to adopt a pro-Russian alignment, a conclusion evident in Kuchma's pro-Russian rhetoric during the 1994 elections and over the past few years as relations with Moscow have strengthened. In this sense, the intensity of internal threats were not constants that Ukrainian leaders were concerned with at all times, unlike Karimov's attitude towards Islamic extremism and domestic political opposition in Uzbekistan. Yet, when they existed, the leader's response, in this case Kuchma on two occasions, entailed strengthening ties with Moscow, although the second shift represented a more tangible and less rhetorical warming to Russia.

As we will see, however, Kuchma's hand-picked successor for the presidency in 2004, Viktor Yanukovich, also adopted a strong pro-Russian alignment, when faced with significant political opposition. This time, though, a galvanizing opposition leader emerged, Viktor Yushchenko, as a result of government manipulation of the 2004 presidential elections. In the end, the popular support for

Yushchenko and the Orange Revolution proved too much for Kuchma, his hand-picked successor, and Moscow.

Another key distinction between Karimov's experience with internal threats and those of Kravchuk and Kuchma is that the latter two gained their positions through a relatively open political system. This provides insight into how CIS leaders pursued their political security under different political conditions. Ukrainian leaders could secure their political positions, with Kuchma infinitely more successful than Kravchuk, but they could not rely on open repression as Karimov did. In fact, it was the overt manipulation of the 2004 presidential elections that gave rise to the galvanizing opposition leader that led to Yanukovich's electoral defeat, despite his pro-Russian inclination. Thus, once Ukrainian authorities crossed this line it opened a pandora's box that they hardly anticipated.

The IT/ED framework acknowledges that a basic analytical difference exists when discussing varying types of political systems. CIS leaders in more democratic systems, or quasi-democratic systems as in Ukraine, tended to form winning coalitions from among various actors within the state, in essence bandwagoning with powerful domestic actors and making sure their political base was strong enough to ensure their position. That is not to suggest a similar practice could not be pursued by leaders in more authoritarian systems, but rather to point out that the option for outright repression was less available, making political bargaining more necessary. This was the most effective and efficient method to prevent the rise of any galvanizing opposition leader or party. However, if such a galvanizing opposition did emerge, this would not prevent leaders from seeking to control such a movement, although the overtness of such actions would have to be minimized in contrast to authoritarian regimes. That is, in more authoritarian political systems leaders tended to undermine any and all political opponents, whether violent, revolutionary, or mainstream, often times through heavy-handed tactics or overt repression.

Once in power, Ukrainian leaders distributed the country's economic resources (both formally and informally) to their political supporters (a political/economic transaction discussed at greater length in the next chapter). In this regard, Ukrainian leaders built a base of political support, or what some have termed the "party of power." This technique is necessary because Ukrainian leaders cannot jail or eliminate their political opponents, as easily as leaders in more authoritarian political systems. Nonetheless, as we will see, Ukrainian leaders were conscious of threats to their positions and attempted to increase their political power. Thus, while the means may differ, the ends are the same: CIS leaders prioritize their political survival and do whatever it takes to ensure it.

Another significant difference between Ukraine and Uzbekistan is that Ukraine has a substantial Russian minority (and Russian-speaking Ukrainians) that live predominantly in the eastern and southern portion of the country. Kravchuk and Kuchma had to walk a tight rope, making sure policies did not drift too far to the West and similarly too far East, since either foreign orientation would isolate a significant portion of the country's population. Kravchuk tended to isolate the

Russian-speaking portions of the population, when he criticized greater integration with Russia. However, Kuchma catered to these groups. While this divide played a significant role in politics during the early 1990s and still remains an important consideration, the East-West divide was far less pronounced in the presidential elections in the fall of 1999 and demonstrated that significant changes had occurred within the overall orientation of Ukraine.[1]

This chapter begins with a brief historical overview of parliamentary and presidential relations within Ukraine. Within the first five years of independence the constitutional powers of the legislature and the presidency were hotly contested, and it was not until the signing of the first post-Soviet constitution in 1996 that the overarching constitutional questions about the balance of institutional power within the government were resolved. The political system in Uzbekistan, on the other hand, remained largely static, with the president dominating the policy making process. Within this discussion the initial political interaction between Kravchuk and Kuchma is highlighted, since the latter served as prime minister under Kravchuk for a limited time.

The chapter then turns to a more explicit examination of who Kravchuk and Kuchma coopted into their party of power (i.e., those political and economic elites that made up the pro-leadership coalition in the government). Following this, the role of domestic political opposition is analyzed in the recent case of Kuchma and the Gongadze scandal. Previously, political opposition to Ukrainian leaders was limited, but in the winter of 2000-01 much of this changed, leading Kuchma to adopt a stronger pro-Russian alignment. The chapter concludes first with a discussion of the March 2002 parliamentary elections, demonstrating the extent and methods available to Kuchma to prevent the rise of any galvanizing opposition leader or party even after Kuchmagate and relatively free elections that year. It then turns to the events of the Orange Revolution in the winter of 2004 to see how internal threats and an alignment with Russia played into Kuchma's and Yanukovich's strategies to maintain power.

Ukrainian Politics: The Early Years

Unlike Karimov in Uzbekistan, Ukrainian leaders faced domestic political opposition throughout the decade and were forced to obtain their office through relatively open elections. In the initial period of independence, other political forces, namely the parliament challenged Ukrainian presidents. This section sketches a brief overview of Ukrainian politics shortly after independence, highlighting the tensions between the president, prime minister, and parliament over the distribution of governmental power and the political interaction of Kravchuk and Kuchma before Kuchma's election in 1994.[2]

Strong executive branches are more the norm, than the exception in the CIS, and Ukraine is no exception.[3] Within the post-Soviet era, two general time frames exist that differentiate executive/legislative tensions. The first period spanned from December 1991 until June 1996. During this phase Ukrainian leaders struggled with the parliament to define the appropriate constitutional powers of their respective political institutions and pass a political and economic agenda that could meet the needs of the leaders (although this did not always coincide with what was best for the Ukrainian people or economy). Once the new constitution was signed in the middle of 1996, however, much of the legal debate concerning the division of power was resolved, although tensions did not disappear altogether between Kuchma and the parliament. The second phase spans roughly from the signing of the 1996 constitution until today, characterized by a stronger Ukrainian presidency.

Shortly before independence, parliamentary elections held in March 1990 performed somewhat of a representative function, as a multi-party system emerged for the first time. But Ukrainian politics did not transform entirely, and opposition political parties had limited participation throughout the country. In 1991, for example, the total membership of all non-Communist political parties was 35,000 to 40,000 out of a population of nearly 52 million. The Communist Party of Ukraine, on the other hand, claimed 2.9 million members at its December 1990 congress.[4] The discrepancies did not end there. The main opposition force within the parliament came from the nationalist-democratic movement, and they were able to garner almost one-third of the seats in the parliament during these elections. However, these parties were unstructured and loosely organized and lacked a substantial parliamentary majority, which made pushing through the national-democratic agenda difficult. What compounded this problem for the nationalist-democratic movement was that party cohesion was near impossible, whereas the Communists voted along party lines, earning them the title of the "Group of 239," or the number of Communists in the parliament (see Table 7.1).

In the last days of the Soviet Union, Kravchuk was primarily concerned with increasing Ukraine's autonomy within the Soviet Union and ensuring the power of the Communist Party of Ukraine. The most significant obstacle to this objective was the interference of Moscow leaders, but in the wake of the failed August pusch in Moscow, centralized power structures weakened. The Ukrainian parliament declared Ukraine's independence on 24 August 1991, with the notion of a federation controlled centrally from Moscow evaporating on 1 December, when Ukrainian voters indicated that 90 percent were in favor of complete independence.[5] The Communist Party of Ukraine was subsequently outlawed at the end of August.[6]

In December 1991 Kravchuk was elected president of Ukraine, with over 60 percent of the vote. For Kravchuk, as we will see below, political support came from the more conservative forces within Ukrainian politics, namely the former Communist Party, although he coopted the nationalists into his initial political coalition by insisting on Ukrainian independence and sovereignty. When the Communist Party of Ukraine was outlawed through the repeal of Article 6 of the 1978 Soviet Constitution, many former Communists quickly organized into the Socialist Party of Ukraine, under the leadership of Oleksandr Moroz, or they remained independent, and remained firmly entrenched in their positions.[7] These individuals still represented the vast majority of parliament based on the pre-independence election held in 1990, and therefore they remained the dominant political force in Ukraine. The IT/ED framework suggests that CIS leaders in more democratic systems are more likely to bandwagon with the most influential actors in the country as opposed to balancing them. This was the precise motivation that drove Kravchuk's political coalition of former Communists and other state apparatchiks.

Table 7.1 Party Representation in the Ukrainian Parliament, 1990-1991[8]

Political Party	Number of Members
Left	239
Communist Party of Ukraine	239
After August 1991	
Socialist Party of Ukraine	38
Peasant Party of Ukraine	44
Independents	157
Moderate Left	40
Party of Democratic Rebirth of Ukraine	36
Social Democratic Party of Ukraine	2
United Social Democratic Party	1
People's Party of Ukraine	1
Nationalist Bloc	78
Rukh	40
Ukrainian Republican Party	12
Democratic Party of Ukraine	23
Ukrainian Conservative Republican Party	1
Ukrainian Christian Democratic Party	1
Statehood and Independence for Ukraine	1
Uncommitted/Independents	87
Total	444

Over the next few years, Kravchuk relied on the political support of the former nomenklatura, or former Soviet officials linked to the state apparatus, and thus reform efforts could not jeopardize the interests of these individuals. If reform threatened their interests, then they would be less likely to support Kravchuk, denying him much-needed political support. As we will see, the inability of Kravchuk to deal with Ukraine's needs in a long-term fashion based on his narrow self-interests of staying in power, ultimately led to his political demise in 1994 as the country plummeted into economic crisis. Indeed, the major difference between Ukraine's initial experience with independence and that of Eastern Europe is that the old regime was not swept away, but rather they reorganized and remained entrenched in their position of political and economic power. Thus, as one commentator notes, the nomenklatura in Ukraine "managed to preserve real power and property quite easily after 1991 by means of a peculiar political deal – by recruiting to its ranks the most conformist leaders of the former counter-elite and by a timely change in its slogans for the sake of a new 'legitimacy.'"[9] This failed transition also played out in tensions between the executive and legislative branches.

Much of the difficulty in Ukraine's transition came from the lack of coordinated policy making and questions over who would make policy decisions, whether it was the parliament, president or prime minister. Initially, Ukraine began with a hybrid premier-presidential system, which has both a prime minister, who depends on the on-going confidence or absence of non-confidence of the parliament, and a popularly elected president.[10] While the president typically has the right to appoint the prime minister, pending parliament's approval, he or she does not have the ability to dismiss the prime minister without the support of the parliament.

Kravchuk did not seek to expand his presidential powers because his political supporters were firmly entrenched in the parliament and it could come at a great political loss if he challenged parliament. Instead, he accepted the division of policy making in Ukraine, while making sure his political supporters would not be influenced adversely. As Charles Wise and Trevor L. Brown conclude:

> While opportunities existed to expand the role and function of the presidency, Kravchuk preferred to work within the boundaries of the executive branch, shoring up his power in the bureaucracy through patronage and kickbacks. Rarely did Kravchuk enter into policy confrontations with the Parliament.[11]

While Kravchuk was nonconfrontational towards the parliament, his view of a subordinate prime minister was much more defined. As he suggested in 1992, "The president should be responsible for building the state, while the prime minister should manage the economy."[12] The obvious implication was that prime ministers were more expendable than the president since their objectives were more narrowly defined than the president's. Initially, Kravchuk chose Vitold Fokin as his prime minister, a former head of the State Planning Committee and much like Kravchuk a former member of the Communist Party of Ukraine's administrative apparatus. Fokin's policies were anything but spectacular, but they were designed to secure economic advantages for Kravchuk's political supporters. Indeed, important governmental and industrial elites relied heavily on their ties to the former state planning apparatus to preserve state subsidies, lobby for favors, and maintain existing privileges.[13] This was necessary for the political trade-off to ensure Kravchuk's position, but did little to secure Fokin's position. Shortsighted policies and rapid economic decline strained the government, and the democratic opposition in parliament, led by Viacheslav Chornovil, forced Fokin out in September 1992.

To replace Fokin, Kravchuk turned to Kuchma, another former Communist official. Kuchma's appointment, however, drew from a different party constituency. He was from the industrial-managerial faction of the Communist Party as opposed to Fokin formerly of the command administrative faction.

During the Soviet era, Kuchma managed the largest rocket manufacturing plant in the Soviet Union, so his ties were rooted deeper in the industrial sector. Kuchma also promised to renew ties with Russia. In his view there was a direct connection between economic decline and anti-Russian policies. By restoring economic ties with Moscow, Kuchma sought to address the growing economic crisis and more specifically Ukraine's dependence on Russian energy supplies. On this latter issue, he was particularly critical of his predecessor. For instance, he argued that Fokin allowed substantial amounts of inexpensive Russian energy (approximately 10-20 percent of world prices in late 1992) to be re-exported at world prices, with corrupt individuals benefiting tremendously while the Ukrainian state accumulated a massive energy debt.[14]

While Kuchma pushed for a more reformist path and was critical of the slow pace of privatization, he did not support shock therapy, preferring a more gradual approach to reform. Initially, he promised to continue Fokin's policies, calling for a process of "evolutionary change" and a search for a "Ukrainian model" of reform.[15] In essence, he assured that the political/economic trade-off occurring between Kravchuk and the former Communist elite would remain unchanged. Parliament ensured this by keeping anti-reform actors in Kuchma's Cabinet of Ministers, including two Fokin appointees, Hryhorii Pialachenko and Vadim Hetman, who kept their positions as the minister of finance and the chairman of the National Bank, respectively. Reform would have to wait until Kuchma returned to power as president in 1994, although even then reform efforts were not without problems.

Once in power (13 October 1992), Kuchma was given ten days to formulate an economic recovery program. One of the boldest steps taken was when he asked parliament for a six-month emergency power "to rule the economy by decree," which was subsequently passed. This enabled Kuchma to forward his economic program, which received broad support in Western financial circles. His initiative was impressive, and it forced Kravchuk to accept reform measures given the momentum of the new government. This also placed Kuchma in the spotlight, a factor that was not wasted on Kravchuk.

Tension between Kravchuk and Kuchma intensified in the spring of 1993 when Kuchma requested an extension to his six-month emergency powers. In an attempt to strengthen his grip on economic policy, Kravchuk issued a decree that would establish an "extraordinary committee" of the cabinet to deal with economic issues and assert the president's control over the government. The political struggle was inflamed by a ten-day strike of coal-miners in the Donbas region of eastern Ukraine, who demanded an increase in wages and a national referendum of confidence in the president and the parliament. Kuchma addressed the strikers by articulating an even more detailed plan of economic reform. Tensions remained high between Kuchma and Kravchuk as economic crisis set on, but parliament was unwilling to accept Kuchma's resignation in hopes of balancing Kuchma off Kravchuk. Nonetheless, by September 1993, Kuchma's resignation was accepted and a no confidence vote was passed on the entire cabinet.

Ultimately, throughout Kuchma's tenure as prime minister, Kravchuk remained unaware of Ukraine's vast economic problems, while he attacked Kuchma's policy of easing relations with Russia.[16] As we will see later, this was a shift that eventually led to Kravchuk's demise and Kuchma's ascendancy. With Kuchma's exit as prime minister, Kravchuk turned to the former mayor of Donetsk, Iukhym Zviahilskyi, to be his new prime minister, but little changed over the next few months except the continued decline of the Ukrainian economy. The greatest change though would occur during the summer presidential elections in 1994.

Kuchma remained in the background of Ukrainian politics, until the presidential elections of 1994. In the first round of elections on 26 June, Kravchuk received 37.7 percent of the vote with Kuchma gaining 31.3 percent, and the Socialist leader, Moroz, obtaining 13.1 percent. However in the runoff election on 10 July, Kuchma picked up the majority of Moroz's supporters and defeated Kravchuk, receiving 52.1 percent of the vote to Kravchuk's 45.1 percent. Kravchuk lost the elections in large part because of the poor economic conditions, but the road ahead for Kuchma was not without obstacles.[17]

The first major difficulty Kuchma faced once in office was the lack of a basic constitution that clearly defined the separation of powers between the president and the parliament. When he was prime minister, Kuchma attempted to expand his power to implement reform, and when he became president he similarly sought to increase the power of the presidency. As we saw above, increasing presidential power was not critical to Kravchuk because he held power in more informal ways through his contacts with conservatives in the parliament. Kuchma, however, sought to strengthen the executive branch.

Kuchma dramatically changed the role of the president in Ukrainian politics. His first tactic came in the form of presidential decrees, which were highly explicit. Much like Yeltsin's successes in Russia, this enabled the president to bypass the parliament's legislative power, in effect turning the president into a law-making entity. His decrees were far-reaching in the areas of privatization, the vertical structure of governance, and the reorganization of the agricultural and energy sectors.

Kuchma remained concerned, however, with the separation of governmental power. Under the existing constitution, the Cabinet of Ministers was accountable to the parliament. Thus, the government (under the guidance of the Cabinet) was responsible to both the president and parliament. This meant that the parliament had the constitutional power to remove an individual or an entire government through a no-confidence vote without the expressed consent of the president. The Speaker of the parliament also was afforded tremendous powers to submit candidates for many leading political institutions, including the Constitutional Court, the National Bank Chairmanship, and the Prosecutor General of Ukraine. In short, policy decisions were shared by the president, prime minister, and speaker of the parliament, although consultation was not necessary for some actions to be taken. This complicated the issue of implementing economic reform because the left dominated the parliament, and they were unwilling to hand over power to the executive branch.

Despite this, by the end of 1994, Kuchma expanded his presidential powers. For starters, Kuchma's relative approval rating was much higher than that of the parliament, and this afforded him a fair degree of political leverage. In early December 1994 he presented the Law on State Power and Local Administration in Ukraine, or the so-called "Power" bill. This served as an interim constitution until the final draft passed. The original version of the "Power" bill eliminated regional parliaments, providing the president with the authority to appoint regional administrators, and it concentrated power at the national level, by allowing the president to appoint a Cabinet and a prime minister without parliamentary approval.

The accord served as a preliminary constitution, but parliament was reluctant to act. In return, Kuchma utilized the bully pulpit. By the end of May 1995, he threatened to hold a national plebiscite on the "Power" bill on national television, only to have the parliament reject it on constitutional grounds. Shortly thereafter, he formalized his plebiscite order in a written decree, and the parliament reconsidered because of a lack of public support in the legislature. According to one poll conducted from 28 April 1995-10 May 1995, Kuchma had on average a 37 percent approval rating and a 37 percent disapproval rating, compared to the parliament, which had on average a ten percent approval and a 64 percent disapproval rating.[18] In the court of public opinion, Kuchma was much more secure, and therefore more willing to engage in political brinkmanship with the parliament. Parliament yielded, and the "Power" bill was passed with a 240-81 vote before any nationwide referendum of confidence could be held on him, or more importantly the parliament.[19] The president obtained the exclusive right to form the government, issue decrees, and overrule local councils that blocked reform. Institutional wrangling between the executive and legislature branched continued, but a basic framework of leadership was established, which provided for a strong executive.

For one year, the accord restricted parliament's formal powers over approval of the budget, ratification of the government's program, and drafting of ordinary legislation. The president, however, gained the exclusive right to form a government, issue decrees, appoint elected chairman of local and regional councils as heads of their respective state administrations, and dismiss the heads of local administrations for violations of the law, Constitution, or presidential decrees. Kuchma's appointment power was unprecedented. He could appoint the prime minister, cabinet, and the heads of power ministries, such as defense, foreign affairs, internal affairs, security service, and so on, without parliamentary confirmation. The prime minister was now subordinate to the president. Parliament could express "no confidence" in the entire government or individual ministries, but they could not appoint successors, which remained within the newly defined presidential powers.[20]

Thus, over the course of the first five years of independence, Ukrainian leaders wrestled with other political institutions within Ukraine, namely the parliament.

Kravchuk was more passive in his confrontation with the parliament, since most of his political supporters comprised the left-leaning parliament. Yet, when Kuchma came into office, he sought to reorganize governmental power, and in the process, establish a strong Ukrainian presidency. With this historical background, the following section examines the political parties Kravchuk and Kuchma coopted to explain where their political support rested. In essence, answering the question how did Ukrainian leaders prevent the rise of galvanizing opposition leaders or parties?

Political Parties and the Party of Power

The IT/ED framework suggests that CIS leaders in more democratic political systems tend to form an alliance with influential domestic actors to provide for their political survival. This contrasts with the more authoritarian systems, like Uzbekistan, in which leaders tend to balance or eliminate political opponents. In the case of Ukraine, Kravchuk and later Kuchma adopted this domestic strategy as they forged winning political coalitions to ensure their political positions. This section focuses more attention on which political parties or factions comprised the pro-leadership coalition.

Throughout much of Central and Eastern Europe, the previous political leadership was replaced with leaders more representative of the interests of the people or the country itself. This was not the case in Ukraine where the former Communist leadership reinvented itself. As Mykola Riabchuk contends, what emerged in Ukraine shortly after independence was a "new nomenklatura" reminiscent of its predecessor under the Soviet system. The new "party of power," or *partiia vlady*, is a group of "pragmatically oriented and de-ideologized high ranking members from the old nomenklatura, including representatives of the state apparat, the mass media, and directors of traditional sectors of industry and agriculture."[21] These political actors wield tremendous influence over Ukrainian politics, but they rarely embrace reform and often seek to undermine it. Those in the party of power, or pro-leadership coalition, gain substantial political and economic advantages, and those that are not are on the fringes of policy making in Ukraine.

Kravchuk's party of power was a timely alliance of convenience. In effect, Kravchuk, a former Communist himself, adopted the strongest position of the nationalists, namely the insistence on Ukrainian independence, and forged a political alliance between these forces and his former Communist colleagues. His most telling success was that he succeeded in co-opting both the Rukh program and its top leaders into the new government through a series of high-level appointments.[22] The nationalists, lacking the institutional support to translate their goal of national independence into a political reality, similarly welcomed this political alliance. Thus, Kravchuk and other former Communists became "national" Communists. As Alexander Motyl writes, Kravchuk transformed himself from "guardian of the Soviet state to guardian of the Ukrainian state, from supporter of all things Soviet to critic of all things Soviet, from enemy of Ukrainian nationalism to Ukrainian nationalist *par excellence*."[23] Unlike other former Communist leaders in Eastern Europe, Kravchuk then was not swept away by the nationalist movement.

Kravchuk's political supporters were primarily his former Communist cronies, and he made sure that he did not undermine the previous system. As Volodymyr Zviglyanich comments, "[U]nder the pretext of moving towards liberal democracy, rule of law and...a market economy, a revamped collectivist elite entrenched itself in power, with Mr. Kravchuk as its leader and symbol."[24] Radical institutional or political reform would only threaten the interests of these entrenched elites, and inherently intensify the level of internal threats to Kravchuk's leadership. The end result is that conservative, anti-reform elements tended to dominate the political arena. In many ways, former Soviet officials merely reinvented themselves. They did not build and develop new institutional relationships, but rather adjusted former practices to the new environment. In the end, ruling elites sought to maintain their positions at all cost and through informal practices and political and economic trade-offs. As one report concluded in 1993:

> Political conditions remain almost the way they were over two years ago (1991) when a minority, in the form of the Communist Party, had uncontrolled and undemocratic monopoly of political, economic, and social power over the people...Now government leaders seek to legitimize their rule by claiming to be "building an independent democratic state." In fact, during the past two years Ukraine has not drawn even one step closer to "real" democracy.[25]

The nationalist dimension of Kravchuk's political base dwindled in late 1992. At the end of 1992, Rukh split, but without an economic power base the party was left at the fringes of the policy making process and became increasingly marginalized politically. As Chornovil, the leader of Rukh, suggested, "the party of power, headed by the President, is straining all its muscles to prevent any reformers from achieving power."[26] Rukh was no longer a part of Kravchuk's political base, which also meant that their political voice would be diminished and therefore less problematic for Kravchuk.[27] To fall out of the pro-leadership coalition only limited the political and economic power of groups in the future.

In the end, Kravchuk adopted a political alliance of convenience between his former Communist colleagues and the more nationalist groups in Western Ukraine that supported Ukrainian independence. Little reform was implemented under his administration (a consideration examined at greater length in Chapter 8) primarily because economic reform threatened the entrenched interests of the new nomenklatura, and threatening these interests only threatened Kravchuk's political supporters. This practice ultimately led to economic crisis in 1993-94, and with it Kravchuk's political demise.

In the 1994 presidential elections, Kuchma defeated Kravchuk by drawing support from the eastern and southern regions of the country, while Kravchuk was more successful in the extreme Western regions.[28] Ultimately, the election came down to the issue of the economy, and as we saw in Chapter 6, Kuchma suggested warming up to both the West and Russia. His message resonated in the western and central parts of the country since he was suggesting the need for greater reform and interaction with the West, while talk of increasing cooperation with Russia reassured those in the other side of the country. Kuchma capitalized on issues that were embraced by both those on the left and right, and in turn he developed a base of support that settled more in the center of the Ukrainian political spectrum.

Beyond the presidential turnover, the parliament itself underwent significant changes, especially since the 1994 election was the first since Ukraine became independent. Not surprisingly, incumbents faired poorly, a form of house cleaning from the Soviet past. Over one-third of the deputies ran for re-election, yet only 66 were re-elected.[29]

A few peculiarities of the Ukrainian party system are worth noting before discussing these results. First, the nature of Ukrainian electoral laws made it more difficult to win a seat in parliament under a recognized political party as opposed to running as an independent. Candidates who ran under a political party had to garner more signatures to participate, as well as support through district branch party conferences, which enabled entrenched party leaders to undermine democratic and nationalist groups. As Bilous and Wilson assert, "it is not in the interests of either the president, the leaders of the military-industrial complex, the heads of the collective farms, or those who work in the government executive to associate themselves with any party."[30] Second and related, because of the multiplicity of political actors within the parliament as well as the number of independents, deputies were encouraged to form and align into factions.[31] The concept of factions is different in Ukrainian politics, than it is in the Western sense of the term. In the West, faction is used to describe a portion of a larger group, but in Ukraine it is used to define an assemblage of parties as a parliamentary group (i.e., bloc), including members from one or more parties and additional independent deputies. This was an attempt to streamline the rather fractured Ukrainian parliament and enhance the process of legislating.[32]

One surprise of the 1994 parliamentary elections was that the left, consisting of the Communists, Socialists, and Agrarians, showed up well, although their support was limited to the southern and eastern regions of the country. The Communist stronghold fell from 239 deputies in the March 1990 parliament to 90 deputies, with other members of the left wing adding some leverage to the bloc (see Table 7.2). As a bloc, the left tends to favor a state-run economy, restoration of the former Soviet Union, and Russian as a second official language. The Socialist and Peasant Parties share similar views, stressing the necessity of subsidies to industry to the agricultural sector, although the Peasant Party does not take any position on the language issue.

The more liberal and nationalist parties hold the opposite view of those on the left. These parties, most notably Rukh, favor Western European parliamentary democracy for Ukraine. They tend to be pro-market, want to leave the CIS in favor of integration within European structures, are concerned with the revival of Ukrainian language and culture, and are against a federal system. Based on the pro-Western orientation it is not surprising that the base of support for these groups is found in Western Ukraine.

Table 7.2 Faction Membership in Ukrainian Parliament, October 1994[33]

Political Party	Number of Members
Left	172
Communists	90
Socialists	30
Peasants (Agrarians)	52
Center	135
Unity	34
Inter-Regional Deputies Group	33
Reforms	31
Center	37
Liberal/Nationalist	55
Rukh	27
Statehood	28
Unaffiliated	31
Total	393

While there are clear distinctions between the left and more liberal political parties, the center is a particularly gray political area in which confusion and complexity are par for the course.[34] A variety of factions made up the center in the 1994-1998 parliament including, the Inter-Regional Deputies Group, Social-Market Choice, Unity, Independents, Center, and Constitutional Center. The center favors close economic ties with Russia, although it opposed greater political and military integration with Russia, and they favor economic reform as well. Language and cultural matters play less of a role in the orientations of these parties. Kuchma gained his greatest support from these centrist forces.

Under most circumstances, centrist forces would be considered a positive for democratic development; however, the center does not always work in positive ways. As Artur Bilous writes, the various centrist factions

> can only be distinguished by their amorphousness and an absence of direction in terms of their political and economic orientation. For this reason, this agglomerate of forces can sooner be described as a gray void than as a political center in the European sense of the term.[35]

Similarly, Rukh chairman, Chornovil, sees the political center in Ukraine as a "parliamentary sludge." As he criticized, "Sometimes they side with the leftists and sometimes with the rightists. They represent what might be called a situational majority, which, unfortunately, does not want to be constructive, and which, in the event of any weakening, disappears."[36] As we will see, Kuchma turned to this burgeoning center for his political support. In many ways, the 1994 election of Kuchma brought to life a new party of power as Kravchuk's gave way. Yet, the implementation of reform was not guaranteed since it similarly threatened many of Kuchma's political allies.[37]

Kuchma's parliamentary support came largely from centrists and democratic reformers, and the primary policy divisions revolved around those that supported his economic reform program and those that opposed it.[38] Kuchma first flirted with the InterRegional Bloc of Reforms and then threw in his lot with the People's Democratic Party and the Agrarians (see Table 7.3). The power of the Agrarians was in the rural communities that tended to vote with the left, thus, Kuchma could enhance his position in the eastern and southern portions of the country traditionally dominated by conservative, Communist politicians. Simultaneously, he suggested the necessity of economic reform and capitalized on the interests of those in the center that sought a greater Western orientation.

Table 7.3 Factions in the Post-March 1998 Ukrainian Parliament[39]

Political Party	Number of Members
Left	167
Communists	120
Left-Center (Socialists/Peasants)	33
Progressive Socialists	14
Center	206
People Democrats	86
Hromada	45
Independents	26
United Social Democrats	25
Greens	24
Liberal/Nationalist	
Rukh	47
Unaffiliated	30
Total	450

As we will see in Chapter 8, Kuchma ensured his political survival in the same way Kravchuk had. The main difference is who benefited from a given leader. Under Kravchuk, it was the former Communists and nomenklatura that were resistant to change and reform. Under Kuchma, it was groups that capitalized on the economic opportunities provided by greater interaction with the West and privatization within the country. In this sense, both leaders required a solid base of political support to ensure their political positions.

What was also common was to place a leader's political allies and friends in political and economic positions to make sure the rank and file did not stray. For example, there was a mass migration of officials from Dnipropetrovsk, where Kuchma served as the director of Pivdenmash, the largest missile factory in the former Soviet Union, to Kyiv upon Kuchma's presidential victory. By one estimate, there were over 60 officials from Dnipropetrovsk in the executive branch by April 1995, with over 160 by the middle of 1996.[40] This was yet another method for obtaining political survival in the CIS, and it falls in line with the traditional neo-patrimonial and nepotistic practices common throughout the post-Soviet political systems.[41]

Kuchma's strategy to prevent the rise of domestic challengers was also evident in his handling of major clans in Ukrainian politics. As discussed above, Kuchma early on in his presidency relied on the support of East Ukrainian industrial elites, many of whom were based in the Dnipropetrovsk region. These individuals had taken control of the large state-owned enterprises after independence. Yet, in the latter part of the decade, after major privatization had occurred, three regionally defined clans of private owners emerged as powerful political and economic actors. The Dnipropetrovsk, Donetsk, and Kyiv clans then competed for influence and support from Kuchma. To this end, all three clans were supported by powerful oligarchs, had their own political parties and parliamentary factions and their own newspapers and television channels, hence, making them well organized for the political arena.

Over the years Kuchma was successful at harnessing the political power of the clans, while balancing them off one another. In his few two years in office, the Dnipropetrovsk clan was dominant politically in Ukraine, although gradually Kuchma understood the desirability of broadening his political support base. And, thus, from approximately 1996 to 2000 the Kyiv clan joined the Dnipropetrovsk clan in its competition for Kuchma's favor and patronage. This inclusion resulted from the financial growth of the Kyiv clan, which made them a dangerous constituency to alienate, as well as the political capital accrued by Kuchma. That is, by having two clans competing for his favor, Kuchma could manage the political competition in a way that inevitably favored himself, thereby strengthening his political position and security. Thus, Kuchma could play the role of arbiter among rival clans and elevate his political power. In 2001 the Donetsk clan reemerged as a political force after a long period of weakness. This position of weakness came from the fact that the clan was closely tied to the Kravchuk administration, and with its ouster in the 1994 elections, their political position was severely curtailed. However, as was seen in the Kyiv clan, a new generation of individuals had risen to financial power in the region, which could then be translated into political power under Kuchma. The greatest achievement of this clan was Viktor Yanukovich's appointment as Prime Minister in November 2002. Thus, by 2001 Kuchma's power base was comprised of these competing clans, and as Mikhail Brodskii noted, "there are no oligarchs in the country that are not part of Kuchma's court."[42]

Since autumn 2002, Kuchma has come to rely more on the Kyiv clan, as evidenced, among other things, by the appointment in June 2002 of the leader of the Kyiv clan, Viktor Medvedchuk, as head of the presidential administration.

Moreover, a number of cadre policy decisions and new decrees in the autumn 2003, and a November 2003 decree which shifted foreign policy authority from the Foreign Ministry to the presidential administration all reinforced the growing power of the Kyiv clan. The clan also benefited from several favorable decisions over privatization deals which strengthened their financial position. Not surprisingly, this has enabled the Kyiv clan to be arguably the most successful clan in installing its members at all levels of executive power in Ukraine. The way in which political deals were struck, especially during the privatization process, will be discussed at greater length in Chapter 8, but the present discussion has sought to underscore and identify some of the most influential political actors Kuchma sought to manage. His successful political wrangling helped Kuchma prevent the rise of any galvanizing opposition leader or party, but this did not prevent public protest of Kuchma in the wake of the "Kuchmagate" scandal. The next section examines more specifically these internal threats in the latter part of the decade, and the impact they had on a stronger pro-Russian alignment.

Internal Threats and Pro-Russian Alignment Patterns

The IT/ED framework suggests that the more internal threats to leaders exist, the more likely a pro-Russian alignment will be adopted to secure the political position of the present leader. As we have seen, internal threats to Ukrainian leaders whether traditional internal threats or domestic political opposition, have been relatively low throughout the decade. This was in large part due to the ability of Ukrainian leaders to form political alliances, which secured their base of political support. But as part of this arrangement, this meant that they had to distribute economic resources to these political backers in exchange for their support. They peaked for Kravchuk in the summer of 1994 and led to his defeat in the presidential elections. On the other hand, as the IT/ED framework would predict, Kuchma came to power promising to strengthen relations with Moscow. As we will see in the next chapter, the root of Kravchuk's internal threats came from the economic crisis that set on by 1993 and domestic dissatisfaction with his pro-Western, anti-Russian orientation.

The second experience with internal threats for Kuchma occurred in the fall of 2000, in the wake of a political scandal surrounding the death of journalist Georgiy Gongadze. Audiotapes were released that allegedly contained the voices of Kuchma, Internal Affairs Minister Yuriy Kravchenko, and Presidential Administration Head Volodymyr Lytvyn. The tapes linked the president and two of his top aides to the disappearance of Gongadze. Gongadze's disappearance and the ensuring scandal led to some of the most outspoken acts of political protest in Ukraine to date. For instance, on 19 December 2000 over 5,000 protesters marched to the parliament and demanded Kuchma's resignation. Since the protests were so massive and included an array of political parties, such as Communists, Socialists, the Christian Democratic Party, extreme nationalist parties and more centrist parties, Kuchma met with the leaders of the movement. During this meeting he agreed to conduct an independent analysis of the audiotapes and seek independent forensic testing on the corpse found outside Kyiv in November, which turned out to be Gongadze's.

Protests continued in Kyiv. Yet as Kuchma intimated, forces within the state were attempting to turn the death of Gongadze into "a political weapon designed to destabilize Ukraine."[43] Accordingly, in two separate incidents, he authorized the removal of protesters who had established a "tent city" on Kyiv's main street and a local park.[44] During a state ceremony at the statue of Ukrainian national poet Taras Shevchenko in early March 2001, police confronted over 200 people when Kuchma arrived to lay ceremonial flowers.[45] On 9 March in response to this incident between 5,000 and 10,000 people protested outside of the presidential administration building in Kyiv, the largest political demonstration since independence.

Similarly, the sacking of Deputy Prime Minister Yulia Tymoshenko in January 2001 demonstrated the extent to which Kuchma favored entrenched interests, sparking further protest against the president. Tymoshenko's dismissal was a response to her efforts to introduce transparent rules in the energy sector, which threatened the interests of Ukrainian oligarchs. Tymoshenko was later arrested and accused of smuggling gas and forging documents by Kuchma. Protests continued outside of the prison in which she was held demanding her release. However, Kuchma dismissed much of this political protest, suggesting that the majority of demonstrators were paid to protest, and therefore do not accurately reflect the interests of the average Ukrainian. Tymoshenko was eventually released, but she continued to be hassled by the Ukrainian government concerning her alleged improprieties when in Kuchma's government.

Thus, as internal threats to Kuchma rose and economic dependence remained high, Kuchma adopted an even stronger alignment with Russia, as outlined the previous chapter. In the words of Taras Stetskyv, a member from the Forum for National Salvation, the recent Putin-Kuchma agreements came about as a result of "the strengthening of the opposition to Kuchma."[46] That is, by cooperating with Russia, Kuchma strengthened his domestic position, particularly since Putin described the Gongadze case as a matter of Ukrainian internal affairs. In this regard, Russia was the only country willing to support Kuchma diplomatically and politically in the face of increased domestic opposition. As we will see below, Russian involvement in supporting Kuchma and his hand-picked successor was consistently felt, with the latter episode prompting a popular revolution against the existing regime after fraudulent presidential elections in November 2004. Thus, as the IT/ED framework would suggest, when threatened or fearful of their political survival, Ukrainian leaders turned to Moscow for assistance, although in the latter case of Yanukovich, there was little more Russia could have done.

March 2002 Parliamentary Elections

The March 2002 parliamentary elections were symbolic of the way in which Kuchma managed the Ukrainian political system in his favor, and they revealed several insights of the political process, notably overt Russian involvement and continued administrative manipulation by the Ukrainian government. For instance, during the elections Russia's Ambassador to Ukraine Viktor Chernomyrdin openly interfered in favor of pro-presidential parties, helped fan the flames of an "anti-nationalist" campaign against pro-Western forces, and criticized Ukrainian officials for their interest in joining the EU, in contrast to the Russian-dominated Eurasian Economic Community.[47] Similarly, the overt use of Russian campaign advisors was another distinct feature of the 2002 elections. The pro-presidential bloc, For a United Ukraine, invited the Russian image company "Nikkolo M" to work for them, while the United Social Democrats employed experts from Gleb Pavlovsky's Fund for Effective Politics, the architects of several of Putin's successful campaigns.[48]

The Ukrainian government itself also carefully orchestrated the political process wherever it could. State- and oligarch-owned media outlets consistently and vocally supported candidates favorable to the regime, whereas on the other hand, Yushchenko rarely received positive air play, and Tymoshenko and Moroz had difficulty even getting on the air. State authorities employed other tactics intended to undermine opposition candidates. For example, "candidate-cloning" – the practice of confusing potential electors by arranging for candidates with the same name to run in a district – was widely used. This technique was complemented by similar efforts at "party cloning" and "bloc cloning."[49]

Despite these efforts, the vote tallies, at least on the side of the proportional party list voting, suggested that the tactics had little effect. Indeed, opposition forces received almost 60 percent of the party list votes, while the two pro-presidential parties (For a United Ukraine and the United Social Democrats) who cleared the 4 percent threshold received only 18 percent of the votes.[50] As Table 7.4 reveals, however, when adding the totals from the single-mandate districts with the party lists, the true power player remained the pro-presidential bloc For a United Ukraine. This was primarily a result of the administrative resources and leverage used in these districts during the elections, and the pressure placed on those individuals that ran as independents after the election to join the pro-presidential group.[51]

Thus, while it seemed that the opposition has scored a resounding success in the elections, the political maneuvering of Kuchma and his political supporters enabled the leader to emerge relatively unscathed, although international criticism of the elections was voiced. Adding to this, Volodymyr Lytvyn, former head of the presidential administration and the first to hold the position on the For a United Ukraine party list, was elected parliamentary speaker by the narrowest of margins. He received the minimum number of votes needed to be elected speaker – 226 out of 450. Having successfully installed a pro-presidential parliamentary leadership, the amorphous For a United Ukraine then splintered into several different factions.

Table 7.4 Results of the 2002 Parliamentary Elections[52]

Parties/Blocs Passing the 4% Threshold	% of Proportional Representation (PR) Vote	Actual Votes for Party Lists	Deputies Voted in on PR Lists	Deputies from Single-Mandate Districts	"Independents" Joining the Parliamentary Faction	Final Total in the Parliamentary Faction	% of Overall Parliament Seats
Our Ukraine	23.52	6,108,088	70	42	5	118	26.2
Communist Party of Ukraine	19.98	5,178,074	59	6	0	64	14.2
For a United Ukraine	11.77	3,051,056	35	85	56	177	39.3
Yulia Tymoshenko's bloc	7.28	1,882,087	22	0	1	23	5.1
Socialist Party of Ukraine	6.87	1,780,642	20	2	0	22	4.9
United Social Democratic Party	6.27	1,626,721	19	8	4	31	6.9
Independents without a faction	—	—	—	11	—	11	2.4

In the end, the March 2002 elections demonstrate a common story under Kuchma. He mastered the political game to his benefit and subsequently prevented the rise of any galvanizing opposition leader or party as the IT/ED framework would predict. This was done because CIS leaders are primarily driven by their desire to secure their political positions, and as a result undermining opposition groups before they pose a threat to the leader is often the best course of action. It could be argued of course that Yushchenko's Our Ukraine does in some form represent a galvanizing opposition leader and party, but at least so far Kuchma has been able to control the threat posed by such a group. What happened in the winter of 2004 would challenge that notion though.

November 2004 Presidential Elections

Much like Shevardnadze's experience in Georgia after the November 2003 parliamentary elections during the Rose Revolution, the logic of the IT/ED framework provides a compelling explanation of Ukraine's alignment behavior. Since independence Ukrainian leaders consistently balanced East and West, but during the presidential elections the choice for Ukraine was in starker contrast. Yanukovich, Kuchma's hand-picked successor, supported a stronger relationship with Russia, while reform-minded Yushchenko promised to bolster ties with the Euro-Atlantic community.

Throughout the election campaign, Yanukovich (as well as Kuchma) saw Yushchenko as a galvanizing opposition leader that threatened his political position. Kuchma had decided not to challenge the constitutional term limits, and thus his presidency was destined to end with these elections. But post-Soviet leaders, as Yeltsin demonstrated himself, were equally concerned with finding a suitable replacement, and more specifically, one that was unlikely to seek any legal or criminal action against the outgoing president – the so-called "golden parachute." Thus, there was still a lot at stake for Kuchma, and his political, economic, and personal well-being would have been safer under Yanukovich than Yushchenko.

Despite the overwhelming support of the Kuchma administration, Yanukovich was unable to mitigate Yushchenko's growing popularity. This was all the more evident when it was projected that Yushchenko would defeat Yanukovich in the November run-off, assuming the elections were conducted in a free and fair manner. The establishment's concern with Yushchenko's dynamism and popular image was one of the reasons for his dioxin poisoning, allegedly linked to Ukrainian authorities close to Kuchma and Yanukovich, which left the presidential hopeful severely disfigured. Indeed, this concern played out during and after the various rounds of elections. In the 31 October first round, Yanukovich and Yushchenko received approximately 39-40 percent a piece. However, in the 21 November run-off, according to official Central Election Commission results, Yanukovich won the election with 49 percent of the vote to Yushchenko's 47 percent. Reliable exits polls projected a nine to eleven point victorious margin for

Yushchenko. As a result, Yushchenko told an ever-growing crowd of supporters on Independence Square that by resorting to massive fraud, primarily in Ukraine's eastern regions, the authorities stole 3.1 million votes from him and consequently his election victory. This was all the more compelling considering the fact that the vote gap between the two candidates as announced by the central Election Commission amounted to some 870,000 votes.

These dubious results prompted widespread criticism from the international community, which placed even greater pressure on Kuchma and Yanukovich. The Organization for Security and Cooperation in Europe (OSCE) International Observation Mission stated in its preliminary conclusions that the vote did not meet a considerable number of democratic election standards. According to the OSCE mission, the Ukrainian executive authorities and the Central Election Commission "displayed a lack of will to conduct a genuine democratic election process."[53] Senator Richard Lugar, serving as Bush's personal representative, complained that the second round was marred by "widespread political intimidation and failure to give equal coverage to candidates in the media. Physical intimidation of voters and illegal use of governmental administrative and legal authorities had been evident and pervasive." He added, "A concerted and forceful program of election day fraud and abuse was enacted with either the leadership or cooperation of government authorities." The White House also released a statement urging Ukrainian authorities to "review the conduct of the election" and not finalize the results "until investigations of organized fraud are resolved." The statement ended by saying, "The United States stands with the Ukrainian people in this difficult time."[54] The only exception to this public condemnation of the November elections came from the CIS Election Observers Mission, a body established in Russia in 2003 that is formed with other CIS member participation. CIS observers reported that the elections were "legitimate and of a nature that reflected democratic standards."[55]

Facing such intense international opposition and domestic protests of tens of thousands of people in Kyiv, Kuchma was forced to strike a deal with Yushchenko, which was accomplished on 8 December. The legislative compromise put forth a restructuring of governmental power and paved the way for another round of elections on 26 December. Lawmakers adopted a constitutional reform bill to limit presidential powers in favor of the prime minister and the parliament, amended the law on presidential elections to safeguard against abuse and fraud, approved a bill of constitutional amendments "in the first reading" to reform local self government, and replaced the Central Election Commission that awarded a dubious victory to Yanukovich in the 21 November runoff.[56] While these measures were significant and helped Yushchenko's bid in the December re-run, they also raised the specter that what he would in fact inherit as president would be a much less powerful institution than that held by previous Ukrainian presidents. In the end, the compromise struck between Kuchma and Yushchenko was a necessary step to enable Kuchma to cede over power willingly, allowing Yushchenko to claim victory in the Orange Revolution. In the 26 December re-run, Yushchenko defeated Yanukovich with 52 percent of the vote to Yanukovich's 44 percent – a resounding victory that more closely paralleled the true will of the Ukrainian people.

As the IT/ED framework would suggest, the threatened leader (the establishment candidate, Yanukovich) would likely align with Russia in an effort to balance his primary internal threat (the galvanizing opposition leader, Yushchenko). This theoretical prediction proved prescient. During the election campaign, Yanukovich's pro-Russian orientation was rewarded with Putin's open and active support. Indeed, the Russian president firmly endorsed Yanukovich during two strategically timed visits to Ukraine days before the elections. Russian political and media strategists close to Putin were also brought on as advisors to the Yanukovich campaign. It is estimated that half of the $600 million spent by the Yanukovich campaign came from Russian sources. Moreover, Putin was the only foreign leader to congratulate Yanukovich on his victory – congratulations that came before the official vote was announced. As Putin stated, "The battle was hard-fought, but open and honest, and his victory was convincing."[57] However, in the face of strong international and domestic opposition, Putin was forced to temper his support. Only a few days after his initial congratulatory remarks, Putin backed down from his previous assurance that the Yanukovich was the clear victor in the November elections. He noted that the election is Ukraine's internal affairs and added that any election disputed should be resolved in a legal manner. "And we know what the legal way is – all claims should be sent to the court," he said.[58]

Despite Russia's continued assistance both before and after the presidential elections, Yanukovich was ultimately unsuccessful in holding onto power and quelling the rising democratic momentum of the Orange Revolution. Nonetheless, the IT/ED framework still provides a revealing glimpse into how a post-Soviet leader sought to secure his political position.

Conclusions

This chapter examined the domestic political setting within Ukraine, and explained how Ukrainian leaders secured their political positions. While leaders in more authoritarian systems are more likely to balance internal threats, leaders in more democratic systems are more likely to align with the strongest political and economic actors. This latter point was evident in the domestic political strategies of Kravchuk and Kuchma, although the political bases differed. Kravchuk relied on his former Communist connections to secure his position, which worked well until Ukraine spiraled into economic decline. Indeed, it is not uncommon for internal threats to rise under conditions of rapid economic decline; such was Kravchuk's experience.

Kuchma pledged to strengthen relations with Russia and the West. This undermined his credibility with the left factions in the parliament, although he was able garner the support of the Agrarians in eastern and southern Ukraine. Kuchma thus aligned with centrist parties, which were willing to work with Russia on economic matters and continue to look West.

In the end, Ukrainian leaders did not eliminate domestic political opposition in an overt manner, but rather they worked around opposition through informal channels based on personal relations with various political groups. However, the political scandal that rocked Ukraine beginning in the fall of 2000, led to a dramatic and unprecedented rise of internal threats to Kuchma, with many groups such as "Ukraine without Kuchma" calling for the leader to step down. Despite this growing opposition, Kuchma and his political supporters were able to prevent these opposition figures from making strong inroads into the political system, as they carefully manipulated the March 2002 parliamentary elections to install a pro-presidential parliamentary majority. The heavy-handed manner with which Kuchma, Yanukovich, and their Russian supporters handled the November 2004 presidential elections, however, opened up a pandora's box. Facing significant international pressure and a galvanizing opposition movement led by Yushchenko, the domestic pressure proved too great for Kuchma and Yanukovich to hold onto their political positions even with the overwhelming support of Putin and the Russian political machine. Indeed, the IT/ED framework posits that the more internal threats to leaders occur, the more likely a strong pro-Russian alignment will be adopted – a proposition that proved true for Kuchma after Kuchmagate and more recently for him and Yanukovich. Beyond this political dimension, economic dependence on Russia also contributed to Kuchma's alignment calculations, a factor examined in the next chapter.

Notes

1. Thomas F. Klobucar, Arthur H. Miller, and Gwyn Erb, "The 1999 Ukrainian Presidential Election: Personalities, Ideology, Partisanship, and the Economy," *Slavic Review* 61, no. 2 (2002): 315-44.
2. For a good overview of these events see, Charles R. Wise and Volodymyr Pigenko, "The Separation of Powers Puzzle in Ukraine: Sorting Out Responsibilities and Relationships between President, Parliament, and the Prime Minister," in *State and Institution Building in Ukraine*, ed. Taras Kuzio, Robert S. Kravchuk, and Paul D'Anieri (New York: St. Martin's Press, 1999); and Paul D'Anieri, Robert Kravchuk, and Taras Kuzio, *Politics and Society in Ukraine* (Boulder, CO: Westview, 1999).
3. Roeder, "Varieties of Post-Soviet Authoritarian Regimes"; and Frye, "A Politics of Institutional Choice."
4. Taras Kuzio, *Ukraine: Perestroika to Independence*, 2nd ed. (New York: St. Martin's Press, 2000), 156.
5. Roman Solchanyk, "Ukraine: From Sovereignty to Independence," *RFE/RL Research Report*, no. 1 (1992): 37.
6. Although it was re-legalized in 1993, the new Communist party did not claim to be the successor to the former Communist Party of the Soviet Union.
7. Article 6 declared the Communist Party the sole means of political representation.
8. Bogdan Szajkowski, *Political Parties of Eastern Europe, Russia, and the Successor States* (Essex: Longman Information & Reference, 1994); and Dominique Arel, "The Parliamentary Blocs in the Ukrainian Supreme Soviet: Who and What Do They Represent?" *Journal of Soviet Nationalities* 1, no. 4 (1990/91): 108-54.

9. Paul D'Anieri, "The Impact of Domestic Divisions on Ukrainian Foreign Policy: Ukraine as a 'Weak State,'" in *State and Institution Building in Ukraine*, ed. Taras Kuzio, Robert S. Kravchuk, and Paul D'Anieri (New York: St. Martin's Press, 1999), 87.
10. M. S. Shugart, "Of Presidents and Parliaments," *East European Constitutional Review*, no. 2 (1993): 30-32.
11. Charles R. Wise and Trevor L. Brown, "Laying the Foundation for Institutionalisation of Democratic Parliaments in the Newly Independent States: The Case of Ukraine," *Journal of Legislative Studies* 2, no. 3 (1996): 231.
12. Ilya Prizel, "Ukraine between Proto-Democracy and 'Soft' Authoritarianism," in *Democratic Changes and Authoritarian Reactions in Russia, Ukraine, Belarus, and Moldova*, ed. Karen Dawisha and Bruce Parrott (Cambridge: Cambridge University Press, 1997), 345.
13. Paul Kubicek, "Post-Soviet Ukraine: In Search of a Constituency for Reform," *Journal of Communist Studies and Transition Politics* 13, no. 3 (1997): 103-26; and Adrian Karatnycky, "Ukraine at the Crossroads," *Journal of Democracy* 6, no. 1 (1995): 117-30.
14. Prizel, "Ukraine between Proto-Democracy," 347.
15. "Dream On," *The Economist*, 17 October 1992, 56.
16. Prizel, "Ukraine between Proto-Democracy," 347.
17. Regional differences also played an important role. Andrew Wilson, "Parties and Presidents in Ukraine and Crimea, 1994," *Journal of Communist Studies and Transition Politics* 11, no. 4 (1995): 362-371.
18. Wise and Brown, "Laying the Foundation," 244.
19. Chrystyna Lapychak, "Showdown Yields Political Reform," *Transition* 1, no. 13 (1995): 3-7; and Taras Kuzio, *Ukraine under Kuchma: Political Reform, Economic Transformation and Security Policy in Independent Ukraine* (New York: St. Martin's Press, 1997), 99-109.
20. For more on parliamentary attitudes towards this separation of power see, Vladimir Pigenko, Charles R. Wise, and Trevor L. Brown, "Elite Attitudes and Democratic Stability: Analysing Legislators' Attitudes towards the Separation of Powers in Ukraine," *Europe-Asia Studies* 54, no. 1 (2002): 87-108.
21. One important distinction between the Soviet and post-Soviet eras is worth noting. That is, the new nomenklatura operates differently than the Soviet one. The Communist Party previously played a "leading and directing" role in policy making, however the new party of power works behind the scenes (and often behind closed doors), while playing a more "manipulative" role than in the past. Riabchuk cited in Paul Kubicek, *Unbroken Ties: The State, Interest Associations, and Corporatism in Post-Soviet Ukraine* (Ann Arbor: University of Michigan Press, 2000), 42. Some Ukrainian observers contend that it is more accurate to call the party of power the "party of chameleons" since individuals are free to change colors as they see fit, and others have drawn distinctions between the "economic nomenklatura" and the "administrative nomenklatura." Kubicek, *Unbroken Ties*, 46-47.
22. Roman Solchanyk, "Ukraine: A Year of Transition," *RFE/RL Research Report*, no. 1 (1993): 59.
23. Alexander Motyl, *Dilemmas of Independence: Ukraine After Totalitarianism* (New York: Council of Foreign Relations Press, 1993), 150.
24. Volodymyr Zviglyanich, "Analysis: Stability and Reform Pose Challenges to New President," *The Ukrainian Weekly*, 16 October 1994, 2.
25. Kubicek, *Unbroken Ties*, 44.

26. V. Skachko, "Vlast' govorit o vyborakh, oppozitsiia – o reformakh" (The authorities are talking about elections, the opposition is talking about reforms), *Nezavisimaia Gazeta*, 4 January 1994, 3.

27. Prizel, "Ukraine between Proto-Democracy," 345.

28. For more on the elections see, Taras Kuzio, "Kravchuk to Kuchma: The Ukrainian Presidential Elections of 1994," *Journal of Communist Studies and Transition Politics* 12, no. 2 (1996): 117-44.

29. Victor Chudowsky, "The Ukrainian Party System," in *State and Nation Building in East Central Europe: Contemporary Perspectives*, ed. John S. Micgiel (New York: Institute on East Central Europe, Columbia University, 1996), 337. Adrian Karatnycky suggested that 56 deputies out of 188 that ran for re-election won. Adrian Karatnycky, "Ukraine at the Crossroads," *Journal of Democracy* 6, no. 1 (1995): 124-25.

30. Andrew Wilson and Artur Bilous, "Political Parties in Ukraine," *Europe-Asia Studies* 45, no. 4 (1993): 693-703.

31. For instance, deputies who organize into factions were afforded office space, staff, technical support, and a seat on the powerful Presidium, while those that continue to work as independents did not. Wise and Brown, "Laying the Foundation," 226-27.

32. For the March 1998 parliamentary elections, a different electoral law was implemented, which was aimed at increasing party cohesion and encouraging party coalitions. In this election, half of the seats of the parliament were elected by proportional representation and individual seats were allotted by the percentage of votes each party received, while parties that received less than 4 percent were excluded. D'Anieri, et al., *Politics and Society in Ukraine*, 156.

33. D'Anieri et al., *Politics and Society in Ukraine*, 157. For other estimates of faction memberships between 1994 and 1998 see, Chudowsky, "The Ukrainian Party System," 340-41; Wise and Brown, "Laying the Foundation," 228; Kataryna Wolczuk, "The Politics of Constitution Making in Ukraine," in *Contemporary Ukraine: Dynamics of Post-Soviet Transformation*, ed. Taras Kuzio (Armonk, NY: M. E. Sharpe, 1998), 126, 128; Wilson, "Parties and Presidents in Ukraine and Crimea, 1994," 362-71; Taras Kuzio, "The 1994 Parliamentary Elections in Ukraine," *Journal of Communist Studies and Transition Politics* 11, no. 4 (1995): 335-61; and Marko Bojcun, "The Ukrainian Parliamentary Elections in March/April 1994," *Europe-Asia Studies* 47, no. 2 (1995): 229-49.

34. In the 1994 elections, as stated above, there were a significant number of deputies that won seats in parliament (218) that did not run under a political party, but rather as independents, joining factions once in office. Non-party members of parliament were represented in every faction, but the centrist (Unity, Reforms, Inter-Regional, and Center) and Agrarians attracted most independents. The Agrarian faction absorbed 16 percent of them, Center gained 16 percent, Independents, 10 percent, Inter-Regional, 12.4 percent, Reforms, 13 percent, and Unity, 14 percent. Few independents chose to the communist, socialist, or Rukh factions. Chudowsky, "The Ukrainian Party System," 341.

35. Bilous is quoted in D'Anieri et al., *Politics and Society in Ukraine*, 159.

36. Ibid.

37. For more on why pro-reform elements are lacking in Ukraine see, Kubicek, "Post-Soviet Ukraine."

38. Wise and Brown, "Laying the Foundation," 224.

39. D'Anieri et al., *Politics and Society in Ukraine*, 158.

40. Sherman W. Garnett, "Like Oil and Water: Ukraine's External Westernization and Internal Stagnation," in *State and Institution Building in Ukraine*, ed. Taras Kuzio, Robert S. Kravchuk, and Paul D'Anieri (New York: St. Martin's Press, 1999), 113.

41. For a good discussion of this point see, Hans Van Zon, "Neo-Patrimonialism as an Impediment to Economic Development: The Case of Ukraine," *Journal of Communist Studies and Transition Politics* 17, no. 3 (2001): 71-95.

42. Interview with Mikhail Brodskii in *Kompanion*, 7 November 2003.

43. *Financial Times*, 27 February 2001.

44. "Ukrainian Police Dismantle Tent City, Arrest Anti-Kuchma Protesters," *RFE/RL Newsline*, 1 March 2001; and "Authorities Sweep Away Second Anti-Kuchma Tent City," *RFE/RL Newsline*, 8 March 2001.

45. "Ukrainian Police Clash with Anti-Kuchma Protesters," *RFE/RL Newsline*, 9 March 2001.

46. *Ukrainian News Agency*, 12-18 February 2001.

47. Taras Kuzio, "National Identities and Virtual Foreign Policies among the Eastern Slavs," *Nationalities Papers* 31, no. 4 (2003), 445.

48. Olexiy Haran' and Rostyslav Pavlenko, "Ukraine on the Eve of Parliamentary Elections: Internal Trends and Security Implications," PONARS Policy Memo. No. 236 (January 2002), 4.

49. Nadia Diuk and Myroslava Gongadze, "Post-Election Blues in Ukraine," *Journal of Democracy* 13, no. 4 (2002), 161.

50. For good overviews of the parties in the election see, Haran' and Pavlenko, "Ukraine on the Eve of Parliamentary Elections," 2-3.

51. As the Organization for Security and Cooperation in Europe noted in its final election report: "Some candidates benefited from office space and transportation directly deriving from their official position in local administrations. Also, local officials put State resources at the disposal of candidates who visited an area. The main, but not exclusive, beneficiary of such violations was For a United Ukraine, which took advantage of State officials to obtain meeting venues and use official events to promote the bloc. For a United Ukraine campaign material was predominant and could be seen throughout the country, often in local administration buildings and even district election commission premises. Furthermore, governors and other officials were seen campaigning in favor of some candidates in direct contravention of the Election Law." Office for Democratic Institutions and Human Rights, OSCE, *Ukraine Parliamentary Elections Final Report* (27 May 2002), 12.

52. Diuk and Gongadze, "Post-Election Blues in Ukraine," 159; and ibid., 24.

53. "Ukraine in Turmoil After Presidential Vote," *RFE/RL Newsline*, 23 November 2004.

54. Taras Kuzio, "International Community Denounces Mass Election Fraud in Ukraine as CIS Upholds Official Results," *Jamestown Eurasia Daily Monitor*, 24 November 2004.

55. Ibid.

56. "Who Won the Orange Revolution?" *RFE/RL Newsline*, 9 December 2004.

57. "Russia's President: Vladimir III?" *The Economist*, 11 December 2004, 46-47; Pavel K. Baev, "Needing a Scapegoat for Fiasco in Ukraine, Moscow Slams OSCE," *Jamestown Eurasia Daily Monitor*, 1 December 2004; and Igor Torbakov, "Ukraine Election Crisis: A Moment of Truth for Russia's Relations with the West," *Jamestown Eurasia Daily Monitor*, 29 November 2004.

58. "Avoiding a New Cold War Over Ukraine," *RFE/RL Newsline*, 1 December 2004.

Chapter 8

Ukraine and Economic Dependence on Russia

This chapter examines Ukrainian economic dependence on Russia and assesses its impact on Ukrainian alignment patterns towards Russia. The IT/ED framework suggests that the more economically dependent a country is on Russia, the more likely a pro-Russian alignment will be adopted. However, when leaders can mitigate or sever this dependence, they are less constrained in their relations towards Russia, allowing for a more independent alignment strategy.

Unlike Uzbekistan, Ukraine has been unable to sever its dependence on Russian trade and energy, which limited Kyiv's foreign policy options. After independence, Kravchuk sought to break ties with Russia, but because his political supporters were conservative, including many former Communists, they did not favor economic reform, which hindered access to Western economic assistance. Thus, his strategy was inherently doomed to fail. Kravchuk wanted to sever ties with Russia, but did not take the appropriate steps to ensure that this objective would succeed in the long-term. After the presidential election in 1994, Kuchma adopted a more balanced approach that combined economic reform, designed to attract Western assistance, and a willingness to expand economic cooperation with Russia. Yet, by the end of the decade, Western assistance dwindled as reform stalled.

This chapter assesses the extent of Ukrainian economic dependence on Russia based on the three indicators outlined in the IT/ED framework: the structure of trade, access to energy supplies, and access to alternative Western economic resources. Ukraine's structure of trade, namely its heavy reliance on Russian energy supplies, served as the most significant factor influencing (and limiting) a pro-independence alignment.

The economic crisis that hit the country in 1993-94, brought on by Ukraine's reliance on subsidized Russian energy supplies, led to the removal (albeit peacefully) of Kravchuk. On the other hand, though, Kuchma was much more successful than Kravchuk at obtaining Western economic resources, primarily because of his initial willingness to implement economic reform. The rest of the decade did not prove as promising, and economic assistance fizzled when the implementation of reform slowed. This exacerbated Ukraine's economic dependence on Russia, prompting a more pro-Russian alignment.

The lack of economic reform is a result of how Ukrainian leaders consolidated their positions. In an effort to prevent any galvanizing opposition leaders or parties from emerging, Ukrainian leaders distributed economic resources to their allies to obtain political support. This political trade-off tended to strengthen conservative forces within Ukraine, who permitted reform but only so far as it could benefit them personally. In the process, Ukrainian leaders facilitated the growth of a powerful anti-reform constituency, such as oligarchic and informal networks, which manipulated the uncertain economic conditions in Ukraine to their financial advantage, often at the expense of the Ukrainian state. Once in office Putin sought to crackdown on the oligarchs in Russia, but the same cannot be said for Kuchma in Ukraine, who thrived and relied on their support.

Economic Relations with Russia and the CIS: The Early Years

As we saw in Chapter 6, Kravchuk was reluctant to cooperate with Russia on security matters, and the same can be said for economic matters. However, after the first year of independence, Ukrainian leaders began to understand the necessity of working with Russia, especially on economic issues. Kuchma's appointment as prime minister in the fall of 1992 underscored the necessity of working with Russia. As he noted in straightforward causal logic, "anti-Russian actions in politics [lead] to anti-Ukrainian economic consequences."[1] Ukraine could not sever all ties with Russia, as Kravchuk had hoped, but rather the country needed to adopt a moderate approach to cooperation with Russia and the CIS.

Accordingly, by late 1992 Ukrainian leaders spoke more about the possibility for greater cooperation within the CIS framework, although economic discussions proved more successful than political and military ones. This was evident at the January 1993 summit. Kravchuk refused to sign the CIS charter, which had been on the table since May 1992.[2] He argued that the agreement was less about improving the situation for the CIS, and more about a ploy by "certain political forces" (i.e., Russia) to exploit the document for political reasons.[3] However, Ukraine signed a number of documents related to economic cooperation at the Minsk summit. Most notably, Ukraine signed a declaration signed by all CIS states, which suggested that the main priority of the organization was economic improvement. Ukraine also signed an agreement, which would establish an "Interstate Economic Bank." This body would help restore trade ties between CIS states. The bank was never established, but it suggested that Ukrainian leaders were more willing to work with Russia to address pressing economic concerns. Furthermore, in April 1993 Ukraine signed the agreement to form the CIS Coordination Consultative Committee, which was prefaced on the understanding that it would be limited to economic issues. Later in September, Ukraine took a half-hearted position towards the creation of the Economic Union, opting for the undefined status of "associate member." Indeed, until early 1994 Ukrainian leaders consistently resisted attempts to create an institutional structure within the CIS, while supporting the idea of loose economic cooperation through the consultative organ of the CIS Inter-Parliamentary assembly.

Much as he had during his term as prime minister, Kuchma emphasized the merits and necessity of strengthening economic ties with Russia when he became president in 1994. As Kuchma stated, "Ukraine no longer looks upon economic cooperation with Russia and the CIS as an unfortunate necessity but as an urgent requirement."[4] Accordingly, he moderated Ukraine's stance towards economic cooperation with Russia and the CIS. In October 1994 he signed on to set up the Interstate Economic Committee (IEC). The IEC dealt with such transnational activities as energy systems, communications, gas and oil pipelines, agriculture, and transportation and helped coordinate economic and social policy, which represented the first supranational organ to be created in the CIS. Afraid of going too far in a pro-Russian direction, however, Ukrainian officials refused to join a proposed monetary union, citing the absence of a common payments system as the reason. Ukraine also signed customs legislation and joined the CIS Common Air Defense Structure in February 1995. To be fair, Ukraine's involvement in the CIS is characterized more accurately as "fake participation." This was clearly evident in the late 1990s, when Ukraine had signed only 130 out of the 910 CIS documents, with its parliament ratifying only 30 of these.[5] But it was in the economic realm that Ukraine most required Russian assistance, and despite his election time rhetoric, as we saw in Chapter 6, Kuchma was no more receptive to political, military, and security cooperation with Russia than Kravchuk. Indeed, Kuchma stated forcefully that he did not become president of Ukraine "in order to become a vassal of Russia."[6] The rest of this chapter turns to a more explicit discussion of the indicators of economic dependence outlined in Chapter 2.

Structure of Trade with Russia

The balance of trade between Ukraine and Russia is the first indicator that Ukraine remained economically dependent on Russia throughout the 1990s. With respect to exports, Ukraine was successful at finding alternative outlets besides Russia. For example, between 1994 1996, Ukraine on average exported about 40 percent of its total exports to Russia (see Table 8.1). This figure improved during the period 1997-2001, where Russia received only 23 percent of Ukrainian exports. Much like Uzbekistan, Ukraine was able to increase its exports to OECD countries to offset the diminished trade to Russia. Trade levels were nominal between 1994-1996, averaging roughly 17 percent of total Ukrainian exports. They rose considerably in the last five years of the decade to approximately 28 percent of exports. The United States specifically played a minor role in importing Ukrainian exports, representing only 3.5 percent of total Ukrainian exports.

While these figures suggest Ukraine has been successful at finding countries willing to accept its exports, the import picture is less optimistic. In 1994 Ukraine imported 54.1 percent of its total imports from Russia (see Table 8.2). This percentage dropped to 37.8 percent in 1995, but for the next six years Ukraine

Table 8.1 Ukrainian Foreign Export Trade, 1994-2001[7] (*millions of US dollars*)

	1994	1995	1996	1997	1998	1999	2000	2001
Total (world)	9,531	15,104	14,400	14,232	12,637	11,582	14,579	14,664
Russia	3,837 (40.2)	6,015 (39.8)	5,577 (38.7)	3,723 (26.2)	2,906 (23.0)	2,396 (20.7)	3,516 (24.1)	3,434 (23.4)
OECD Countries	1,509 (15.8)	2,740 (18.1)	2,639 (18.3)	2,976 (20.9)	3,560 (28.2)	3,446 (29.8)	4,267 (29.3)	4,562 (31.1)
United States	336 (3.5)	429 (2.8)	380 (2.6)	302 (2.1)	502 (4.0)	436 (3.8)	727 (5.0)	696 (4.7)

Table 8.2 Ukrainian Foreign Import Trade, 1994-2001[8] *(millions of US dollars)*

	1994	1995	1996	1997	1998	1999	2000	2001
Total (world)	11,082	20,077	17,586	17,114	14,676	11,844	13,955	16,860
Russia	5,998 (54.1)	7,588 (37.8)	8,817 (50.1)	7,838 (45.8)	7,064 (48.1)	5,592 (47.2)	5,825 (41.7)	5,424 (32.2)
OECD Countries	1419 (12.8)	3,742 (18.6)	3,776 (21.5)	4,560 (26.6)	4,194 (28.6)	3,214 (27.1)	3,848 (27.6)	5,723 (33.9)
United States	185 (1.7)	245 (1.2)	570 (3.2)	651 (3.8)	590 (4.0)	402 (3.4)	361 (2.6)	226 (1.3)

imported on average 44 percent of its total imports from Russia. Thus, Ukraine's economic dependence on trade with Russia is extensive, with Russia receiving approximately a quarter of total Ukrainian exports and responsible for just under half of its total imports. Imports from OECD countries gradually increased over the decade from an average of 16 percent between 1994-1995, to 26 percent between 1996-1998, and up to 30 percent between 1999-2001.

The real vulnerability for Ukraine rests not only in the overall balance of trade, but also in *what* goods are traded. Russia is the dominant trading partner of Ukraine, not unlike many CIS states, but Ukraine suffers from one of the most strategic vulnerabilities, the lack of indigenous oil and gas supplies (discussed at greater length in the next section). For instance, in 1997 Russia supplied Ukraine with 100 percent of its oil, 81 percent of gas supplies, and 50 percent of its raw materials.[9] While Ukrainian exports are not as concentrated as imports, Russia still serves as the most important market for Ukrainian goods accounting for 63.7 percent of food exports, 51.4 percent of machinery and equipment exports, 37.3 percent of vehicles, and 21.3 percent of chemicals.[10]

Not surprisingly, throughout the 1990s, trade tensions emerged between Kyiv and Moscow. For instance, in January 1996 Kuchma complained that Russia continued to levy a value-added tax of 20 percent, and an additional special tax of 3 percent on its exports to Ukraine. As a result of this policy, raw materials imported from Russia were sold in Ukraine at a price 50 percent above the domestic price in Russia. In retaliation, the Ukrainian government increased excise duties on vodka, cigarettes, and pipe tobacco imported from Russia. Due to high import taxes, Ukrainian exports to Russia in the first eight months of 1997 fell by more than 27 percent compared to the same period of 1996.

To alleviate such economic tension a more moderate pro-Russian approach was needed. This led to an agreement signed by Russia and Ukraine in March 1997, which allowed Russia to use two Soviet-era ballistic-missile radar stations located in Ukraine in exchange for spare parts for Ukraine's military sector.[11] Later in the year, Russia also announced that it would import an annual quota of 600,000 tons of Ukrainian sugar. Within the quota framework, Ukrainian sugar was exempted from the 25 percent duty on imported sugar introduced by Russia in March 1997. In a further attempt to improve trade relations between the two countries, Ukraine and Russia concluded the Interstate Economic Treaty in March 1998. In accordance with the agreement, the two countries dropped the VAT and other trade barriers between them. It was anticipated that this agreement would help expand trade between the two countries by some 10-15 percent.[12]

By the end of the decade, Ukrainian trade dependence served as a major constraint on Ukrainian foreign policy. Indeed, Ukraine's trade deficit with Russia grew from an estimated $1.4 billion in late 1992 to over $12.5 billion by the end of 1998.[13] There was little that could be done because the root of the problem rested in Ukraine's inability to find alternative energy suppliers other than Russia. This dilemma is examined below.

Strategic Goods

By 1993-94 Kravchuk, and later Kuchma, was forced to contend with a severe energy crisis. The problem came with Kravchuk's decision to sever economic ties with Russia, which meant an end to subsidies. This decision proved perilous, and the importance of energy subsidies became increasingly evident. Previously, Russia subsidized Ukraine by supplying around 50 million tons of oil and a substantial amount of gas each year at a fraction of world prices. Since Ukraine could not meet its energy needs domestically, it imported 30 to 35 million tons of oil and 85 billion to 90 billion cubic meters of gas per year. These purchases required allocation of $9 billion to $15 billion for this purpose annually.[14] Considering that oil and gas prices within the former Soviet system were roughly 35-45 percent of world prices, Russia's removal of energy subsidies to Ukraine had a series of negative economic consequences for Ukraine, most notably the creation of sizable trade deficits to Russia.

By 1993 Ukrainian leaders were aware of the inherent flaws of attempting to sever economic ties with Russia. Kravchuk suggested that miscalculations were made in the initial days of independence, drawing attention to Ukraine's underlying dependence on Russia. In the spring of 1993 he stated:

> Working out the economic strategy, we obviously underestimated the capabilities of the Ukrainian economy, and did not consider that it structurally was built on the principle of incompleteness, was deprived of integrity, harmony, completion. We were not aware also of the great degree of dependence on the economies of the other states of the former Union. From this arose the energy and payments crisis, which today are the most dangerous factors. We also with tardiness realized the danger of dependence of the monetary system of Ukraine on the unified emissions bank in the borders of the CIS, and thereby on the new monetary policy of Russia.[15]

This dependence was in large part due to a lack of sufficient energy sources within Ukraine itself. In his speech to the Supreme Council in 1993, Kuchma stated bluntly that Ukraine must face the fact of "total dependence" on Russia, which was "a key factor in Ukraine's economic development."[16]

If Ukraine relied on Russian energy imports and was therefore significantly dependent on Russia, the IT/ED framework predicts that a leader would either try to promote domestic production or conservation or would try to find alternative trading partners willing to provide the necessary energy supplies. Unlike Uzbekistan, which had proven energy reserves, Ukraine was unable to increase energy production. Whereas Ukraine produced twice as much oil as Uzbekistan did in 1991 (4.9 million tons to 2.8), by 1998 Uzbekistan completely reversed this figure, in that Uzbek oil production had increased to 8.1 million tons while Ukrainian production declined to 3.9 million tons, falling to 3.7 million tons by 2000.[17] Thus, with limited reserves at home, Ukraine was forced to look abroad to find energy, which inexplicably meant working with Russia (and to a lesser extent Turkmenistan).

Russia remained the primary supplier of energy to Ukraine after independence.[18] Coupled with the fact that Russia accounted for more than 54 percent of total Ukrainian imports and Ukraine had no alternative port or pipeline facilities to import oil from other sources, this placed Ukraine in a highly dependent position. Moreover, Russia was willing to continue to extend credits to Ukraine allowing a massive debt to accumulate. There was one factor, however, that favored Ukraine.

While Russia enhanced its power through pipelines and transit routes, Ukraine, at times, could exert counter-pressure on Russia, given its position between Europe and Russia and its extensive pipeline infrastructure. Indeed, Ukraine tried to exploit Russia's dependence on Ukrainian pipelines, since 90 percent of Russia's natural gas exports ran through its territory. This is not surprising, as Albert Hirschman points out, because countries that handle transit trade have the ability to gain influence through trade, provided the commodity traded is indispensable and it only superficially affects the state profiting from this transit trade.[19] Ukraine could always secure 50 million to 80 million cubic meters of gas daily as a transit fee because a full shutoff was too costly. When Russia cut off gas to Ukraine in March 1994, Ukrainian leaders openly warned that a cutoff might result in the siphoning of pipelines.[20] Ukrainian leaders continued to negotiate with Russian policy makers over the issue of pipelines and more specifically the siphoning of gas throughout discussions over Ukraine's energy debt to Russia.

Since Ukraine lacked domestic energy reserves, the only other option open to Ukrainian leaders was to find alternative sources of energy, with Turkmenistan, Iran, and Uzbekistan being the most likely candidates although they were not always the most willing and receptive. Attempts were made, such as from Turkmenistan, but this could not bring any significant results because full payment for energy supplies could not always be assured.[21] At times, such as in March 1992 and February 1994, Turkmenistan too halted gas deliveries to Ukraine because of outstanding debt. Possibilities of working with Iran and Uzbekistan also fizzled as the Ukrainian government moved slowly at building its own port and pipeline facilities at Odessa, without which Ukraine remained dependent on Russian pipelines.

Kravchuk failed to address the energy dependence on Russia, which led to an energy crisis by 1993 and the amassing of a sizable debt to Russia. This influenced his policies towards Russia in a way predicted by the IT/ED framework. That is, when a country is economically dependent on Russia, there is a greater likelihood that leaders will adopt a more pro-Russian alignment.

Kravchuk first attempted to deal with Ukraine's energy needs in a pragmatic fashion at the September 1993 Massandra summit. At the meeting Kravchuk reportedly agreed to surrender the BSF to Russia in return for the forgiveness of Ukraine's energy debt to Russia. The deal proved too costly domestically for Kravchuk, as many Ukrainians looked to the issue of Crimea as an important litmus test for Russian-Ukrainian relations and were unwilling to give strategic assets away hastily.

However, this demonstrated that while Kravchuk was unable to find alternative sources of energy, he did attempt to address the issue on some instances, and by his actions, demonstrated that economic dependence on energy was a primary factor shaping Ukrainian-Russian relations.

The emergence of GUUAM in 1996 also represents an attempt by Kuchma to confront Ukraine's energy dependence on Russia through more multilateral initiatives. GUUAM was seen as an important element in deepening economic and energy cooperation among its members, with priority given to gaining access to Caspian oil and gas. However, GUUAM cooperation is at best a long-term solution to the economic dependence Ukraine retains on Russian energy supplies.

In an attempt to foster even greater economic ties between GUUAM members (a consideration that would presumably increase Ukrainian access to non-Russian economic resources), Kuchma stressed the need to create a free trade zone within GUUAM at the June 2001 Yalta summit of GUUAM presidents. Yet, while this proposal was not accepted at the meeting due to minor "formalities," GUUAM members did sign a formal charter that stressed the goals of socio-economic development of its members, resolution of regional security problems, and the fight against international crime and the narcotics trade.[22] What became apparent was that Kuchma could not find a quick fix for Ukraine's economic situation through immediate GUUAM cooperation and was forced to continue his pro-Russian orientation.

Little progress has been made in alleviating Ukraine's energy dependence on Russia, which according to the IT/ED framework, leads to a more pro-Russian alignment. What has begun to occur is that Ukraine will make significant concessions in a variety of realms to Russia and Russian companies to alleviate debt problems associated with energy imports. Indeed, this has been a mainstay of economic relations between Moscow and Kyiv, and unfortunately for the long-term prospects of Ukraine, Russian capital finds the Ukrainian economy very attractive but not always in ways that will benefit the overall development of the country. In 1999, for example, Russian officials attempting to resolve the gas debt problem provided a Ukrainian delegation with a list of Ukrainian enterprises that Russia, in exchange for writing off part of the energy debts, was interested in seeing privatized and in which it could later acquire shares.[23] Thus, Ukraine's indebtedness potentially opens the Ukrainian economy to Russian companies seeking to become major stockholders. This setting creates favorable conditions for Russian oligarchic networks interested in Ukrainian enterprises and could have serious long-term consequences.[24] Officials have also stated that Ukraine may provide up to one-third of its fuel-pipeline network as a "concession" to Russia.[25] Similarly, Ukraine softened its approach towards Russia on some military matters. For example, in 1999 Ukraine gave Russia eight Blackjack TU-160 and three Bear TU-95 strategic bombers along with 674 cruise missiles in exchange for writing off $285 million of Ukraine's natural gas debts.[26] In this regard, the causal connection between Ukraine's energy dependence, its staggering debt, and its willingness to acquiesce to Russian interests is relatively straightforward.

Staving off more serious steps, Ukraine and Russia reached a breakthrough agreement on the debt issue in early November 2000. Ukraine agreed to stop siphoning Russian natural gas piped through its territory in exchange for a Russian agreement to defer collecting Ukraine's gas debt for 10 years, while maintaining a low rate of interest. Moreover, Russia agreed to give Ukraine an eight-to-ten year break on debt payments for half of future gas supplies, if Ukraine pays for the remaining half in cash and stops siphoning off gas.[27]

In the end, Ukraine remains heavily dependent on Russian energy, and this picture has changed little over the years. The subsequent section examines how effective Kravchuk and Kuchma were at obtaining Western economic resources. As we will see, Kuchma was more successful, which in the middle of the 1990s enabled him to adopt a more independent foreign policy.

Alternative Resources from the West

The IT/ED framework suggests that CIS leaders can turn to Western countries and financial institutions for economic assistance, but aid is largely conditioned of promises to both enact and implement economic reform. During the 1990s, economic reform in Ukraine progressed and regressed, which had an adverse influence on the availability of Western economic resources. Much of this is a result of Ukrainian leaders and their domestic political strategies that led them to distribute economic resources to their political supporters.

Without economic reform, a leader's access to Western resources is likely to be more limited; such was the case during the Kravchuk years. As we saw in Chapter 6, some of Kravchuk's difficulties were the result of Washington's insistence that Ukraine relinquish its nuclear weapons and its Russo-centric outlook towards the former Soviet Union. Nonetheless, Kravchuk was unable to obtain significant Western economic resources because of a general apathy towards economic reform. As a result, this undermined his strategy to sever economic ties with Russia, while forging new ones with the West. In many ways, Kravchuk's foreign policy priorities (independence from Russia and a pro-Western orientation) took precedence over internal reform, for instance, in the case of foreign trade liberalization, which ran far ahead of domestic liberalization.[28] This made sense, as we saw in the last chapter, because it shored up Kravchuk's political support and ensured his position. The practices that sealed this trade-off were also the primary reasons why Western economic assistance to Ukraine remained limited.

Kravchuk's political supporters preferred rentier capitalism and economic instability because of their ability to convert political positions from the previous system into financial and economic power in the new transition economy.[29] As Oleh Havrylyshyn notes:

> The so called "new" rentier capitalists are an amorphous and ill-defined group including Directors of enterprises, kolhosps and radhosps, heads of trade groups and

new private, "commercial" group entities formed as spin-offs from state enterprises...Illegal actions occur, of course, but they have been incidental or they have been built upon the main tendency of earning large "rents" from having a privileged position to obtain large credits and special licenses to trade or export.[30]

The privatization process in eastern Ukraine during 1992-1994 was indicative of how Kravchuk and the elites who supported him benefited during the economic transition. A large majority of privatization in the region was done by local political and economic elites, with 80 percent of these privatizations acquired through a lease-to-buy system (in contrast to full-scale privatization) and the majority of them obtained despite legal violations.[31] As Paul Hare, Mohammed Ishaq, and Saul Estrin conclude: "Privatization is often about power and the distribution of property to those already close to power – the nomenklatura."[32] This distribution occurred in myriad ways under Kravchuk.

Anti-reform elements within Ukraine based their relationships on informal networks institutionalized under the Soviet system, and acquired many mechanisms to pursue private gains through official channels. Indeed, Ukraine's first two years of independence were marked by massive credits to heavy industry and the agricultural sector, with regulations on foreign trade allowing top government officials and other members of informal networks to enrich themselves.[33]

For instance, substantial administrative control over exports allowed bureaucrats to continue extracting rents through a complicated set of licenses and quotas designed to control trade and access to hard currency. Particularly attractive for personal enrichment were the energy supplies since prices of oil and gas charged by Russia for the former Soviet republics in 1991 were approximately 35-45 percent of the corresponding world levels. This allowed bureaucrats and their cronies to purchase gas and oil from Russia at subsidized prices and then re-sell it to the West at world prices.[34] Naturally, the quotas and permissions for trading the energy supplies were provided to a limited number of actors who maintained personal ties with the political leadership.

One of the most widespread devices was to spin off private "daughter companies," owned by managers and their close allies. Such companies acquired the output of the enterprise and sold it at market prices; meanwhile, the main enterprises accumulated debt, withheld taxes, and delayed wages. Particularly impressive in its "achievements" was the symbiosis of corrupted state bureaucrats and entrepreneurs operating on the energy market. In the absence of transparent rules regulating the energy market, the companies operating on this market were not only protected from potential competitors but also were granted a tax-free status. This resulted in billions hryvnas lost for the state budget. In one instance, a former head of the Parliament was in the management of a company that received an $80 million credit for purchase of agricultural equipment under government guarantees. The company ultimately went bankrupt and the money was never returned.[35]

Kravchuk also provided capital to inefficient state enterprises to keep them afloat. Instead of adjusting to market reforms, managers of these enterprises began to incur debt. The solution to the debt problem was usually socialist in spirit: managers of large inefficient state enterprises, relying on their informal contacts with state banks, received credits at the expense of new private and potentially more efficient enterprises. The informal links were also widely exploited in the horizontal inter-firm relations where suppliers extended credits to their customers with a purpose of protecting their markets, while customers made loans to suppliers to guarantee the flow of necessary supplies. As a result, enterprises were engaged in complex cross-indebtedness relations where delay or postponement of past-due payments was a common practice.

As the Ukrainian economy plummeted, Kravchuk sought to renew the command economy in late 1993. State orders and contracts were issued for certain critical goods and consumer products. Kravchuk's goal was to stabilize production. However in the process, he contributed to greater capital flight as the government supported inefficient firms. Much like Soviet times, enterprises that met state goals received fuel, raw materials, and other privileges.[36] Thus, in the end, economic reform was not a top priority for Kravchuk, which limited access to alternative Western economic resources because it would only jeopardize the economic interests of his political supporters. As we saw previously, his economic strategy placed Ukraine in a position of massive debt to Russia, and with the election of Kuchma in the summer of 1994 the situation appeared more optimistic. Indeed, unlike Kravchuk, Kuchma appeared willing to reform the Ukrainian economy is significant ways, which would presumably enhance Kyiv's prospects for obtaining Western economic resources.

The probability that economic reform would be implemented increased dramatically in 1994 with the onset of economic crisis. Kuchma reassessed the potential security consequences of preserving the economic status quo, suggesting that only radical economic reform could assure Ukraine's sovereignty.[37]

Compared to those of his predecessor, Kuchma's efforts in economic reform were serious and warranted the attention of Western countries and financial institutions. His reform program was characterized by cuts in state subsidies, gradual progress on privatization, the deregulation of many prices, reductions in government spending, the reduction of heavy tax burdens, and the establishment of markets for state securities including bonds.[38] These measures fell in line with the conventional logic emanating from Washington and other international financial institutions and helped Kuchma attract much needed Western economic resources, despite the fact that reform fell short of what would be identified as radical reform in the spirit of shock therapy.[39]

By the fall of 1994 Western financial institutions began to extend Ukraine much needed economic assistance. A marked turn in the Western attitude toward Ukraine was evident at the October 1994 G-7 meeting in Winnipeg, where Ukraine was promised $4 billion in aid. This contrasted sharply with the April 1993 Vancouver summit, where Russia was offered $1.6 billion in U.S. aid and Ukraine nothing. The IMF approved a $371 million stabilization loan on 26 October and the World Bank approved a $500 million credit on 22 December to support ambitious plans for economic reform, including price liberalization, quicker privatization, and banking reform announced on 11 October. The World Bank also supported a comprehensive privatization program, including the creation of investment funds, the launch of mass privatization and acceleration of small-scale privatization with a rehabilitation loan in 1994. The approval of the 1995 Ukrainian budget, by both the Ukrainian parliament and the IMF, also paved the way for the IMF to release almost $2 billion in aid, which consisted of a one-year Stabilization Fund ($1.5 billion), to be given in conditional tranches, and the second portion of the Systematic Transformation Facility ($392 million, the first half of which was released in October 1994).[40]

However, by the following spring, the initial economic measures that Kuchma announced as a part of his fall 1994 reform program (measures that largely followed the prescriptions of Western financial institutions) were openly criticized by Ukrainian leaders. Instead of adhering to the blind monetarist policy prescribed by Western institutions, Kuchma increasingly saw the need for a more state-regulated transition. Addressing parliament in early April 1995, he stated that economic reform should be state-regulated, more gradual, and should provide a greater social safety net.[41] A few months later, Kuchma disregarded IMF conditions, when he outlined a fundamental policy correction that dropped the IMF target of 1 or 2 percent monthly inflation to 4 or 5 percent by the end of the year.[42] While Kuchma continued to speak about ensuring that economic reform was irreversible, his more gradualist approach was accepted overwhelmingly by parliament in October 1995. Indeed, ever since this "correction," economic reform in Ukraine has failed to get back on track, although several major reforms were implemented after 1995, such as the establishment of a new currency in September 1996 and large-scale privatization completed between 1996-98.

Privatization was slow going in Ukraine, since as we saw in the previous section, both Kravchuk and Kuchma engaged in trade-offs between the distribution of economic resources and political support from important elites in the country. The overall pace of privatization remained low during the Kravchuk years. As a World Bank study found, the total number of privatized objects was approximately 11,852 during 1992-94, while in 1995 (after Kuchma's efforts at reform) 16,227 enterprises were privatized, with 19,487 privatized in 1996.[43] These were not favorable figures if Kravchuk hoped to obtain greater Western economic resources, but they demonstrated Kuchma's willingness to privatize.

Kuchma was more effective in some aspects of the privatization process, but less so in others. The real successes came in small-scale privatization, such as that of shops, restaurants, small service establishments, in which existing managers and employee groups sought to purchase small enterprises. For instance, by 1997 over 90 percent of the estimated 45,000 small enterprises in Ukraine were privatized. The same cannot be said for medium- and large-scale enterprises, since by mid 1997 only 9,649 of the over 18,000 medium and large firms had entered the preprivatization stage, and only 5,087 had transferred more than 70 percent of their shares to private hands.[44]

As we saw in the previous chapter, parliament also had a hand in slowing the privatization process down. The left-leaning parliament sought to block further privatization in the wake of Kuchma's election by voting to suspend the process, enacting a moratorium on the sale of medium and large firms. Parliament also refused to lift the moratorium unless "strategically important" firms were earmarked and exempt from privatization, of which many were in the energy, transportation, and communications sectors. While the moratorium lasted four months until the cabinet excluded the best industries of the economy, immense debate ensued as to which types of firms should be included on the list, just as the sheer numbers of firms fluctuated over time.[45]

In the fall of 1996, the IMF actively worked with the Ukrainian government and the National Bank of Ukraine on its new reform package. These reforms became the basis of the Extended Fund Facility (EFF), a three-year loan program targeted at both macroeconomic and structural reform. However, it became increasingly apparent by the summer of 1997 that neither the Ukrainian government nor parliament was interested in the implementation of such reform. Aware of this, the IMF concluded a minor one-year stand-by agreement with few conditions and dollars attached (slightly under $400 million). As some observers have noted, by the summer of 1997, Ukrainian authorities became strangely seized by a sense that financial constraints were easing, at a time when Western institutions were suggesting continued conditionality.[46]

The death of the EFF agreement by the summer of 1997 and Ukraine's inability to meet IMF conditions also blocked World Bank funding, which in 1996 totaled over $1 billion. The majority of World Bank assistance went to projects in the sectors of electricity power and energy development, agriculture, mining (related to coal adjustment), and the private sector. In line with the approach of the IMF, the World Bank released no monies to Ukraine during 1997, and it was not until well into 1998 that other assistance was extended.

The deadlock over economic reform continued, and little Western assistance was extended during the first half of 1998. Yet, on 18 June Kuchma ended the stalemate and declared that given parliament's paralysis over the question of reform, he would adopt several presidential decrees, among them reduction of the tax burden, elimination of arrears in the budget sector, and measures aimed at encouraging business activity.[47] Many of these decrees had been part of the initial economic reform package outlined in 1996. Thus, in the span of one month Kuchma was able to accomplish many of the reforms sought for the past several years. The IMF deemed the reform efforts sufficient for the conclusion of an EFF agreement during the summer of 1998, one that would replace the aborted agreement of spring 1997. The agreement was eventually completed in September 1998 and provided just under $2 billion in assistance. However, the trajectory of reform continued to decline and with it so has access to Western resources.

The IT/ED framework suggests that access to Western economic resources enables leaders to adopt more independent alignments because of the ability of leaders to lessen their country's economic dependence on Russia. Such a foreign policy is largely conditioned by a leader's willingness to implement economic reform. In this regard, Kuchma's implementation of economic reform upon his election in 1994 brought about much needed aid. However, his inability to continue the reform process led Western institutions to slow their assistance programs.

Several factors led to a suspension of IMF funds. First, many conditions placed on IMF funding never came to fruition, including stalled discussions over the gas sector, restructuring the bank sector, the privatization process, and the writing off of debts and unpaid taxes by the Ukrainian government.[48] The lack of reform led the IMF to suspend the disbursement of funds to Ukraine in September 1999. Although lending was resumed after a 14-month break in December 2000, the IMF chose not to extend a scheduled March 2001 tranche.[49]

Another factor leading to the suspension of IMF aid is that IMF officials became aware that between 1996 and 1998 Ukraine's Central Bank conducted almost $1 billion worth of transactions that moved several hundreds of million of dollars through Credit Suisse First Boston, a Swiss-owned investment bank. These transactions gave a false impression of healthy currency reserves, and Ukraine received funding that otherwise would have been withheld. Ukraine's interaction with the IMF has changed substantially from the mid-1990s, in that assistance has been less forthcoming (see Table 8.3).

Table 8.3 IMF Disbursements and Repayments to Ukraine[50] (*in SDRs*)

| Year | General Resources Account (GRA) | |
	Disbursements	Repurchases
1994	249,325,000	0
1995	787,975,000	0
1996	536,000,000	0
1997	207,262,000	0
1998	281,815,500	77,331,250
1999	466,600,000	407,031,249
2000	190,070,000	643,491,270
2001	290,780,000	361,231,584
2002	0	140,748,392
2003	0	62,016,666

In reality, the relationship between IMF/World Bank assistance and economic reform is not clear-cut. Indeed, as critics point out, repeated failures of post-Soviet states (with much of the attention focusing on Russia) to meet the conditions of Western institutions were only met with temporary delays in funding, during which time monetary commitments were scaled back or delayed (but rarely cancelled) to allow these states time to substantiate claims that they had met particular conditions.[51] As one former top Russian official in several Yeltsin administrations stated cynically: "The IMF was pretending that it was seeing a lot of reforms [while] Russia was pretending to conduct reform."[52]

With respect to Ukraine in a geopolitical sense, the United States through its leadership position in the IMF and World Bank, supported Kuchma, provided that he steered clear of Russia, regardless of the seriousness of Ukrainian reform. U.S. willingness to tolerate corruption and a lack of reform is considerably lower than Russia's. This gives Russia a geopolitical advantage, but the difference is one of degree, not of category.[53] Nonetheless, the IMF still strongly links reform to continued aid, as it demonstrated recently by not releasing expected tranches in 2001. Thus, faced with IMF delays, Kuchma began to question the usefulness of the IMF, suggesting that the need for assistance has passed and that Ukraine could live without it.[54] When leaders fail to implement economic reform, their access to Western resources diminishes and as a result their foreign policy is more likely to shift in a pro-Russian direction. This shift has become increasingly apparent in Kuchma's foreign policy towards Russia.

In addition to the events outlined in Chapter 6, there are other indicators that substantiate an increasingly pro-Russian orientation, many of which are linked to Kuchma's unwillingness to implement economic reform. In September 2000, for instance, pro-Western Foreign Minister, Borys Tarasyuk, who Moscow disliked, was removed. As one observer noted, Tarasyuk dismissal was a "major concession to Russia and a slap to the West."[55] In a similar manner, the sacking of Energy Minister Tymoshenko in January 2001 demonstrated the extent to which Kuchma favored anti-reform interests in Ukraine. Her dismissal was a response to efforts to introduce transparent rules in the energy sector, which threatened oligarchic interests. As Oleksandr Turchynov, Batkivschyna Party faction leader, concludes, Tymoshenko's dismissal was a result of oligarchic activities rooted in one of the most corrupt sectors of the economy.[56] In May 2001 the replacement of the pro-reformist premier Yushchenko with Anatoliy Kinakh led many in the West to question the sincerity of Ukrainian leaders' commitment to continued reform, not to mention their overall orientation towards Europe. These developments were complemented by Putin's appointment of former Russian Premier Viktor Chernomyrdin as Russian Ambassador to Ukraine. This appointment is seen by critics as a further attempt to promote Russian interests in Ukraine (presumably to the detriment of Ukrainian interests).[57] Thus, in a variety of ways, Kuchma began to adopt a more pro-Russian alignment in response to both a rise in his internal threats, as seen in the last chapter, and the long-standing economic dependence on Russia.

Conclusions

This chapter has assessed Ukrainian economic dependence on Russia based on the indicators presented in Chapter 2. The findings of this chapter reveal that Ukraine has remained heavily dependent on Russia in its trade relations, especially in the import of Russian energy supplies. The dependence on energy contributed to billions of dollars of debt owed to Russia, which fundamentally constrained the alignment choices of Ukrainian leaders. In the initial days of independence, while Ukraine remained economically dependent on Russia, Kravchuk attempted to sever economic ties with Russia. In this regard, the reality of Ukraine's dependence was underestimated by Kravchuk and thus the prediction of the IT/ED framework did not play out – that Ukraine would be more constrained and adopt a more pro-Russian alignment. That is, despite Ukraine's dependence, Kravchuk gambled that he could find substitutes in the West, which could lessen the existing dependence on Russia. The energy crisis of 1993-94, however, was the most telling example of this gross miscalculation and the failure of this strategy.

Perhaps the underlying issue with Ukrainian dependence on Russia is that Ukrainian leaders failed to address the dependence in any long-term fashion, and instead did what was necessary to secure their political positions in the short-term, which inherently meant distributing economic resources and benefits to political allies. This tendency, as we saw in Chapter 7, undermined Ukraine's fledgling democracy, and its ability to reorient its economy towards the West.

Ultimately, Ukraine faced a common problem when leaders have difficulties mobilizing support, both popular and among the most powerful elites, for economic reform. Without a pro-reform constituency in Ukraine, it makes the deeper penetration and implementation of reform less effective because powerful domestic actors have a vested interest in maintaining the status quo. The unofficial or shadow economy of Ukraine has also been difficult to curb, contributing to the loss of sizable sums of taxable income.

The dominance of anti-reform actors also undermined the development of transparent institutions, since transparency only threatened existing and established informal networks. Oligarchs and other anti-reform actors shaped the pattern and character of reform in Ukraine and made sure that reforms got stuck at the first stage and did not proceed too far in terms of deregulation.[58] Privatization enhanced the power of anti-reform actors tremendously, where bureaucrats and oligarchs became the new owners. They then benefited from favourable interpretations of the privatization process and stripped the best assets of the former Soviet economy for their own narrow interests. New owners continued to exploit their good connections with their old bureaucratic allies to get subsidized credits, tax breaks and other privileges.

In short, even though Kuchma came to power in 1994 promising reform, the reality of the political game was that Kuchma's supporters, similar to those of Kravchuk, were interested in controlling the economic status quo or making sure that any reform measures would serve their interests. In this regard, widespread corruption, a lack of rule of law, inadequate protection of property rights, a lack of transparency and predictability in state's policy decisions, and all other arrangements that can be qualified as informal institutions reflected the dominance of anti-reform actors on the Ukrainian political scene. Informal practices meant that oversight and accountability would be much more elusive and allow strategically positioned individuals the opportunity to amass tremendous wealth.

By the end of the decade the lack of economic reform coupled with the political crisis in the fall of 2000 meant that the West was no longer a receptive audience, and were less willing and less trustworthy of Kuchma's talk of reform and change. This led Ukraine back to the East and continued cooperation (and dependence) on Russia.

Notes

1. Solchanyk, "Ukraine, Russia, and the CIS," 29.
2. O. Oliinyk, "Pry Iedynii Dii. Do Pidsumkiv Vizytu Delegatsii Verkhovnoi Rady Rosii do Kyieva" (Joint activities. Summarizing the results of the Supreme Soviet visit of Russia to Kiev), *Uriadovyi Kur'ier*, 23 March 1993, 1.
3. Hale, "Statehood at Stake," 321.
4. Taras Kuzio, *Ukraine: Back From the Brink* (London: Institute for European Defense and Strategic Studies, 1995), 31.
5. Kuzio, "Geopolitical Pluralism in the CIS," 84.
6. V. Skachko, "Ia ne budu nich'im vassalom" (I will not become anybody's vassal), *Nezavisimaia Gazeta*, 28 October 1994, 3.
7. IMF, *Direction of Trade Statistics Yearbook* (2000), 466-67; and IMF, *Direction of Trade Statistics Yearbook* (2002), 472-73. Primary sources are largely consistent with these figures. CIS Interstate Statistical Committee, *Sodruzhestvo Nezavisimykh Gosudarstv i strani mira. Statisticheskii Sbornik* (Commonwealth of Independent States in the world. Statistical yearbook) (Moscow: CIS Interstate Statistical Committee, 1999), 280, 292; State Statistics Committee of Ukraine, *Shchorichnyk Ukrainy za 1998 rik* (Ukraine yearbook for 1998) (Kyiv: State Statistics Committee of Ukraine, 1999), 289; State Statistics Committee of Ukraine, *Statystychnyi Shchorichnyk Ukrainy za 1996 rik* (Statistical yearbook of Ukraine for 1996) (Kiev: State Statistics Committee of Ukraine, 1997), 327; and CIS Interstate Statistical Committee, *Sodruzhestvo Nezavisimykh Gosudarstv v 1994 godu* (Commonwealth of Independent States in 1994) (Moscow: CIS Interstate Statistical Committee, 1995), 65.
8. IMF, *Direction of Trade Statistics Yearbook* (2000), 466-67; and IMF, *Direction of Trade Statistics Yearbook* (2002), 472-73.
9. D'Anieri, et. al, *Politics and Society in Ukraine*, 174; and Gregory V. Krasnov and Josef C. Brada, "Implicit Subsidies in Russian-Ukrainian Energy Trade," *Europe-Asia Studies* 49, no. 5 (1997): 825-43.
10. Oleksandr Bilotserkivets, "Ukraine's Foreign Trade: Structure and Developments," *Ukrainian Economic Monitor*, no. 6-7 (1998): 23-28.
11. "Chronicle of Events," *The Ukrainian Quarterly* (Spring-Summer 1997), 173.
12. D'Anieri, et. al., *Politics and Society in Ukraine*, 175.
13. Ibid., 176.
14. Ustina Markus, "Debt and Desperation," *Transition*, 14 April 1995, 14.
15. Quoted in Hale, "Statehood at Stake," 320.
16. Oles M. Smolansky, "Ukraine's Quest for Independence: The Fuel Factor," *Europe-Asia Studies* 47, no. 1 (1995): 80.
17. CIS Interstate Statistical Committee, *Sodruzhestvo Nezavisimykh Gosudartsv v 2001 godu*, 146-47; and CIS Interstate Statistical Committee, *Deciat' Let Sodruzhestva Nezavisimykh Gosudartsv (1991-2000)*, 46-47.
18. D'Anieri, *Economic Interdependence in Ukrainian-Russian Relations*, 73.

19. Hirschman, *National Power and the Structure of Foreign Trade*, 33-34.
20. "Russia Cutting Fuel to Neighbors," *New York Times*, 4 March 1994, A6.
21. Prime Minister Leonid Kuchma emphasized this fact in 1993. "Ne Plutaimo S'ogodnishni Zlydni z Nashym Realnym Potenzialom. Vystup Prem'ier-Ministra Ukrainy L.D. Kuchmy na Zasidanni Verkhovnoi Rady Ukrainy 31 Serpnia 1993 r." (Do not mix present impoverishment with our real potential. The speech of the prime minister of Ukraine L.D. Kuchma at the session of Verkhovna Rada on 31 August 1993), *Uriadovyi Kur'ier*, 2 September 1993, 5.
22. "GUUAM Countries Sign Charter But Fail to Adopt Free Trade Accord," *RFE/RL Newsline*, 8 June 2001.
23. A list of enterprises Russia expressed its interest in can be found in "Zhenu Otdai Diade, a Sam Idi k ... Tete?" (Give your wife to your uncle and yourself to ... the aunt?) *Zerkalo Nedeli*, 11-17 December 1999, 1.
24. See, for example, Hirschman's discussion of the "commercial fifth column" that evolves through extensive trade. Hirschman, *National Power and the Structure of Foreign Trade*, 29.
25. Peter Byrne, "Report: Kyiv May Toss Moscow a Pipeline," *Kyiv Post*, 3 August 2000.
26. "Sales of Bombers Irk US," *Kyiv Post*, 10 August 2000.
27. "Ukraine, Russia Reach 'Breakthrough' Deal on Gas Debts," *RFE/RL Newsline*, 4 December 2000.
28. Neil Malcolm, "Introduction: Economic and Society," in *Contemporary Ukraine: Dynamics of Post-Soviet Transition*, ed. Taras Kuzio (Armonk, NY: M. E. Sharpe 1998), 161.
29. R. Shpek, "Zhuttia Stane Krashchym" (Life would become better), *Uriadovyi Kur'ier*, 4 February 1995, 1.
30. Quoted in Prizel, "Ukraine between Proto-Democracy," 348.
31. Kuzio, *Ukraine under Kuchma*, 157.
32. Paul Hare, Mohammed Ishaq, Saul Estrin, "Ukraine: The Legacies of Central Planning and the Transition to a Market Economy," in *Contemporary Ukraine*, 194.
33. John Jaworsky, *Ukraine: Stability and Instability*, McNair Paper, no. 42 (Washington, D.C.: Institute for National Strategic Studies, 1995), 8.
34. V. Il'chenko, "Teche Nafta v Ukrainu, ale i Vytikaie" (Oil flows to Ukraine, but flows out as well), *Uriadovyi Kur'ier*, 9 December 1992, 1.
35. Kateryna Fonkych, "Rent-Seeking and Interest Groups in Ukrainian Transition," *Ukrainian Journal Economist* (March 2000): 58.
36. D'Anieri, et. al., *Politics and Society in Ukraine*, 194.
37. "Glyboki Ekonomichni Reformy—Shliakh do Vidrodzhennia Ekonomiky, Zabezpechennia Suverenitetu Ukrainy. Vystup Prezudenta Ukrainy Leonida Kuchmy na naradi u L'vovi 13 liutogo ts.r." (Radical economic reform—the way of restoring the economy, securing sovereignty of Ukraine. The speech of the president of Ukraine Leonid Kuchma at the meeting in Lviv on 13 February), *Uriadovyi Kur'ier*, 16 February 1995, 3-4.
38. Hare, et. al, "Ukraine," 188-91; and D'Anieri, et. al., *Politics and Society in Ukraine*, 195.
39. Alexander Motyl reasons that Ukraine was not in a position to enact shock therapy: "The structural legacy of the USSR's collapse, in particular, the kinds of elite Ukraine inherited and its resource endowment, has kept Ukraine on the path of evolutionary change." Alexander J. Motyl, "Structural Constraints and Starting Points: The Logic of

Systemic Change in Ukraine and Russia," *Comparative Politics* 29, no. 4 (1997): 435.

40. For an excellent overview of these events see, Kuzio, *Ukraine under Kuchma*, chap. 5.

41. "Zvernennia Prezydenta Ukrainy Leonida Kuchmy do Verkhovnoi Rady Ukrainy 4 kvitnia 1995 roku" (The address of the president of Ukraine Leonid Kuchma to the Verkhovna Rada of Ukraine on 4 April 1995), *Holos Ukrainy*, 6 April 1995, 3.

42. "Vid Politychnoi do Ekonomichnoi Stabilizatsii: Vystup Prezydenta Ukrainy Leonida Kuchmy v Uzhhorodi na Urochystomu Zasidanni z Nagody 50-i Richnytsi Vozz'iednannia Zakarpattia z Ukrainoiu" (From political to economic stabilization: The speech of the president of Ukraine Leonid Kuchma in Uzhorod during the anniversary meeting dedicated to the 50th anniversary of the reunification of Zakrpattia with Ukraine), *Uriadovyi Kur'ier*, 1 July 1995, 2-4.

43. World Bank, *Ukraine: Restoring Growth with Equity, A Participatory Country Economic Memorandum* (Washington, D.C.: World Bank, 1999), 205.

44. D'Anieri, et. al., *Politics and Society in Ukraine*, 185.

45. For instance, in February 1995 the cabinet expanded the list to 5,600 entities; in March 1995, the list was increased to 6,102; by November 1996 the number increased again to 7,111; only to decline again in early 1997 to 5,125. Ibid., 186, n. 59.

46. Anders Aslund and Georges de Menil, "The Dilemmas of Ukrainian Economic Reform," in *Economic Reform in Ukraine: The Unfinished Agenda*, ed. Anders Aslund and Georges de Menil (Armonk, NY: M. E. Sharpe, 2000), 12.

47. "Zvernennia Prezydenta Ukrainy L.D. Kuchmy do Ukrains'kogo Narodu vid 18 chervnia 1998 roku" (The address of the president of Ukraine L. D. Kuchma to the Ukrainian people on 18 June 1998), *Uriadovyi Kur'ier*, 20 July 1998, 1-3.

48. "IMF Unlikely to Give Money to Ukraine in March," *RFE/RL Newsline*, 8 February 2001. See also Aslund and Menil, *Economic Reform in Ukraine*.

49. "IMF Withholds Loan Tranche to Kyiv," *RFE/RL Newsline*, 19 February 2001.

50. "Ukraine: Transactions with the Fund to June 30, 2003," www.imf.org/external/country/UKR/index.htm.

51. For good recent studies see, Cohen, *Failed Crusade*; Wedel, *Collision and Collusion*; and Peter Reddaway and Dmitri Glinski, *The Tragedy of Russia's Reforms: Market Bolshevism Against Democracy* (Washington, D.C.: U.S. Institute of Peace Press, 2001).

52. Boris Fyodorov is quoted in Cohen, *Failed Crusade*, 59.

53. I am indebted to Paul D'Anieri for suggesting this point.

54. "Kuchma Wants Ukraine to Learn to Live Without IMF," *RFE/RL Newsline*, 6 April 2001.

55. Quoted in Oleksandr Pavliuk, "An Unfulfilling Partnership: Ukraine and the West, 1991-2001," *European Security* 11, no. 1 (2002): 88.

56. "Prazdnik na Ulitse Oligarkhov" (Celebration on the street of oligarchs), *Zerkalo Nedeli*, 20-26 January 2001, 3.

57. "Moscow to Step Up Economic Pressure on Kyiv Following Chernomyrdin's Appointment?" *RFE/RL Newsline*, 11 May 2001.

58. Anders Aslund, "Why Has Ukraine Failed to Achieve Economic Growth?" in *Economic Reform in Ukraine: The Unfinished Agenda*, ed. Anders Aslund and Georges de Menil (Armonk, NY: M. E. Sharpe, 2000), 268.

Chapter 9

Conclusions

This chapter has three interrelated objectives. Initially it examines the empirical findings of the two case studies based on the IT/ED framework. I begin by outlining the theoretical argument and how the empirical evidence supported the causal explanation. Having offered this framework as an alternative to traditional alignment theories, the second objective is to distill the theoretical and empirical insights of the work. I conclude with a discussion of the policy implications of these insights.

Findings of the IT/ED Framework

Chapter 2 hypothesized that when internal threats to leaders are high and economic dependence on Russia is severe, leaders adopt strong pro-Russian alignments. Reciprocally, when internal threats to leaders do not exist and the level of economic dependence is low, leaders adopt more pro-independent (often anti-Russian) alignment patterns. When the values of the independent variables were mixed, leaders adopted moderate or weak pro-Russian alignments.

Internal threats to leaders are a variable that acknowledge the centrality of CIS leaders in the decision-making process. CIS leaders were, more often than not, able to accomplish their goals, especially those of securing their political positions, through their ability to leverage and manipulate the political process. Few institutional constraints existed capable of curbing their power, such as strong legislative and judicial branches. And the public by and large played a minor role in the decision-making processes, which were dominated by former Soviet bureaucrats, state officials, and newly emerging oligarchs. In the more authoritarian systems, leaders tended to balance or eliminate their political opponents; whereas in the quasi-democratic regimes, leaders tended to forge political coalitions or bandwagon with the most powerful groups in society.

However, CIS leaders could not always outmaneuver political opponents or eradicate them through outright repression. This was most evident when leaders faced traditional internal threats like those outlined by David, such as assassination attempts, secessionist movements, civil conflict, and religious extremism. The presence and intensity of these internal threats often meant, especially in the early days of independence, that Russia was the only state willing or able to assist these leaders in the pursuit of their political survival. Moreover, in some instances, Russia actually instigated and actively supported secessionist movements, a strategy designed to destabilize regimes and ultimately lead to active requests for Russian involvement.

The second independent variable is economic dependence on Russia. This dependence and asymmetry between CIS countries and Russia was largely rooted in the Soviet experience. Under the Soviet system, former republics were tied to the command economy to such an extent that few were capable of pursuing a path free from Russian assistance after independence. This was especially true for states that lacked domestic energy resources. By and large, Russia subsidized CIS states both before and after the Soviet collapse in return for a willingness to cooperate more with Russia.

The empirical findings in the cases of Uzbekistan and Ukraine are robust in light of the theoretical propositions of the IT/ED framework. In particular, when internal threats to leaders were high, the strongest pro-Russian alignments were observed. Yet, both variables are necessary to explain alignment outcomes and variations in the strength of a given alignment.

Internal threats influenced alignment patterns in predicted ways in both cases. For Karimov this was particularly clear at two different times. The first was in the initial days of independence when civil war erupted in Tajikistan. Karimov did not fear that Tajikistan would invade Uzbekistan, but rather that the local intercommunal conflict could spread into Uzbekistan itself – a consideration evidenced by previous unrest in 1989, 1990, and 1992. An additional concern was that this unstable environment could become an ideal breeding ground for religious extremism, which might seep into Uzbekistan from Tajikistan and Afghanistan. Thus, he did not fear threats from other states, as balance of power and balance of threat theories would suggest, but rather that regional instability could exacerbate and give rise to more pressing and dangerous internal threats.

From Karimov's perspective, these factors threatened his political position, and therefore measures needed to be taken to stabilize the region. While Uzbekistan played an important role in the stabilization of Tajikistan, Russia was the only state powerful enough to secure the Tajik-Afghan border and quell the situation in the country. As a result, Karimov joined the CIS CST and forged a strong alignment towards Russia. However, as the instability in neighboring Tajikistan waned by 1997, the necessity of stronger security relations with Russia declined. By this time, Karimov had also eliminated other domestic political threats, both religious and secular, to his position through outright repression. Coupled with a severing of economic dependence on Russia, this enabled the Uzbek leader to adopt a more independent alignment. But the threat from religious extremism would reignite cooperation with Moscow by decade's end.

The second moment of rising internal threats to Karimov came shortly thereafter. The first indication of a reemergence of political threats was the February 1999 assassination attempt on Karimov. Moreover, when Islamic extremists began to operate out of Tajikistan and Afghanistan in the areas of southern Kyrgyzstan and the Ferghana Valley in Uzbekistan in the summers of 1999 and 2000, increasing security cooperation with Russia became more necessary. This led Karimov to soften his stance towards Russia and adopt a moderate pro-Russian alignment. Although what changed in the post 11 September security environment is that the United States was willing to assist regional leaders against Islamic extremism, thereby lessening the importance of Russia as a guarantor of regional stability. This issue will be discussed in greater detail below.

While comparatively different in nature (i.e., the lack of traditional potentially violent domestic threats), internal threats also motivated Ukrainian leaders to adopt alignments in line with the IT/ED framework. Immediately after independence, Kravchuk was highly successful at bandwagoning with other powerful groups, namely former Communist, to ensure his political position. This meant that he faced few internal threats to his position. But his failure to address Ukraine's economic priorities and his decision to sever economic ties with Russia propelled the country into a dire economic crisis by 1993-94. This economic mismanagement, while suitable for securing his position in the short-term, ultimately led to Kravchuk's political demise in the 1994 presidential elections. Kuchma came to power, as the IT/ED framework would suggest, by promising to strengthen relations with Russia, capitalizing on the anti-Western sentiment widespread in the eastern and southern portions of the country. In contrast to Karimov in Uzbekistan, Kuchma (as Kravchuk did before him) bandwagoned with powerful groups in Ukraine, promising behind the scenes to distribute economic resources to these groups in exchange for their continued political support. Thus, for the majority of his tenure, Kuchma faced few internal threats.

Bandwagoning with domestic groups proved successful for Kuchma, as outright repression would have undermined his quest for political survival. However, in the wake of "Kuchmagate," the scandal linking Kuchma to the death of a Ukrainian journalist in the winter of 2000, political protest emerged in an unprecedented fashion as discussed in Chapter 7. Hence, with a rise in the level of internal threats to his leadership, Kuchma turned to Russia for greater assistance, as the IT/ED framework would suggest. Indeed, the scandal tainted Kuchma's image in the West and seeking international recognition (and support) to buffer him from the adverse effect of increasingly outspoken opposition groups, Kuchma had few places to turn but back to Russia.

Economic dependence on Russia also influenced alignment patterns in predicted ways. The IT/ED framework suggests that when economic dependence is high, leaders are more likely to adopt pro-Russian alignments. This was true in Uzbekistan in the early 1990s. Karimov initially favored stronger economic ties with Russia in hopes of continuing economic subsidies obtained during the Soviet system. Yet, as Russia altered the terms for economic cooperation, the asymmetrical nature of relations became more apparent. Karimov became acutely aware that continued economic cooperation would come at a lofty price. Accordingly, he addressed the most significant aspect of Uzbek economic dependence, namely its reliance on Russian oil supplies, through the development and production of domestic oil supplies. The strategy proved highly effective, and by 1995 Uzbekistan no longer relied on Russian oil imports. Indeed, Karimov's economic approach was targeted at self-sufficiency, and despite his lack of economic reform, which undermined Uzbekistan's ability to garner Western economic resources, the country maintained a degree of economic autarky, although economic growth was limited. This coupled with the declining level of internal threats enabled Karimov to adopt a strong pro-independence alignment by the late 1990s. However, as we saw above, a more moderate alignment emerged when Islamic extremism reemerged as a threat to Karimov's regime.

In the case of Ukraine, economic dependence on Russia was a much greater impediment to a more independent alignment. Most importantly, Ukraine was unable to sever its dependence on Russian energy imports. Attempts to find substitute trading partners proved futile since Ukraine was often unable to pay for energy deliveries. Coupled with a lack of domestic energy reserves, Ukraine remained dependent on Russian energy. The staggering energy debt that accrued over the decade exacerbated Ukrainian dependence on Russia, and opened the country up to greater economic penetration by Russian capital and businesses.

Similar to Uzbekistan, Ukraine had difficulty obtaining continuous Western economic assistance, although Western involvement was much greater than in Uzbekistan. Kravchuk failed to implement economic reform, and it was not until Kuchma came into power in 1994 that reform measures were taken in line with IMF prescriptions. Access was short-lived, however. By the spring of 1995, reform efforts slowed, and within a few years they ground to a halt. This led to a suspension of IMF and World Bank funds to Ukraine, and by the end of the decade Kuchma strengthened economic ties with Russia, especially given Ukrainian dependence on Russian energy supplies.

In the alignment patterns of Uzbekistan and Ukraine, the IT/ED framework provides compelling explanations as to why leaders cooperated with Russia under certain circumstances and others did not. Uzbekistan went from a strong pro-Russian alignment in the early 1990s (H1) to a strong pro-independent alignment in the mid 1990s (H4), and then to a more moderate Russian alignment by 2000 (H2). The main driver in the Uzbek alignment patterns was Karimov's concerns with internal threats emanating from regional instability in and around Tajikistan, and later the resurgence of Islamic extremism. But economic dependence on Russia still constrained his alignment options immediately after independence, although by 1995 Uzbekistan had successfully severed its dependence on Russian imports, especially those related to energy.

On the other hand, Ukraine went from a strong pro-independent alignment in the early 1990s (H4), to a weak pro-Russian alignment in the mid 1990s (H3), and then to a strong pro-Russian alignment beginning in 2000 (H1). Economic dependence on Russia proved to be the most constraining variable influencing Ukraine's alignment patters toward Russia, although by the end of the decade Kuchma's concerns with a rise in internal threats to his position began to shape a more pro-Russian alignment.

One important qualification of this first period, depicted as a moment of pro-independence for Ukraine, is worth noting. While it is true that Ukraine was economically dependent on Russia at the time of independence, Kravchuk attempted to sever these ties and forge a more independent alignment. As Kravchuk acknowledged a few years later, he grossly underestimated the extent of this dependence. The IT/ED framework does not account for a leader's misperception or miscalculation of these variables. However, it does note that leaders may attempt to sever economic dependence on Russia through a variety of methods, some more radical than others (i.e., self-sufficiency or engaging in economic reform to attract Western economic resources). In this regard, Kravchuk adopted a foreign alignment based on his belief that economic dependence on Russia was not that significant and could easily be overcome. He was wrong in this instance, and thus the economic crisis that led to his downfall was really a result of his failed policies and miscalculation of Ukraine's economic position.

		Internal Political Threats	
		High	Low
Economic Dependence on Russia	High	**H1** *Strong Pro-Russian* Uzbekistan (1991) Ukraine (2000)	**H3** *Weak Pro-Russian* Ukraine (1994)
	Low	**H2** *Moderate Pro-Russian* Uzbekistan (2000)	**H4** *Strong Pro-Independent* Ukraine (1991) Uzbekistan (1995)

Figure 9.1 Alignment Outcomes for Uzbekistan and Ukraine

Theoretical and Empirical Implications of the IT/ED Framework

One work is unlikely to capture all the trends and patterns in the international relations of the CIS. But the IT/ED framework provides us with a short cut for understanding critical aspects of these relations as well as highlighting under what conditions CIS leaders are most likely to cooperate with Russia. This book began with a straightforward puzzle about alignment patterns between CIS states and Russia. Balance of power and balance of threat theories suggest that states are more likely to balance power/threats, in this case Russia, than they are to bandwagon with it, and both were highlighted given their prominence in the field of security studies. However, their theoretical logic does not accurately depict alignment patterns in the cases of Uzbekistan and Ukraine. In the case of Ukraine, it actually relinquished its nuclear weapons in the early 1990s and then adopted strong pro-Russian policies by decade's end. In the case of Uzbekistan, the country at times bandwagoned with Russia to meet its security requirements, but these concerns were not linked to fears of Russia's power or perceptions of threat. Instead, Karimov was driven more by concerns over domestic stability and its impact on his political survival.

Balance of threat theory has similar shortcomings. The theory conceptualizes the notion of external threat (i.e., aggregate power, geographic proximity, offensive capabilities, and aggressive intentions) in a way that is less compelling in the context of the CIS. For instance, in the Uzbek case such a conceptualization would miss the threat posed by Islamic extremism, since this would score low according to Walt's definition. Walt's theory is also primarily state-centric, and would have difficulty accounting for transnational threats. And in fact, it was these threats and their influence on domestic threat perception that had the greatest impact on Uzbek alignment patterns. In the end, the IT/ED framework offers a more accurate explanation for alignment outcomes as these leaders were less concerned with Russian power and external threat perceptions and more concerned with securing their own political positions from domestic threats, while managing economic dependence on Russia.

Indeed, the IT/ED framework developed and tested in this book has argued in favor of refining parsimonious traditional alignment theories, like balance of power and balance of threat theories, in favor of one that incorporates domestic political and economic threats that influence alignment patterns. This does not suggest that traditional alignment theories are void of any merit, but when refinements can be made that greatly enhance the explanatory capability of a theory, such attempts should be encouraged. Indeed, the core logic of traditional alignment theories as well as the IT/ED framework is threat-based. Balance of power focuses on the most powerful states, whereas balance of threat theory suggests that states balance the most threatening states, especially those that demonstrate aggressive international behavior. Much like David argued, the IT/ED framework confirms that alignments are primarily a response to threats, but it disagrees as to where the most pressing threats originate – in this instance from domestic threats as opposed to international threats. Moreover, it argues that traditional alignment theories should not necessarily disregard economic variables in alignment explanations, especially when those economic factors have a direct impact on a leader's threat perception.

In the end, although this two-case comparison is not sufficient to establish causality, the evidence offered in this article suggests that more research along this argumentative line is worthwhile and compelling. That is, the confirmatory evidence offered by the cases of Uzbekistan and Ukraine can be seen as plausibility studies. If, for instance, the IT/ED framework did not provide sufficient evidence in these cases, then the applicability of the framework would be questionable. Yet, since it offers ample evidence in explaining Uzbek and Ukrainian alignment patterns, the framework carries more theoretical weight in explaining the empirical behavior of CIS states.

By highlighting the influence of internal threats and economic dependence on alignment outcomes, the present framework sheds light on a different aspect of CIS domestic and international politics. What would be useful in the future is more rigorous testing of the IT/ED framework throughout the CIS to examine cases that may not fit neatly with the argument. For instance, some CIS leaders, such as those in Moldova, Georgia, and Azerbaijan, faced internal threats but failed to align with Russia in any sincere fashion. A preliminary assessment of these cases suggests unique circumstances, however. The internal threats to leaders in these instances were so intense and, more important, Russian involvement was so overt that it was nearly impossible for these leaders to align with Russia, as David might predict.[1] If these leaders had aligned with Russia, this would only have heightened their internal threats and potentially toppled their governments altogether. It should be noted, though, that some of these leaders, such as those in Georgia and Azerbaijan, did at times overlook this fact and align with Russia formally to seek assistance in confronting their internal threats.[2] Greater theorizing about the foreign relations of the CIS in general is also needed, as the region continues to redefine its relations not only within itself but also in relation to the larger international system.

Ultimately, traditional alignment theories are less successful in explaining CIS alignment patterns vis-à-vis Russia because they fail to recognize contextual and situational factors often more influential in a leader's alignment calculations. Two contextual factors are most illustrative. First, the former Soviet Union as a region is not one in which systemic anarchy prevails, but rather given the extensive connections and historical relations between Russia and its former republics, the region is defined more by hierarchy than anarchy.[3] In this regard, the political, economic, social, cultural, and especially military ties established under the Soviet Union were not quick to change after independence. More importantly, Russia saw the former Soviet Union as its unique sphere of influence, and tried to exert its influence whenever and wherever possible. Indeed, the international community tended to grant Russia a free hand in stabilizing various regions that erupted into conflict, for instance, in the widespread use of Russian-led CIS peacekeeping forces. As a result, for many leaders, Russia was the logical state to turn to when assistance was needed, and often it was the only state available and willing to assist CIS leaders in the pursuit of their political survival.

Second, CIS leaders were dominant players in the policy making process within these countries because of the lack of political institutionalization and state-dominated Soviet legacy. Accordingly, the IT/ED framework built on and refined the work of Steven David, who placed the analytical focus on leaders when explaining alignment patterns in Third World or "quasi-states" that lack much of the political institutionalization found in the Western world.[4] As evidenced by the findings of this book, this theoretical nuance provides greater insight into alignment patterns within the CIS, than traditional alignment theories. Beyond this theoretical contribution, the insights generated from the IT/ED framework touch on other compelling issues that are of interest to academic and policy circles. The theme that resonates most is that CIS leaders tended to prioritize their own personal security over the security of the state, and thus the analytical focus on leaders is both justified and informative.

The fall of the Soviet empire brought with it tremendous change in the way in which CIS states organized their newly independent political and economic systems. To capitalize on this unique moment in history, the Clinton administration focused a great deal of attention and Western funds on the large-scale nation-building enterprise throughout the CIS, especially in Russia. Western assistance and guidance fueled this process, but by the end of decade it had proven largely futile in the development of more transparent political and economic institutions. In this regard, the billions of dollars of Western assistance channeled through bilateral and multilateral means did not always bring about the intended results. This was largely because these international institutions were unable to accept CIS states for what they were and instead focused naively on what they thought they could become. The end result was that tremendous sums of money, especially in the case of Russia and Ukraine, was wasted and directly and indirectly channeled to individuals who manipulated the political process for their own narrow benefit.

This book sheds light on this nation-building effort as it underscores the dilemma that CIS leaders were the primary actors in post-Soviet politics and sought to ensure their positions at all costs. Few in the West in the beginning of the 1990s fully appreciated the power of CIS leaders in the post-Soviet political systems, and more specifically, their willingness to do whatever it took to maintain their political positions. This in turn led to development strategies that were not tailored to post-Soviet realities, but rather ones that were generated based on the presumed wisdom of past development successes. Indeed, by the end of the decade leaders in both the IMF and World Bank openly acknowledged their failure in adjusting preconceived notions of what would work in favor of ideas of what could work in the post-Soviet context. This is also an institutional concern for these organizations because as many in the IMF structure will reveal the IMF does not attempt to solve these domestic issues. While these international organizations cannot be tasked with every conceivable objective, they nonetheless played a role in the post-Soviet transition that at times was counter-productive.

The lessons derived from the nation-building enterprise offer additional insight. Not surprisingly, in those countries that embraced political and economic reform, the role of Western assistance proved very effective. This is especially true in the context of transitions in Eastern Europe with many of these states looking more actively to Europe, first in the form of NATO enlargement, and second in the more difficult path to EU accession. Yet, this book is about the CIS and there are far fewer examples of success in this context. While not part of the CIS, the sole examples in the former Soviet Union are the Baltic states, who willingly tackled reform efforts often to the detriment of a particular leader's political survival. As Abraham Lowenthal noted in a sweeping study of efforts to export democracy to Latin America, democratic consolidation was only possible when conditions within a country were propitious.[5] Thus, without a sincere desire to follow through on reform measures, little political change can occur, and little did occur throughout the CIS over the past decade.

In the end, nation-building efforts were thwarted from within. CIS leaders were primarily concerned with securing their own political positions and such an assumption undermines the capacity to reform a political system, since reform would likely threaten a leader's political position. As Joel Hellman points out, in those post-Soviet countries where the governments were most susceptible to the threat of an electoral backlash, reform efforts were adopted and comprehensive reform programs flourished.[6] Thus, the desire to transform CIS states into more open, politically free, and transparent societies was untenable from the beginning because few political leaders were willing to relinquish it for such an endeavor.

This also raises a related concern about the politics of economic reform, and the ability to implement economic reform. Traditional logic in international political economy suggests that leaders need to be insulated from those parties that would most likely suffer from reform measures. That is to say, the short-term losers of economic reform, such as striking workers, resentful former state officials, impoverished pensioners, or masses of unemployed, are the greatest threats to debunking reform because they are the groups most likely to suffer the greatest costs.[7] Traditional thinking is that leaders must be protected and insulated from these groups and if they are not, then these groups are likely to push for regime change, which could ultimately lead to the collapse of the reform effort.[8]

When applied to the CIS, such logic proved counter-productive because it only fed the interests of those leaders that were already in power. CIS leaders did not want an electoral backlash, which would threaten their positions, and often, as we saw in the case of Ukraine, leaders ensured their political survival by trading economic resources for the political support of powerful elites within the society. In short, as Hellman argues, the greatest threat to economic reform in the post-Soviet context came not from the short-term losers, but rather the short-term winners, or those individuals that benefited from an unstable and highly volatile economy.[9] The short-term winners, such as enterprise insiders, commercial bankers, local corrupt officials, and the mafia, manipulated the reform process for their own advantage and stripped their respective countries of valuable assets that ultimately left the country worse off than when it started to implement reform, while increasing their personal coffers.[10] The IT/ED framework addresses this phenomenon in its analysis of how CIS leaders maintained their political positions, especially as we saw in the case of Ukraine.

Policy Implications of the IT/ED Framework

The events of 11 September and the subsequent U.S.-led war on terrorism did not alter the primary motivation of CIS leaders – namely the pursuit of their political survival – but it did fundamentally change their strategic calculations. The most significant development was that the United States was now willing to assist leaders against Islamic extremism and terrorism (and hence their own internal threats), a role traditionally held by Russia before 11 September.

In his speech to Congress on 20 September 2001, Bush offered a harbinger of his efforts to come: "Our war on terror begins with al Qaeda, but it does not end there. It will not end until every terrorist group of global reach has been found, stopped, and defeated."[11] Given the focus on Afghanistan, Bush's mention of the links between al Qaeda and the Taliban and the IMU in his speech was also purposeful. He was beginning to align his security objectives with those that plagued the Karimov regime as well as other Central Asian governments (i.e, Islamic extremism and terrorism in the form of the IMU), and in the process lay the foundation for a new strategic partnership with Central Asia, especially Uzbekistan, a country that would quickly become Washington's key regional partner.

As discussed previously in Chapter 1, to support the war on terrorism, and specifically military operations in Afghanistan, Washington looked to regional leaders for assistance. On that mark, they were forthcoming albeit to varying degrees. Uzbekistan and Kyrgyzstan featured prominently in these calculations with the temporary basing of U.S. and coalition forces at airbases in Karshi Khanabad and Manas, respectively. Similarly, the South Caucasus states, namely Georgia and Azerbaijan, were equally vital for logistical purposes. Coalition aircraft en route to Afghanistan and Central Asia were allowed to overfly and refuel in the Caucasus states, providing the only realistic air corridor through which military aircraft could travel.

As a result of 11 September, leaders in Central Asia and the Caucasus benefited from U.S. interest in the region. Financial and military assistance was more forthcoming, and perhaps most importantly, the United States became a significant player in the geopolitics of the region for the first time. This was welcome relief, especially to Karimov, as it gave the Uzbek leader more options in his efforts to balance the Islamic extremist element in the region. Where Russia was once the only state willing to assist leaders against their internal threats, now Washington had entered the scene.

The specter of international terrorism also had profound significance for overall U.S. thinking towards the region. Indeed, while the importance of Central Asia and the Caucasus for conducting operations in Afghanistan cannot be understated, increasingly U.S. defense planners began to recast their strategic view of the entire region in light of the changing security environment after the Cold war and especially 11 September. As Ilan Berman noted, "If Afghanistan prompted Washington's initial interest in Central Asia and the Caucasus, the Pentagon's strategic transformation has preserved its attention."[12]

Throughout the 1990s, the strategic priorities of the U.S. military remained largely static. While the Soviet collapse fundamentally altered the international system after 1991, U.S. defense planners altered their priorities little over the years, simply substituting Russia for the Soviet Union as the primary adversary. The 11 September terrorist attacks shattered this strategic rationale, demanding a fundamental reassessment of U.S. military strategy. Indeed, the 70,000 troops stationed in Germany were still poised to counter a Soviet land invasion. Moreover, nearly 80 percent of U.S. forces deployed to Europe were in Germany, while three-quarters of U.S. troops in Asia remained in bases in South Korea and Japan. As one observer noted, this pattern represents a "network of U.S. forward deployment locations created to counter a threat now long gone."[13]

To address this strategic discrepancy, the Bush administration has identified new priorities for U.S. military strategy. As part of the 2001 Quadrennial Defense Review, the new strategy and force structure should be aimed as developing capabilities to assure allies, dissuade adversaries, deter aggression, and, if necessary, decisively defeat undeterred enemies.[14] The underlying assumption of this review was that the U.S. military needed to move away from an adversary-based approach to military planning toward a capabilities-based approach designed to achieve assurance, dissuasion, deterrence, and defense against any potential adversary in any environment. During the Cold War, it was easy to define the adversary (i.e., the Soviet Union), but in the post-Cold War era and especially after 11 September, it was much more difficult to maintain such an adversary-based model, simply because the United States could not plan as easily for an unpredictable threat like Islamic terrorism that could strike anywhere in the world with little notice. As the White House argued in its September 2002 National Security Strategy: "[a] military structured to deter massive Cold War-era armies must be transformed to focus more on how an adversary might fight rather than where or when a war might occur."[15]

The post-Soviet space emerged as one of the newest fronts in this transformational effort. The rationale was simple: many of the new emerging threats originate in or near the region, therefore, requiring greater U.S. involvement and action. In his 2002 report to the president and Congress, Rumsfeld argued that, "[a]long a broad arc of instability that stretches from the Middle East to Northeast Asia, there exists a volatile mix of rising and declining regional powers."[16] Accordingly, U.S. defense planners began to launch a global realignment of its defense posture aimed at gaining strategic control of this arc through an expanded military presence in those theaters.[17] The military engagement in Central Asia and the Caucasus that resulted from 11 September was a key part of this strategy. Indeed, as U.S. Undersecretary of Defense Douglas Feith noted in 2003, "everything is going to move everywhere...there is no place in the world where [U.S. military presence] is going to be the same as it was."[18] Hence, the new strategy was to "create a web of far-flung, austere forward operation bases, maintained normally only by small support units, with the fighting forces deploying from the United States if necessary."[19]

The Bush administration's war on terrorism and its global posture review has fundamentally reshaped the geostrategic landscape of the former Soviet Union – a reshaping that CIS leaders have been able to capitalize on in the pursuit of their continued political survival. But this new strategic calculus is not without significant pitfalls for U.S. policy makers. Most prominently, the tension between the pursuit of U.S. security objectives in the war of terror and the advancement of political and economic reform as well as the burgeoning geopolitical competition between the United States, Russia, and China will continue to confront U.S. decisions makers in the short and long term.

Security Interests vs. Democratization and Reform

The United States should be wary of narrowly focusing on security cooperation with CIS states. In Central Asia and the Caucasus, for example, the Bush administration prioritized its war on terrorism, which indirectly aided these leaders against their internal threats. In the long-term such security cooperation may prove counter-productive because it props up authoritarian regimes that stifle political and economic reform. As the United States witnessed in other places, especially during the Cold War, the backlash from such a narrowly focused policy may not emerge in the short-term, but could lead to more significant long-term challenges. U.S. support for the shah of Iran is a case in point, which in time led to the 1979 Iranian revolution and fundamentally altered the balance of power and U.S. interests in the Persian Gulf. The stability of many parts of the CIS is not assured in the future, and providing for regime security could prompt leaders to continue their long-established practice of repression to ensure their political survival.

As a result, U.S. policy should continue to stress human rights and political and economic reform in addition to security cooperation. Without this type of broader engagement, the United States may face an even more dangerous and unstable security environment as the short sightedness and corruption of many CIS leaders contributes to entrenching poverty and economic disparity. Moreover, the United States should recognize that terrorism is not an isolated problem in and of itself, but often times is a symptom of deeper societal crisis. In this regard, to truly deal a blow to terrorism the United States must also confront the economic roots of terrorism, which stem from the lack of economic development and widespread poverty common throughout many of these regions. Furthermore, the lack of political expression in many of these countries and pervasive repression only fuels reactionary forces. That is not to suggest that Islamic extremism should be offered a legitimate political outlet, but it does imply that state policies towards Islam and political expression, or lack thereof, in general may also contribute to these terrorist organizations. Indeed, many of the members of IMU that returned to Uzbekistan and Kyrgyzstan in 1999 and 2000 were those individuals that were repressed and forced to flee the country, as a result of Karimov's domestic crackdown in the early 1990s. Thus, defeating terrorist organizations alone will prove inefficient because many of the underlying causes of that animosity will still exist, especially in the CIS context.

In the challenging case of Uzbekistan, however, the Bush administration has been reluctant to suspend existing military and economic assistance to the country for fear that it could further destabilize Karimov's regime and push Tashkent out of the U.S. coalition fighting the war on terrorism, especially in light of the U.S. military base in the country.[20] This juggling act between security concerns and human rights has prompted U.S. officials to send mixed signals to Karimov. For instance, the United States withheld $18 million in aid in July 2004 when Secretary of State Colin Powell decided that Tashkent had not fulfilled the terms of its 2002 Strategic Partnership Framework that mandated "substantial and continuing progress" on democratization. Yet the very next month, General Richard Myers, chairman of the Joint Chiefs of Staff, announced that Washington would be giving an additional $24 million in military aid in a show of support for Tashkent's antiterrorism efforts.[21]

More recently, Bush himself has put forth loftier goals of democratization that do not appear to find traction in actual policy towards Tashkent. In the aftermath of the Andijon massacre in May 2005, during a speech at the International Republican Institute in Washington, D.C., Bush signaled that the United States would increase its global democratization efforts: "We are seeing the rise of a new generation whose hearts burn for freedom – and they will have it."[22] But this political rhetoric has not been backed with concrete and firm messages to Karimov, especially in light of the leader's repressive and bloody crackdown on unarmed civilian protesters that same month. In a 16 June briefing, Secretary of State Condoleezza Rice offered a more sober assessment of the challenges Uzbekistan pose to U.S. policy makers, while stressing the uneasy balance between U.S. perceived security interests and its desire to promote democratization. "We have arrangements with the Uzbek government and we continue to hope that we can use those arrangements," she noted, referencing the basing agreement for Karshi Khanabad. She added that for the last several years the administration has been "urging the Karimov government to do something about the openness of its political system. The answer to the potential threat of extremism in a country is not to close the system down, but rather to open it up to legitimate and more moderate voices in the political system."[23]

Yet, as the IT/ED framework suggests, and as Karimov's behavior has consistently supported, the Uzbek leader is unwilling to take any measures that may threaten his political position or give rise to opposition forces within the country. In the end, Washington must continue to stress broader engagement of these countries that emphasizes both legitimate security interests as well as its goals for political and economic reform to ensure stability and security in the long-term, although this will continue to tax U.S. decision makers with difficult and often times impossible choices. But while the United States struggles with these realpolitik and moral issues, other regional actors are under no such constraints.

The Rise of Geopolitical Competition

Initially, Moscow and Beijing did not greet the entrance of the U.S. military into Central Asia with much concern. Moscow has struggled with its own terrorist problem stemming from instability in the North Caucasus and its military campaign to subjugate Chechnya. Similarly, China remains concerned that Uighur separatists, struggling for greater autonomy in Xinjiang, could capitalize on any instability in the region to further radicalize the Uighur opposition movement. Thus, the fight against terrorism was warmly received and supported immediately after 11 September. However, as the U.S. military presence began to solidify in the years after 2001, and especially after the conclusion of combat operations in Afghanistan, Russian and Chinese leaders began to jockey for geopolitical position.

Traditionally, Moscow has viewed competition with other great powers in its former empire as a zero-sum game, in that a gain for one country inherently implies a loss for another. While Putin has stressed the positive aspects of the U.S. military presence in Central Asia in its efforts against the Taliban in Afghanistan, other Russian officials have questioned U.S. intentions. In late 2003, for instance, Defense Minister Sergei Ivanov stated that Russia accepted U.S. military bases in Central Asia solely for the purpose and duration of anti-terrorist operations in Afghanistan.[24] The underlying intimation, thus, was that once these operations had been completed the rationale for the U.S. military presence will have expired as well. Similarly, when Secretary of State Colin Powell remarked in Moscow in January 2004 that the U.S. global defense posture review suggested shifting military bases eastward, speculation ran rampant in the Russian media as to the possibility of permanent bases in the region, providing fresh skepticism about U.S. long-term intentions.[25] Indeed, the Manichean viewpoint that Russian must not lose its geopolitical position in the region was the topic of discussion for Putin in his comments at an extraordinary session of the country's Security Council in July 2004: "We are facing an alternative – either we'll achieve a qualitative strengthening of the CIS and create on its basis an effectively functioning and influential regional organization, or else we'll inevitably see the erosion of the geopolitical space." The latter, Putin stressed, "should not be allowed to happen."[26]

Accordingly, Moscow has sought to secure its foothold in the region. At the April 2003 Dushanbe summit of CIS CST members, the body was transformed into a new political-military body: the Collective Security Treaty Organization (CSTO). Members agreed to establish a headquarters in Moscow, and the charter contained a NATO-like provision calling for the joint response to aggression against any member state, of which a similar provision was provided for the original CST signed in Tashkent in 1992. Moscow agreed to fund 50 percent of the CSTO's activities, with the other five members contributing 10 percent a piece. The Collective Rapid Deployment Force (CRDF), created under the CST in May 2001, was also placed under Russian command. Indeed, although the CRDF was to be based on the respective military capabilities of its members (Kazakhstan, Kyrgyzstan, Tajikistan, and Russia), in practice the force is built around the existing presence of Russia's 201st Motorized Division already stationed in Tajikistan; non-Russian participation initially totaled 1,300 personnel which were added to a battalion of the existing Russian force.[27] In short, the multilateral façade of the new CSTO does not eclipse the reality of Russia's preeminence in the military organization.

Similarly, and undoubtedly as a response to the U.S. military presence, Russia secured access to military bases in Kyrgyzstan and Tajikistan. In an effort to strengthen the CRDF, Russia reached an agreement with Kyrgyzstan for use of a joint base at Kant, just outside of Bishkek and nearby the existing U.S. airbase at Manas. Elements of the Russian air force first deployed to Kant in late 2002 to test the facilities before the official opening of the base in October 2003. The base will operate for 15 years, and the lease could then be renewed in 5-year increments. Putin was quick to point out the importance of this additional Russian military presence. During discussions with Kyrgyz President Askar Akaev concerning the base, he noted: "While the situation [in Kyrgyzstan] is stable, it is not simple. Our military presence is something both we and out CIS partners need." At the October base opening, he added that the new airbase would help "strengthen the security of a region whose stability is a growing factor in the international situation." Then in late 2004, during an official state visit by Putin to Dushanbe, a far-reaching strategic agreement was reached with the Tajik government. The centerpiece of the agreement provided for the permanent basing of 5,000 Russian troops to Tajikistan "on a free of charge and open-ended basis."[28]   Much like his comments at the opening of the Kant airbase in Kyrgyzstan, Putin stressed that "the base will boost peace and stability in Central Asia and throughout the former Soviet republics." According to a Moscow daily, a more aggressive interpretation could also be forwarded: the base, the paper wrote, will act as "a firm fist to protest Russian interests abroad."[29]

While not as overt, China has similarly broadened its engagement with Central Asian states for myriad reasons. Security fears over the spread of extremism and separatism, an expanding thirst for Central Asia energy resources, the desire to curb U.S. power in the region, and the pursuit of additional markets for domestic goods add up to a significant stake for Beijing in the region. The SCO, created in its current form in 2001, has been China's primary diplomatic entry into regional politics. The organization has provided opportunities to expand security cooperation and engage in multilateral military exercise among member states as well as gave rise to a SCO regional anti-terrorism center to be based in Tashkent that will work closely with its CSTO counterpart. Not surprisingly, Moscow and Beijing have a similar strategic objective for the SCO, namely the creation of a joint sphere of influence that will curb U.S. regional power. In a July 2005 meeting between Putin and Chinese President Hu Jintao, the leaders agreed to such an implicit vision. Advancing their vision of geopolitical multipolarity, which includes a diminishing of U.S. power in the region, the leaders issued a joint declaration on "world order" rejecting efforts by any powers to achieve a "monopoly in world affairs," divide the world into "leaders and followers," and "impose models of social development" on other countries.[30]

The most important geopolitical opening for Moscow and Beijing, however, came with the Andijon massacre in Uzbekistan, which led to a cooling of relations between Washington and Tashkent. Both powers seized this window of opportunity to advance their positions and attempt to push the United States out of the region. As we saw in Chapter 4, Russian officials defended Karimov's actions suggesting that the protesters had ties to larger international terrorist networks in Afghanistan. Beijing was also the first country to welcome Karimov after the events. During the trip, Karimov signed a treaty on "friendly and cooperative partnership" with Chinese President Hu as well as a number of technical and economic cooperation agreements, including a $600-million oil joint venture.[31] Addressing the crackdown, a spokesman for China's Foreign Ministry said, "This is fundamentally an Uzbek domestic matter. We've always staunchly supported the Uzbek government's attacks on the three forces – separatism, terrorism and extremism."[32] Then during a summit of the SCO on 5 July in Kazakhstan, the organization's members provocatively requested U.S.-led anti-terrorist coalition forces set a date for leaving its military bases in Uzbekistan and Kyrgyzstan, arguing that military operations had ended in Afghanistan, and thus with it the raison e'tre of the U.S. military presence.[33]   Thus, while Washington scrambled for an acceptable policy position that factored in its security interests, while not implicitly condoning the repression, Moscow and Beijing defended and supported Karimov in his time of international need.   This was welcome support, as the IT/ED framework would suggest, because Karimov was primarily concerned with which outside power(s) were most likely to ensure his political position and combat his internal threats.   Shortly thereafter, in response to U.S. support for a United Nations evacuation of refugees that had fled the violence in Andijon to neighboring Kyrgyzstan, Karimov gave the U.S. military 180 days to withdraw from its base at Karshi Khanabad.   Ultimately, Russia and China have proven their willingness to support any regional leader, especially those that have no tolerance for extremism and political opposition and those that are willing to snub the United States.

The infusion of U.S. military power into the former Soviet Union as a result of 11 September has had the effect of displacing Russian political and economic power and influence in many instances.   The long-term effects of this shift remain unclear, but the balance of power in the region has shifted in remarkable ways that would have been unlikely before 11 September.   In the end, the key for successful policy (and theoretical explanation) will rest on the correct determination of which factors – especially internal threats to leaders and economic dependence on Russia – are driving alignment dynamics.

Notes

1.   For good overviews see Thomas Goltz, "Letter from Eurasia: The Hidden Russian Hand," *Foreign Policy*, no. 92 (1993): 92–116; Fiona Hill and Pamela Jewett, *Back in the USSR: Russia's Intervention in the Internal Affairs of the Former Soviet Republics and the Implications for United States Policy toward Russia* (Cambridge: Strengthening Democratic Institutions Project, Harvard University, January 1994); Stuart J. Kaufman, "Spiraling to Ethnic War: Elites, Masses, and Moscow in Moldova's Civil War," *International Security* 21, no. 2 (1996): 108–38; and Lynch, *Russian Peacekeeping Strategies in the CIS*.

2.   Georgia signed the CST in 1993 and shortly thereafter an agreement with Russia over access to military bases in the country—an issue which complicates Georgian-Russian relations today – in an effort to coax Russia to curb its support for Abkhazian separatists. Similarly, Azerbaijan joined the CST in 1993 hoping Russia would curtail its involvement in the Nagorno-Karabakh conflict.

3.   David A. Lake, "Anarchy, Hierarchy, and the Variety of International Relations," *International Organization* 50, no. 1 (1996): 1-34.

4.   Jackson, *Quasi-States*.

5.   Abraham Lowenthal, *Exporting Democracy: The United States and Latin America* (Baltimore: Johns Hopkins University Press, 1991).

6. Hellman, "Winners Take All," 232.
7. For a good overview of the literature see, Hector E. Schamis, "Distributional Coalitions and the Politics of Economic Reform in Latin America," *World Politics* 51, no. 2 (1999): 236-68.
8. Variations of this theme stress the merits of autonomous states in Peter Evans, "The State as Problem and Solution: Predation, Embedded Autonomy, and Structural Change," in *The Politics of Economic Adjustment*, ed. Stephen Haggard and Robert R. Kaufman (Princeton: Princeton University Press, 1992); powerful executives in Haggard and Kaufman, *The Political Economy of Democratic Transitions*; and insulated technocrats in John Williamson, "In Search of a Manual for Technopols," in *The Political Economy of Policy Reform*, ed. John Williamson (Washington, D.C.: Institute for International Studies, 1994).
9. Hellman, "Winners Take All."
10. For good overviews see, David E. Hoffman, *The Oligarchs: Wealth and Power in the New Russia* (New York: Public Affairs, 2002); and Chrystia Freeland, *Sale of the Century: Russia's Wild Ride from Communism to Capitalism* (New York: Crown, 2000).
11. "Address to a Joint Session of Congress and the American People," 20 September 2001, http://www.whitehouse.gov/news/releases/2001/09/20010920-8.html.
12. Berman, "The New Battleground," 60.
13. P. Grier, "Lighter Footprint, Longer Range," *Air Force Magazine* (October 2003): 50.
14. Department of Defense, *Quadrennial Defense Review Report*, 30 September 2001, 11-13.
15. The White House, *National Security Strategy of the United States of America* (September 2002): 29.
16. U.S. Department of Defense, "2002 Annual Report to the President and the Congress," Washington, D.C., 2002.
17. Douglas J. Feith, "Transforming the Global Defense Posture," remarks at the Center for Strategic and International Studies, Washington, D.C., 3 December 2003.
18. E. Schrader, "U.S. to Realign Troops in Asia," *Los Angeles Times*, 29 May 2003, 1; Paul D. Wolfowitz, Statement before House Armed Forces Committee, U.S. House of Representatives, Washington, D.C., 18 June 2003.
19. C. Robinson, "Worldwide Reorientation of U.S. Military Basing in Prospect," Center for Defense Information, Military Reform Project, 19 September 2003, 1; and Kurt M. Campbell and Celeste Johnson Ward, "New Battle Stations?" *Foreign Affairs* 82, no. 5 (2003): 95-103.
20. Ariel Cohen, "Bush Administration Backs Uzbek Response to March Militant Attacks," *Eurasianet*, 14 April 2004.
21. "Top US General Tours Central Asian Capitals, Dispenses Aid to Uzbekistan," *Eurasianet*, 13 August 2004.
22. Igor Torbakov, "Despite Shared Interest in Stability, Russia and United States Unlikely to Cooperate on Uzbekistan," *Eurasianet*, 26 May 2005.
23. "Uzbek Government adds 'So-Called Democrats' to Its Enemies List," *Eurasianet*, 17 June 2005.
24. Thom Shanker, "Russian Official Cautions U.S. on Use of Central Asian Bases," *New York Times*, 9 October 2003, A9.
25. Wishnick, *Strategic Consequences of the Iraq War*, 21.
26. Igor Torbakov, "Putin Urges Shift in Russia's CIS Policies," *Jamestown Eurasia Daily Monitor*, 27 July 2004.

27. Roger N. McDermott, *Countering Global Terrorism: Developing the Antiterrorist Capabilities of the Central Asian Militaries* (Carlisle, PA: Strategic Studies Institute, U.S. Army War College, February 2004), 13.
28. Valery Zhukov, "Russian Military Base in Tajikistan Big Achievement – Armitage," Itar-TASS News Service, 17 July 2004; and Arun Sahgal, "Growing Russian Influence in Central Asia," *Eurasianet*, 8 November 2004.
29. Kambiz Arman, "Russia and Tajikistan: Friends Again," *Eurasianet*, 28 October 2004.
30. Michael A. Weinstein, "Intelligence Brief: Shanghai Cooperation Organization," *Power and Interest News Report*, 12 July 2005.
31. "Uzbek President Begins Visit to China," *RFE/RL Newsline*, 26 May 2005.
32. Chris Buckley, "China Opens Arms to Uzbek Chief," *International Herald Tribune*, 26 May 2005.
33. Vladimir Socor, "SCO Asks Washington to Set a Date for Withdrawal of Forces," *Jamestown Eurasia Daily Monitor*, 6 July 2005.

Bibliography

Documents and Official Sources

Bush, George. *Public Papers of the Presidents of the United States: 1991*. Vol. 2. Washington, D.C.: U.S. Government Printing Office, 1992.

Commission on Security and Cooperation in Europe. *Human Rights and Democratization in Uzbekistan and Turkmenistan*. 106th Cong., 2nd sess., 2000.

_____. *Democratization and Human Rights in Uzbekistan: Hearing before the Commission on Security and Cooperation in Europe*. 106th Cong., 1st sess., 18 October 1999.

Commonwealth of Independent States Interstate Statistical Committee, *Sodruzhestvo Nezavisimykh Gosudartsv v 2001 godu: Statisticheskii Spravochnik* (Commonwealth of Independent States in 2001: Statistical Abstract). Moscow: CIS Interstate Statistical Committee, 2002.

_____. *Deciat' Let Sodruzhestva Nezavisimykh Gosudartsv (1991-2000): Statisticheskii Sbornik* (Ten Years of the Commonwealth of Independent States, 1991-2000: Statistical Abstract). Moscow: CIS Interstate Statistical Committee, 2001.

_____. *Sodruzhestvo Nezavisimykh Gosudarstv i strani mira. Statisticheskii Sbornik* (Commonwealth of Independent States and the World. Statistical yearbook). Moscow: CIS Interstate Statistical Committee, 1999.

_____. *Sodruzhestvo Nezavisimykh Gosudarstv v 1994 godu* (Commonwealth of Independent States in 1994). Moscow: CIS Interstate Statistical Committee, 1995.

Foreign Ministry of the Russian Federation. *Diplomaticheskii Vestnik* (Diplomatic Bulletin), no. 7 (1995): 43-46.

_____. *Diplomaticheskii Vestnik* (Diplomatic Bulletin), no. 9-10 (1994): 46-47.

International Monetary Fund. *Direction of Trade Statistics Yearbook*. Washington, D.C.: International Monetary Fund, 2002.

_____. *Direction of Trade Statistics Yearbook*. Washington, D.C.: International Monetary Fund, 2000.

_____. *Uzbekistan: IMF Economic Reviews*, no. 4 (1994).

Karimov, Islam. *Uzbekistan on the Threshold of the Twenty-First Century*. Cambridge, Mass., 1998.

_____. *Uzbekistan: Sobstvennaia model' perekhoda na rynochnye otnosheniia* (Uzbekistan: Its own model for transition to a market economy). Tashkent: Uzbekiston Publishers, 1993.

_____. *Uzbekistan: Svoi put' obnovlenniia i progressa* (Uzbekistan: The Road of Renewal and Progress). Tashkent: Uzbekistan, 1992.

Office for Democratic Institutions and Human Rights, Organization for Security and Cooperation in Europe. *Ukraine Parliamentary Elections Final Report. 21* May 2002.

State Statistics Committee of Ukraine. *Schorichnuk Ukrainu za 1998 rik* (Ukraine yearbook for 1998). Kyiv: State Statistics Committee of Ukraine, 1999.

_____. *Statustuchnyi Schorichnuk Ukrainu za 1996 rik* (Statistical yearbook of Ukraine for 1996). Kyiv: State Statistics Committee of Ukraine, 1997.

The White House. *National Security Strategy of the United States of America* (September 2002).

U.S. Department of Defense. *Quadrennial Defense Review Report*, 30 September 2001.

World Bank. *Ukraine: Restoring Growth with Equity, A Participatory Country Economic Memorandum*. Washington, D.C.: World Bank, 1999.

Newspapers and Serials

Current Digest of the Post-Soviet Press.
Economist.
Eurasianet.
Financial Times.
Foreign Broadcast Information Service.
Holos Ukrainu (Kiev).
International Herald Tribune.
Izvestiia (Moscow).
Jamestown Eurasia Daily Monitor.
Kommersant' Daily (Moscow).
Komsomol'skaia Pravda (Moscow).
Krasnaia Zvezda (Moscow).
Kyiv Post (Kyiv).
Los Angeles Times.
New York Times.
Nezavisimaia Gazeta (Moscow).
Pravda (Moscow).
Pravda Vostoka (Tashkent).
Radio Free Europe/Radio Liberty Central Asia Report.
Radio Free Europe/Radio Liberty Newsline.
Rossiiskaia gazeta (Moscow).
Segodnia (Moscow).
Sovetskaia Rossiia (Moscow).
Uriadovyi Kur'ier (Kiev).
Wall Street Journal.
Washington Post.
Zerkalo Nedeli (Kiev).

Monographs

Abdelal, Rawi. *National Purpose in the World Economy: Post-Soviet States in Comparative Perspective*. Ithaca: Cornell University Press, 2001.

Allison, Roy, and Lena Jonson, ed. *Central Asian Security: The New International Context*. Washington, D.C.: Brookings Institution Press, 2001.

Allworth, Edward. *The Modern Uzbeks: From the Fourteenth Century to the Present*. Stanford: Hoover Institution Press, 1990.

Anderson, Lisa, ed. *Transitions to Democracy*. New York: Columbia University Press, 1999.

Atlantic Council of the United States. *The Future of Ukrainian-American Relations: Joint Policy Statement with Joint Policy Recommendations.* Washington, D.C.: Atlantic Council of the United States, 1995.

Baker, III, James A., with Thomas M. DeFrank. *The Politics of Diplomacy: Revolution, War & Peace, 1989-1992.* New York: G. P. Putnam's Sons, 1995.

Baldwin, David A. *Economic Statecraft.* Princeton: Princeton University Press, 1985.

Beissinger, Mark R. *Nationalist Mobilization and the Collapse of the Soviet State.* Cambridge: Cambridge University Press, 2002.

Blanchard, Jean-Marc F., Edward D. Mansfield, and Norrin M. Ripsman, ed. *Power and the Purse: Economic Statecraft, Interdependence, and National Security.* London: Frank Cass, 2000.

Blank, Stephen J. *Proliferation and Non-Proliferation in Ukraine, Implications for European and U.S. Security.* Carlisle, PA: Strategic Studies Institute, U.S. Army War College, 1994.

Bohr, Annette. *Uzbekistan: Politics and Foreign Policy.* London: Royal Institute of International Affairs, 1998.

Boycko, Maxim, Andrei Shleifer, and Robert Vishny. *Privatizing Russia.* Cambridge: MIT Press, 1995.

Bremmer, Ian, and Ray Taras, ed., *Nations and Politics in the Soviet Successor States.* Cambridge: Cambridge University Press, 1993.

Breslauer, George W. *Gorbachev and Yeltsin as Leaders.* Cambridge: Cambridge University Press, 2002.

Brown, Archie, and Liliia Fedorovna Shevtsova. *Gorbachev, Yeltsin, and Putin: Political Leadership in Russia's Transition.* Washington, D.C.: Carnegie Endowment for International Peace, 2001.

Brown, Michael E., Sean M. Lynn-Jones, and Steven E. Miller, ed. *Debating the Democratic Peace.* Cambridge: MIT Press, 1996.

Bueno de Mesquita, Bruce, and David Lalman. *War and Reason: Domestic and International Imperatives.* New Haven: Yale University Press, 1992.

Churchill, Winston. *The Second World War.* Vol. 1. Boston: Houghton Mifflin, 1948.

Cohen, Ariel, ed. *Eurasia in Balance: The U.S. and the Regional Power Shift.* Aldershot, UK: Ashgate Publishing, 2005.

Cohen, Raymond. *Threat Perception in International Crisis.* Madison: University of Wisconsin Press, 1979

Cohen, Stephen F. *Failed Crusade: America and the Tragedy of Post-Communist Russia.* New York: W.W. Norton & Company, 2000.

D'Anieri, Paul J. *Economic Interdependence in Ukrainian-Russian Relations.* Albany: State University of New York Press, 1999.

D'Anieri, Paul, Robert Kravchuk, and Taras Kuzio. *Politics and Society in Ukraine.* Boulder, CO: Westview, 1999.

David, Steven R. *Choosing Sides: Alignment and Realignment in the Third World.* Baltimore: Johns Hopkins University Press, 1991.

Dawisha, Adeed, and Karen Dawisha. *The Making of Foreign Policy in Russia and the New States of Eurasia.* Armonk, NY: M. E. Sharpe, 1995.

Dawisha, Karen, and Bruce Parrott. *Russia and the New States of Eurasia.* Cambridge: Cambridge University Press, 1994.

Deutscher, Isaac. *Stalin: A Political Biography.* London: Pelican Books, 1966.

Drezner, Daniel W. *The Sanctions Paradox: Economic Statecraft and International Relations.* Cambridge: Cambridge University Press, 1999.

Dyczok, Marta. *Ukraine: Movement without Change, Change without Movement.* Singapore: Harwood Academic Publishers, 2000.

Ebel, Robert E. *Energy Choices in the Near Abroad: The Haves and Have-nots Face the Future.* Washington, D.C.: Center for Strategic and International Studies, 1997.

Freeland, Chrystia. *Sale of the Century: Russia's Wild Ride from Communism to Capitalism.* New York: Crown, 2000.

Garnett, Sherman. *Keystone in the Arch: Ukraine in the Emerging Security Environment in Central and Eastern Europe.* Washington: Carnegie Endowment for International Peace, 1997.

Gilpin, Robert. *War and Change in World Politics.* Cambridge: Cambridge University Press, 1981.

Gourevitch, Peter. *Politics in Hard Times.* Ithaca: Cornell University Press, 1986.

Gregory, Paul, and Robert Stuart. *Soviet and Post-Soviet Economic Structure and Performance.* 5th ed. New York: Harper Collins, 1994.

Gurr, Ted Robert. *People Versus States: Minorities at Risk in the New Century.* Washington, D.C.: U.S. Institute of Peace Press, 2000.

Haggard, Stephen, and Robert Kaufman. *The Political Economy of Democratic Transitions.* Princeton: Princeton University Press, 1995.

Haghayeghi, Mehrdad. *Islam and Politics in Central Asia.* New York: St. Martin's Press, 1995.

Hill, Fiona, and Pamela Jewett. *Back in the USSR: Russia's Intervention in the Internal Affairs of the Former Soviet Republics and the Implications for United States Policy toward Russia.* Cambridge: Strengthening Democratic Institutions Project, Harvard University, January 1994.

Hiro, Dilip. *Between Marx and Muhammad: The Changing Face of Central Asia.* London: Harper Collins, 1996.

Hirschman, Albert O. *National Power and the Structure of Foreign Trade.* Berkeley: University of California Press, 1969.

Hoffman, David E. *The Oligarchs: Wealth and Power in the New Russia.* New York: Public Affairs, 2002.

Hollifield, James F., and Calvin Jillson, ed. *Pathways to Democracy: The Political Economy of Democratic Transitions.* New York: Routledge, 2000.

Huntington, Samuel P. *The Clash of Civilizations and the Remaking of World Order.* New York: Simon & Schuster, 1996.

International Institute for Strategic Studies. *The Military Balance, 2000-2001.* London: IISS, 2000.

_____. *The Military Balance, 1995-1996.* London: IISS, 1995.

Jackson, Robert H. *Quasi-States: Sovereignty, International Relations, and the Third World.* Cambridge: Cambridge University Press, 1990.

Jaworsky, John. *Ukraine: Stability and Instability.* McNair Paper, no. 42. Washington, D.C.: Institute for National Strategic Studies, 1995.

Jervis, Robert, and Jack Snyder, ed. *Dominoes and Bandwagons: Strategic Beliefs and Great Power Competition in the Eurasian Rimland.* New York: Oxford University Press, 1991.

Kaiser, Robert J. *The Geography of Nationalism in Russia and the USSR.* Princeton: Princeton University Press, 1994.

Kaser, Michael. *The Economies of Kazakhstan and Uzbekistan.* London: Royal Institute of International Affairs, 1997.

Kennedy, Paul. *The Rise and Fall of Great Powers: Economic Change and Military Conflict from 1500 to 2000.* New York: Random House, 1987.

Keohane, Robert O., and Joseph S. Nye. *Power and Interdependence*. 3rd ed. New York: Longman, 2001.

King, Gary, Robert O. Keohane, and Sidney Verba. *Designing Social Inquiry: Scientific Inference in Qualitative Research*. Princeton: Princeton University Press, 1994.

Knight, Amy. *Spies without Cloaks: The KGB's Successors*. Princeton: Princeton University Press, 1996.

Knorr, Klaus Eugen. *Power and Wealth: The Political Economy of International Power*. New York: Basic Books, 1973.

Knorr, Klaus, and Frank N. Trager, ed. *Economic Issues and National Security*. Lawrence, KS: Regents Press of Kansas, 1977.

Kubicek, Paul. *Unbroken Ties: The State, Interest Associations, and Corporatism in Post-Soviet Ukraine*. Ann Arbor: University of Michigan Press, 2000.

Kuzio, Taras. *Ukraine: Perestroika to Independence*. 2nd ed. New York: St. Martin's Press, 2000.

_____. *Ukraine under Kuchma: Political Reform, Economic Transformation and Security Policy in Independent Ukraine*. New York: St Martin's Press, 1997.

_____. *Ukraine: Back From the Brink*. London: Institute for European Defense and Strategic Studies, 1995.

Ledeneva, Alena V. *Russia's Economy of Favours: Blat, Networking, and Informal Exchange*. New York: Cambridge University Press, 1998.

Lipton, David, and Jeffrey Sachs. *Privatization in Eastern Europe: The Case of Poland*. Brookings Papers on Economic Activity, no. 2. Washington, D.C.: Brookings Institution, 1990.

_____. *Creating a Market Economy in Eastern Europe: The Case of Poland*. Brookings Papers on Economic Activity, no. 1. Washington D.C.: Brookings Institution, 1990.

Lowenthal, Abraham. *Exporting Democracy: The United States and Latin America*. Baltimore: Johns Hopkins University Press, 1991.

Luong, Pauline Jones. *Institutional Change and Political Continuity in Post-SovietCentral Asia: Power, Perceptions, and Pacts*. Cambridge: Cambridge University Press, 2002.

Lynch, Dov. *Russian Peacekeeping Strategies in the CIS: The Cases of Moldova, Georgia and Tajikistan*. New York: St. Martin's Press, 2000.

McDermott, Roger N. *Countering Global Terrorism: Developing the Antiterrorist Capabilities of the Central Asian Militaries*. Carlisle, PA: Strategic Studies Institute, U.S. Army War College, 2004.

Mearsheimer, John J. *The Tragedy of Great Power Politics*. New York: W.W. Norton, 2003.

Menon, Rajan, Yuri E. Fedorov, and Ghia Nodia, ed. *Russia, the Caucasus, and Central Asia: The 21st Century Security Environment*. Armonk, NY: M. E. Sharpe, 1999.

Miyamoto, Akira. *Natural Gas in Central Asia: Industries, Markets and Export Options of Kazakstan, Turkmenistan, and Uzbekistan*. London: Royal Institute of International Affairs, 1997.

Morgenthau, Hans J., and Kenneth W. Thompson. *Politics Among Nations: The Struggle for Power and Peace*. New York: Knopf, 1985.

Moroney, Jennifer D. P., Taras Kuzio, and Mikhail Molchanov, ed. Ukrainian Foreign and Security Policy: Theoretical and Comparative Perspectives. Westport, CT: Praeger, 2002.

Motyl, Alexander J. *Dilemmas of Independence: Ukraine After Totalitarianism*. New York: Council of Foreign Relations Press, 1993.

Nove, Alev. *The Soviet Economic System*. Boston: Allen & Unwin, 1986.

Olcott, Martha Brill. *Central Asia's New States: Independence, Foreign Policy, and*

Regional Security. Washington, D.C.: U.S. Institute of Peace Press, 1996.

Olcott, Martha Brill, Anders Aslund, and Sherman W. Garnett. *Getting It Wrong: Regional Cooperation and the Commonwealth of Independent States*. Washington, D.C.: Carnegie Endowment for International Peace, 1999.

Papayoanou, Paul A. *Power Ties: Interdependence, Balancing, and War*. Ann Arbor: University of Michigan Press, 1999.

Posen, Barry R. *The Sources of Military Doctrine: France, Britain, and Germany between the World Wars*. Ithaca: Cornell University Press, 1984.

Prizel, Ilya. *National Identity and Foreign Policy: Nationalism and Leadership in Poland, Russia, and Ukraine*. Cambridge: Cambridge University Press, 1998.

Rashid, Ahmed. *The Resurgence of Central Asia: Islam or Nationalism?* London: Zed Books, 1994.

Reddaway, Peter and Dmitri Glinski. *The Tragedy of Russia's Reforms: Market Bolshevism Against Democracy*. Washington, D.C.: U.S. Institute of Peace Press 2001.

Rosecrance, Richard, and Arthur A. Stein, ed. *The Domestic Bases of Grand Strategy*. Ithaca: Cornell University Press, 1993.

Rothstein, Robert L. *Alliances and Small Powers*. New York: Columbia University Press, 1968.

Sanders, Deborah. *Security Co-operation between Russia and Ukraine in the Post-Soviet Era*. London: Palgrave, 2001.

Shleifer, Andrei, and Daniel Triesman. *Without a Map: Political Tactics and Economic Reform in Russia*. Cambridge: MIT Press, 2000.

Siverson, Randolph M., ed. *Strategic Politicians, Institutions, and Foreign Policy*. Ann Arbor: University of Michigan Press, 1998.

Skidmore, David, and Valerie Hudson, ed. *The Limits of State Autonomy: Societal Groups and Foreign Policy Formulation*. Boulder, CO: Westview, 1993.

Snyder, Jack. *Myths of Empire: Domestic Politics and International Ambitions*. Ithaca: Cornell University Press, 1991.

Solchanyk, Roman. *Ukraine and Russia: The Post-Soviet Transition*. Lanham: Rowman & Littlefield Publishers, 2001.

Szajkowski, Bogdan. *Political Parties of Eastern Europe, Russia, and the Successor States*. Essex: Longman Information & Reference, 1994.

Tabyshalieva, Anara. *The Challenges of Regional Cooperation in Central Asia: Preventing Ethnic Conflict in the Ferghana Valley*. U.S. Institute of Peace Peaceworks, no. 28. Washington, D.C.: U.S. Institute of Peace Press, 1999.

Tsygankov, Andrei P. *Pathways After Empire: National Identity and Foreign Economic Policy in the Post Soviet World*. Lanham: Rowman & Littlefield, 2002.

Ulam, Adam B. *Expansion and Coexistance*. New York: Praeger, 1972.

Van Evera, Steven. *Causes of War*, Vol. 1, *The Structure of Power and the Roots of War*. Ithaca: Cornell University Press, 1999.

Wagner, Steven. *Public Opinion in Uzbekistan, 1996*. Washington, D.C.: IFES, 1997.

Walt, Stephen M. *Origins of Alliances*. Ithaca: Cornell University Press, 1987.

Waltz, Kenneth N. *Theory of International Politics*. Reading, MA: Addison-Wesley, 1979.

Webber, Mark. *CIS Integration Trends: Russia and the Former Soviet South*. London: Royal Institute of International Affairs, 1997.

Wedel, Janine R. *Collision and Collusion: The Strange Case of Western Aid to Eastern Europe, 1989-1998*. New York: St. Martin's Press, 1998.

Wejnert, Barbara, ed. *Transition to Democracy in Eastern Europe and Russia: Impact on Politics, Economy, and Culture*. Westport, CT: Praeger, 2002.

Wishnick, Elizabeth. *Strategic Consequences of the Iraq War: U.S. Security Interests in*

Central Asia Reassessed. Carlisle, PA: Strategic Studies Institute, U.S. Army War College, 2004.

Wolf, John B. *The Emergence of the Great Powers, 1685-1715*. New York: Harper, 1951.

Wolfers, Arnold. *Discord and Collaboration: Essays on International Politics*. Baltimore: Johns Hopkins University Press, 1962.

Zakaria, Fareed. *From Wealth to Power: The Unusual Origins of America's World Role*. Princeton: Princeton University Press, 1998.

Articles, Essays, and Chapters

Arel, Dominique. "The Parliamentary Blocs in the Ukrainian Supreme Soviet: Who and What do They Represent?" *Journal of Soviet Nationalities* 1, no. 4 (1990/91): 108-54.

Aslund, Anders. "Why Has Ukraine Failed to Achieve Economic Growth?" In *Economic Reform in Ukraine: The Unfinished Agenda*, edited by Anders Aslund and Georges de Menil. Armonk, NY: M. E. Sharpe, 2000.

Aslund, Anders, and Georges de Menil. "The Dilemmas of Ukrainian Economic Reform." In *Economic Reform in Ukraine: The Unfinished Agenda*, edited by Anders Aslund and Georges de Menil. Armonk, NY: M. E. Sharpe, 2000.

Babadzhanov, Bakhtiyar. "On the Activities of Hizb-ut-Tahrir in Uzbekistan." In *Islam in the Post-Soviet Newly Independent States: The View from Within*, edited by Alexei Malashenko and Martha Brill Olcott. Moscow: Carnegie Moscow Center, 2001.

Baldwin, David A. "Interdependence and Power: A Conceptual Analysis." *International Organization* 34, no. 4 (1980): 471-506.

Barnett, Michael N., and Jack S. Levy. "Domestic Sources of Alliances and Alignments: The Case of Egypt, 1962-1973." *International Organization* 45, no. 3 (1991): 369-95.

Berman, Ilan. "The New Battleground: Central Asia and the Caucasus." *Washington Quarterly* 28, no. 1 (2004-05): 59-69.

Bilinsky, Yaroslav. "Basic Factors in the Foreign Policy of Ukraine." In *The Legacy of History in Russia and the New States of Eurasia*, edited by S. Frederick Starr. Armonk, NY: M. E. Sharpe, 1994.

Bilotserkivets, Oleksandr. "Ukraine's Foreign Trade: Structure and Developments." *Ukrainian Economic Monitor*, no. 6-7 (1998): 23-28.

Bojcun, Marko. "The Ukrainian Parliamentary Elections in March/April 1994." *Europe-Asia Studies* 47, no. 2 (1995): 229-49.

Botobekov, Uran. "Spreading the Ideas of the Hizb-ut-Tahrir in South Kyrgyzstan." In *Islam in the Post-Soviet Newly Independent States: The View from Within*, edited by Alexei Malashenko and Martha Brill Olcott. Moscow: Carnegie Moscow Center, 2001.

Brand, Laurie A. "Economics and Shifting Alliances: Jordan's Relations with Syria and Iraq, 1975-1981." *International Journal of Middle East Studies* 26, no. 3 (1994): 393-413.

Breuning, Marijke, and John T. Ishiyama. "Aiding the (Former) Enemy: Testing Explanations for Foreign Assistance to Eastern Europe and the FSU." *International Politics* 36, no. 3 (1999): 357-71.

Brown, Aurel. "All Quiet on the Russian Front? Russia, Its Neighbors, and the Russian Diaspora." In *The New European Diasporas: National Minorities and Conflict in Eastern Europe*, edited by Michael Mandelbaum. New York: Council of Foreign Relations Press, 2000.

Brown, Bess. "Whither Tajikistan?" *Radio Free Europe/Radio Liberty Research Report*, no.

24 (1992): 1-6.

_____. "Tajik Civil War Prompts Crackdown in Uzbekistan." *Radio Free Europe/Radio Liberty Research Report*, no. 11 (1993): 1-6.

Brown, Michael E. "Introduction." In *The International Dimensions of Internal Conflict*, edited by Michael E. Brown. Cambridge: MIT Press, 1996.

Brzezinski, Zbigniew. "The Premature Partnership." *Foreign Affairs* 73, no. 2 (1994): 67-82.

Bueno de Mesquita, Bruce. "Domestic Politics and International Relations." *International Studies Quarterly* 46, no. 1 (2002): 1-9.

Bueno de Mesquita, Bruce, and Randolph M. Siverson. "War and the Survival of Political Leaders: A Comparative Study of Regime Types and Political Accountability." *American Political Science Review* 89, no. 4 (1995): 841-55.

Byman, Daniel L., and Kenneth M. Pollack. "Let Us Now Praise Great Men: Bringing the Statesman Back In." *International Security* 25, no. 4 (2001): 107-46.

Campbell, Kurt M., and Celeste Johnson Ward. "New Battle Stations?" *Foreign Affairs* 82, no. 5 (2003): 95-103.

Caporaso, James A. "Dependence, Dependency, and Power in the Global System: A Structural and Behavioral Analysis." *International Organization* 32, no. 1 (1978): 13-43.

Carlisle, Donald S. "Islam Karimov and Uzbekistan: Back to the Future?" In *Patterns in Post-Soviet Leadership*, edited by Timothy J. Colton and Robert C. Tucker. Boulder, CO: Westview, 1995.

"Chronicle of Events." *The Ukrainian Quarterly* (Spring/Summer 1997): 173.

Chudowsky, Victor. "The Limits of Realism: Ukrainian Policy toward the CIS." In *Ukrainian Foreign and Security Policy: Theoretical and Comparative Perspectives*, edited by Jennifer D. P. Moroney, Taras Kuzio, and Mikhail Molchanov. Westport, CT: Praeger, 2002.

_____. "The Ukrainian Party System." In *State and Nation Building in East Central Europe: Contemporary Perspectives*, edited by John S. Micgiel. New York: Institute on East Central Europe, Columbia University, 1996.

Clark, Susan. "The Central Asian States: Defining Security Priorities and Developing Military Forces." In *Central Asia and the World*, edited by Michael Mandelbaum. New York: Council of Foreign Relations Press, 1994.

Colton, Timothy J. "Professional Engagement and Role Definition among Post-Soviet Deputies." In *Parliaments in Transition*, edited by T. F. Remington. Boulder, CO: Westview, 1994.

Cooley, Alexander. "Depoliticizing Manas: The Domestic Consequences of the U.S. Military Presence in Kyrgyzstan." PONARS Policy Memo 362 (February 2005).

_____. "International Aid to the Former Soviet States: Agent of Change or Guardian of the Status Quo?" *Problems of Post-Communism* 47, no 4 (2000): 34-44.

Copeland, Dale C. "Economic Interdependence and War: A Theory of Trade Expectations." *International Security* 20, no. 4 (1996): 5-41.

Cornell, Svante E. "The United States and Central Asia: In the Steppes to Stay?" *Cambridge Review of International Affairs* 17, no. 2 (2004): 239-54.

Cornell, Svante E., and Regine A. Spector. "Central Asia: More than Islamic Extremists." *Washington Quarterly* 25, no. 1 (2002): 193-206.

D'Anieri, Paul. "The Impact of Domestic Divisions on Ukrainian Foreign Policy: Ukraine as a 'Weak State.'" In *State and Institution Building in Ukraine*, edited by Taras Kuzio, Robert S. Kravchuk, and Paul D'Anieri. New York: St. Martin's Press, 1999.

_____. "International Cooperation Among Unequal Partners: The Emergence of

Bilateralism in the Former Soviet Union." *International Politics* 34, no. 4 (1997): 417-48.

David, Steven R. "Explaining Third World Alignment." *World Politics* 43, no. 2 (1991): 233-57.

Dawisha, Karen. "Constructing and Deconstructing Empire in the Post-Soviet Space." In *The End of Empire? The Transformation of the USSR in Comparative Perspective*, edited by Karen Dawisha and Bruce Parrott. Armonk, NY: M. E. Sharpe, 1997.

Dingman, Robert V. "Theories of, and Approaches to, Alliance Politics." In *Diplomacy: New Approaches in Theory, History, and Policy*, edited by Paul Gordon Lauren. New York: Free Press, 1979.

Elman, Colin. "Horses for Courses: Why *Not* Neorealist Theories of Foreign Policy." *Security Studies* 6, no. 1 (1996): 7-53.

Evangelista, Matthew. "Issue-Area and Foreign Policy Revisited." *International Organization* 43, no. 1 (1989): 147-71.

Evans, Peter. "The State as Problem and Solution: Predation, Embedded Autonomy, and Structural Change." In *The Politics of Economic Adjustment*, edited by Stephen Haggard and Robert R. Kaufman. Princeton: Princeton University Press, 1992.

Fonkych, Kateryna. "Rent-Seeking and Interest Groups in Ukrainian Transition." *Ukrainian Journal Economist* (March 2000): 58.

Franklin, James. "IMF Conditionality, Threat Perception, and Political Repression: A Cross-National Analysis." *Comparative Political Studies* 30, no. 5 (1997): 576-606.

Frye, Timothy. "A Politics of Institutional Choice: Post-Communist Presidencies." *Comparative Political Studies* 30, no. 5 (1997): 523-52.

Fukuyama, Francis. "The End of History?" *The National Interest*, no. 16 (1989): 3-18.

Garnett, Sherman W. "Like Oil and Water: Ukraine's External Westernization and Internal Stagnation." In *State and Institution Building in Ukraine*, edited by Taras Kuzio, Robert S. Kravchuk, and Paul D'Anieri. New York: St. Martin's Press, 1999.

_____. "Ukraine's Decision to Join the NPT." *Arms Control Today* 25, no. 1 (1995): 7-12.

Garthoff, Raymond L. "Russian Military Doctrine and Deployment." In *State Building and Military Power in Russia and the New States of Eurasia*, edited by Bruce Parrott. London: M.E. Sharpe, 1995.

Gartzke, Erik, Quan Li, and Charles Boehmer. "Investing in the Peace: Economic Interdependence and International Conflict." *International Organization* 55, no. 2 (2001): 391-438.

George, Alexander L. "Case Studies and Theory Development: The Method of Structured, Focused Comparison." In *Diplomacy: New Approaches in History, Theory, and Policy*, edited by Paul Gordon Lauren. New York: Free Press, 1979.

Glaser, Charles L. "Realists as Optimists: Cooperation as Self-Help." *International Security* 19, no. 3 (1994/95): 50-90.

Gleason, Gregory. "Uzbekistan: From Statehood to Nationhood." In *Nations & Politics in the Soviet Successor States*, edited by Ian Bremmer and Ray Taras. Cambridge: Cambridge University Press, 1993.

Goltz, Thomas. "Letter from Eurasia: The Hidden Russian Hand." *Foreign Policy*, no. 92 (1993): 92–116.

Hale, Henry E. "Democracy and Revolution in the Postcommunist World: From Chasing Events to Building Theory." PONARS Working Paper no. 24 (April 2005).

_____. "Statehood at Stake: Democratization, Secession, and the Collapse of the Union of Soviet Socialist Republics." Ph.D. diss., Harvard University, 1998.

_____. "Islam, State-Building, and Uzbekistan Foreign Policy." In *The New*

Geopolitics of Central Asia and Its Borderlands, edited by Ali Banuazizi and Myron Weiner. Bloomington, IN: Indiana University Press, 1994.

Haran, Olexiy, and Rostyslav Pavlenko. "The Paradoxes of Kuchma's Russian Policy." PONARS Policy Memo No. 291 (September 2003).

_____. "Ukraine on the Eve of Parliamentary Elections: Internal Trends and Security Implications." PONARS Policy Memo. No. 236 (January 2002).

Hare, Paul, Mohammed Ishaq, and Saul Estrin. "Ukraine: The Legacies of Central Planning and the Transition to a Market Economy." In *Contemporary Ukraine: Dynamics of Post-Soviet Transition*, edited by Taras Kuzio. Armonk, NY: M. E. Sharpe 1998.

Harknett, Richard J., and Jeffrey A. VanDenBerg. "Alignment Theory and Interrelated Threats: Jordan and the Persian Gulf Crisis." *Security Studies* 6, no. 3 (1997): 112-53.

Hellman, Joel S. "Winners Take All: The Politics of Partial Reform in Postcommunist Transitions." *World Politics* 50, no. 2 (1998): 203-34.

Hill, Fiona, and Florence Fee. "Fueling the Future: The Prospects for Russian Oil and Gas." Demokratizatsiya 10, no. 4 (2002): 462-87.

Horbulin, Volodymyr. "Ukraine's Contribution to Security and Stability in Europe." *NATO Review* 46, no. 3 (1998): 9-12.

Hyman, Anthony. "Moving Out of Moscow's Orbit: The Outlook for Central Asia." *International Affairs* 69, no. 2 (1993): 289-304.

Ikenberry, G. John. "The State and Strategies of International Adjustment." *World Politics* 39, no. 1 (1986): 53-77.

Jackson, Robert H., and Carl G. Rosberg. "Why Africa's Weak States Persist: The Empirical and Juridical in Statehood." *World Politics* 35 (1982): 1-24.

Jaworsky, John. "Ukraine's Armed Forces and Military Policy." In *Ukraine in the World: Studies in the International Relations and Security Structure of a New Independent State*, edited by Lubomyr A. Hajda. Cambridge: Harvard University Press, 1998.

Kaminiski, Bartlomiej. "Introduction." In *Economic Transition in Russia and the New States of Eurasia*, edited by Bartlomiej Kaminiski. Armonk, NY: M. E. Sharpe 1996.

Kangas, Roger. "The Heirs of Tamerlane." In *Building Democracy: The OMRI Annual Survey of Eastern Europe and the Former Soviet Union*. Armonk, NY: M. E. Sharpe, 1996.

Kann, Robert A. "Alliances versus Ententes." *World Politics* 28, no. 4 (1976): 611-21.

Karatnycky, Adrian. "Ukraine at the Crossroads." *Journal of Democracy* 6, no. 1 (1995): 117-30.

Katzenstein, Peter. "International Relations and Domestic Structures." *International Organization* 30, no. 1 (1976): 1-45.

Kaufman, Robert G. "To Balance or to Bandwagon? Alignment Decisions in 1930s Europe." *Security Studies* 1, no. 3 (1992): 417-47.

Kaufman, Stuart J. "Spiraling to Ethnic War: Elites, Masses, and Moscow in Moldova's Civil War." *International Security* 21, no. 2 (1996): 108–38.

Khmelko, Valeri, and Andrew Wilson. "Regionalism and Ethnic and Linguistic Cleavages in Ukraine." In *Contemporary Ukraine: Dynamics of Post-Soviet Transformation*, edited by Taras Kuzio. Armonk, NY: M. E. Sharpe, 1998.

Klobucar, Thomas F., Arthur H. Miller, and Gwyn Erb. "The 1999 Ukrainian Presidential Election: Personalities, Ideology, Partisanship, and the Economy." *Slavic Review* 61, no. 2 (2002): 315-44.

Kolomayets, Marta. "Ukraine to Seek Special Partnership with NATO." *The Ukrainian Weekly*, no. 26 (1996): 1-2.

Kopylenko, Maria. "Ukraine: Between NATO and Russia." In *Enlarging NATO: The National Debates*, edited by Gale A. Mattox and Arthur R. Rachwald. Boulder, CO:

Lynne Rienner, 2001.

Krasnov, Gregory V., and Josef C. Brada. "Implicit Subsidies in Russian-Ukrainian Energy Trade." *Europe-Asia Studies* 49, no. 5 (1997): 825-43.

Kubicek, Paul. "Post-Soviet Ukraine: In Search of a Constituency for Reform." *Journal of Communist Studies and Transition Politics* 13, no. 3 (1997): 103-26.

Kuzio, Taras. "National Identities and Virtual Foreign Policies among the Eastern Slavs." *Nationalities Papers* 31, no. 4 (2003): 431-52.

_____. "European, Eastern Slavic, and Eurasian: National Identity, Transformation, and Ukrainian Foreign Policy." In *Ukrainian Foreign and Security Policy: Theoretical and Comparative Perspectives*, edited by Jennifer D. P. Moroney, Taras Kuzio, and Mikhail Molchanov. Westport, CT: Praeger, 2002.

_____. "Geopolitical Pluralism in the CIS: The Emergence of GUUAM." *European Security* 9, no. 2 (2000): 81-114.

_____. "Kravchuk to Kuchma: The Ukrainian Presidential Elections of 1994." *Journal of Communist Studies and Transition Politics* 12, no. 2 (1996): 117-44.

_____. "The 1994 Parliamentary Elections in Ukraine." *Journal of Communist Studies and Transition Politics* 11, no. 4 (1995): 335-61.

Labs, Eric J. "Beyond Victory: Offensive Realism and the Expansion of War Aims." *Security Studies* 6, no. 4 (1997): 1-49.

Lake, David A. "Anarchy, Hierarchy, and the Variety of International Relations." *International Organization* 50, no. 1 (1996): 1-34.

Lapychak, Chrystyna. "Showdown Yields Political Reform." *Transition* 1, no. 13 (1995): 3-7.

Layne, Christopher. "The Unipolar Illusion: Why New Great Powers Will Rise." *International Security* 17, no. 4 (1993): 5-51.

Levy, Jack S., and Michael N. Barnett. "Alliance Formation, Domestic Political Economy, and Third World Security." *Jerusalem Journal of International Relations* 14, no. 4 (1992): 19-40.

Makarenko, Tamara, and Daphne Billouri. "Central Asian States to Pay the Price of US Strikes." *Jane's Intelligence Review*, 19 October 2001.

Malcolm, Neil. "Introduction: Economic and Society." In *Contemporary Ukraine: Dynamics of Post-Soviet Transition*, edited by Taras Kuzio. Armonk, NY: M. E. Sharpe, 1998.

Markus, Ustina. "Black Sea Fleet Dispute Apparently Over." *Transition*, 28 July 1995, 31-34.

_____. "Debt and Desperation." *Transition*, 14 April 1995, 14.

Mastanduno, Michael. "Preserving the Unipolar Moment: Realist Theories and U.S. Grand Strategy after the Cold War." *International Security* 21, no. 4 (1997): 5-58.

McFaul, Michael. "The Fourth Wave of Democracy and Dictatorship: Noncooperative Transitions in the Postcommunist World." *World Politics* 54, no. 2 (2002): 212-44.

Mearsheimer, John J. "The Case for a Ukrainian Nuclear Deterrent." *Foreign Affairs* 72, no. 3 (1993): 50-66.

_____. "Back to the Future: Instability in Europe After the Cold War." *International Security* 15, no. 1 (1990): 5-56.

Menon, Rajan. "In the Shadow of the Bear: Security in Post-Soviet Central Asia." *International Security* 20, no. 1 (1995): 149-81.

Menon, Rajan, and Hendrik Spruyt. "Possibilities for Conflict and Conflict Resolution in Post-Soviet Central Asia." In *Post-Soviet Political Order: Conflict and State Building*, edited by Jack Snyder and Barnett R. Rubin. London: Routledge, 1998.

Miller, Eric A. "Smelling the Roses: Eduard Shevardnadze's End and Georgia's Future."

Problems of Post-Communism 51, no. 2 (2004): 12-21.

_____. "Morale of U.S. Trained Troops in Georgia is High, But U.S. Advisors Concerned About Sustainability." *Eurasianet*, 5 May 2003.

Miller, Eric A., and Victor Zaborksy. "Curbing Arms Industry is Vital for Ukraine's NATO Ambitions." *Jane's Intelligence Review* (July 2005): 51-53.

Modelski, George. "The Study of Alliances: A Review." In *Alliance in International Politics*, edited by Julien Friedman, Christopher Bladen, and Steven Rosen. Boston: Allyn and Bacon, 1970.

Morse, Edward L., and James Richard. "The Battle for Energy Dominance." *Foreign Affairs* 81, no. 2 (2002): 16-31.

Motyl, Alexander J. "Structural Constraints and Starting Points: The Logic of Systemic Change in Ukraine and Russia." *Comparative Politics* 29, no. 4 (1997): 433-47.

Murell, Peter. "What is Shock Therapy? What Did it Do in Poland and Russia?" *Post-Soviet Affairs* 9, no. 2 (1993): 111-40.

Mzoz, Edwin, and Oleksandr Pavliuk. "Ukraine: Europe's Lynchpin." *Foreign Affairs* 75, no. 3 (1996): 52–62.

Olcott, Martha Brill. "Central Asia's Catapult to Independence." *Foreign Affairs* 71, no. 3 (1992): 108-30.

Olynyk, Stephen D. "The State of Ukrainian Armed Forces: ROA National Security Report." *The Officer* (November 1997): 27.

Papayoanou, Paul A. "Economic Interdependence and the Balance of Power." *International Studies Quarterly* 41, no. 1 (1997): 113-40.

Pascual, Carlos, and Steven Pifer. "Ukraine's Bid for a Decisive Place in History." *Washington Quarterly* 25, no. 1 (2002): 175-92.

Pavliuk, Oleksandr. "An Unfulfilling Partnership: Ukraine and the West, 1991-2001." *European Security* 11, no. 1 (2002): 81-101.

Pigenko, Vladimir, Charles R. Wise, and Trevor L. Brown. "Elite Attitudes and Democratic Stability: Analysing Legislators' Attitudes towards the Separation of Powers in Ukraine." *Europe-Asia Studies* 54, no. 1 (2002): 87-108.

Pipes, Daniel. "The Event of Our Era: Former Soviet Muslim Republics Change the Middle East." In *Central Asia and the World*, edited by Michael Mandelbaum. New York: Council of Foreign Relations Press, 1994.

Priess, David. "Balance-of-Threat Theory and the Genesis of the Gulf Cooperation Council: An Interpretive Case Study." *Security Studies* 5, no. 4 (1996): 143-71.

Prizel, Ilya. "Ukraine between Proto-Democracy and 'Soft' Authoritarianism." In *Democratic Changes and Authoritarian Reactions in Russia, Ukraine, Belarus, and Moldova*, edited by Karen Dawisha and Bruce Parrott. Cambridge: Cambridge University Press, 1997.

Putnam, Robert D. "Diplomacy and Domestic Politics: The Logic of Two-Level Games." *International Organization* 42, no. 3 (1988): 427-60.

Raphael, Therese, Claudia Rosett, and Suzanne Crow. "An Interview with Russian Foreign Minister Andrei Kozyrev." *Radio Free Europe/Radio Liberty Research Report*, no. 28 (1994): 36-42.

Reuveny, Rafael. "Bilateral Import, Export, and Conflict/Cooperation Simultaneity." *International Studies Quarterly* 45, no. 1 (2001): 131-58.

Robins, Philip. "Between Sentiment and Self-Interest: Turkey's Policy Toward Azerbaijan and the Central Asian States." *Middle East Journal* 47, no. 4 (1993): 593-610.

Roeder, Philip G. "From Hierarchy to Hegemony: The Post-Soviet Security Complex." In *Regional Orders*, edited by David A. Lake and Patrick M. Morgan. University Park, PA: Pennsylvania State University Press, 1997.

_____. "Varieties of Post-Soviet Authoritarian Regimes." *Post-Soviet Affairs* 10, no. 1 (1994): 61-101.

Rose, Gideon. "Neoclassical Realism and Theories of Foreign Policy." *World Politics* 51, no. 1 (1998): 144-72.

Rouhana, Nadim N., and Susan T. Fiske. "Perception of Power, Threat, and Conflict Intensity in Asymmetric Intergroup Conflict: Arab and Jewish Citizens of Israel." *Journal of Conflict Resolution* 39, no. 1 (1995): 49-81.

Rubin, Barnett R. "Tajikistan: From Soviet Republic to Russian-Uzbek Protectorate." In *Central Asia and the World*, edited by Michael Mandelbaum. New York: Council of Foreign Relations Press, 1994.

Rupert, James. "Dateline Tashkent: Post-Soviet Central Asia." *Foreign Policy*, no. 87 (1992): 175-95.

Sagan, Scott D. "Why Do States Build Nuclear Weapons? Three Models in Search of a Bomb." *International Security* 21, no. 3 (1996/97): 54-86.

Schamis, Hector E. "Distributional Coalitions and the Politics of Economic Reform in Latin America." *World Politics* 51, no. 2 (1999): 236 68.

Schweller, Randall L. "Bandwagoning for Profit: Bringing the Revisionist State Back In." *International Security* 19, no. 1 (1994): 72-107.

Shugart, M. S. "Of Presidents and Parliaments." *East European Constitutional Review*, no. 2 (1993): 30-32.

Smolansky, Oles M. "Ukraine's Quest for Independence: The Fuel Factor." *Europe-Asia Studies* 47, no. 1 (1995): 67-90.

Solchanyk, Roman. "Ukraine, Russia, and the CIS," In *Ukraine in the World: Studies in the International Relations and Security Structure of a New Independent State*, edited by Lubomyr A. Hajda. Cambridge: Harvard University Press, 1998.

_____. "Ukraine: A Year of Transition." *Radio Free Europe/Radio Liberty Research Report*, no. 1 (1993): 58-63.

_____. "Ukraine: From Sovereignty to Independence." *Radio Free Europe/Radio Liberty Research Report*, no. 1 (1992): 35-38.

Spruyt, Hendrik. "The Prospects for Neo-Imperial and Nonimperial Outcomes in the Former Soviet Space." In *The End of Empire? The Transformation of the USSR in Comparative Perspective*, edited by Karen Dawisha and Bruce Parrott. Armonk, NY: M. E. Sharpe, 1997.

Starr, S. Frederick. "Making Eurasia Stable." *Foreign Affairs* 75, no. 1 (1996): 80–92.

Thacker, Strom Cronan. "The High Politics of IMF Lending." *World Politics* 52, no. 1 (1999): 38-75.

Tolstov, Serhiy. "Ukrainian Foreign Policy Formation in the Context of NATO Enlargement." *The Ukrainian Review* 44, no. 2 (1997): 9-11.

Trushin, Eshref F. "Uzbekistan: Foreign Economic Activity." In *Central Asia: The Challenges of Independence*, edited by Boris Rumer and Stanislav Zhukov. Armonk, NY: M. E. Sharpe, 1998.

Trushin, Eskender. "Uzbekistan: Problems of Development and Reform in the Agrarian Sector." In *Central Asia: The Challenges of Independence*, edited by Boris Rumer and Stanislav Zhukov. Armonk, NY: M. E. Sharpe, 1998.

Wagner, R. Harrison. "Economic Interdependence, Bargaining Power, and Political Influence." *International Organization* 42, no. 3 (1988): 461-83.

Walt, Stephen M. "Testing Theories of Alliance Formation: The Case of Southeast Asia." *International Organization* 42, no. 2 (1988): 275-316.

Waltz, Kenneth N. "The Emerging Structure of International Politics." *International Security* 18, no. 2 (1993): 45-73.

Williamson, John. "In Search of a Manual for Technopols." In *The Political Economy of Policy Reform*, edited by John Williamson. Washington, D.C.: Institute for International Studies, 1994.

Wilson, Andrew. "Parties and Presidents in Ukraine and Crimea, 1994." *Journal of Communist Studies and Transition Politics* 11, no. 4 (1995): 362-371.

Wilson, Andrew, and Artur Bilous. "Political Parties in Ukraine." *Europe-Asia Studies* 45, no. 4 (1993): 693-703.

Wise, Charles R., and Trevor L. Brown. "Laying the Foundation for Institutionalisation of Democratic Parliaments in the Newly Independent States: The Case of Ukraine." *Journal of Legislative Studies* 2, no. 3 (1996): 216-44.

Wise, Charles R., and Volodymyr Pigenko. "The Separation of Powers Puzzle in Ukraine: Sorting Out Responsibilities and Relationships between President, Parliament, and the Prime Minister." In *State and Institution Building in Ukraine*, edited by Taras Kuzio, Robert S. Kravchuk, and Paul D'Anieri. New York: St. Martin's Press, 1999.

Wolczuk, Kataryna. "The Politics of Constitution Making in Ukraine." In *Contemporary Ukraine: Dynamics of Post-Soviet Transformation*, edited by Taras Kuzio. Armonk, NY: M. E. Sharpe, 1998.

Wright, Robin. "Islam, Democracy, and the West." *Foreign Affairs* 71, no. 3 (1992): 131-45.

Zakaria, Fareed. "The Rise of Illiberal Democracy." *Foreign Affairs* 76, no. 6 (1997): 22-43.

_____. "Realism and Domestic Politics: A Review Essay." *International Security* 17, no. 1 (1992): 177-98.

Zon, Hans Van. "Neo-Patrimonialism as an Impediment to Economic Development: The Case of Ukraine." *Journal of Communist Studies and Transition Politics* 17, no. 3 (2001): 71-95.

Zviglyanich, Volodymyr. "Analysis: Stability and Reform Pose Challenges to New President." *The Ukrainian Weekly*, 16 October 1994, 2.

Index